Recovering Disability in Early Modern England

EDITED BY
ALLISON P. HOBGOOD AND
DAVID HOUSTON WOOD

THE OHIO STATE UNIVERSITY PRESS | COLUMBUS

Library of Congress Cataloging-in-Publication Data

Recovering disability in early modern England / Edited by Allison P. Hobgood and
David Houston Wood.
p. cm.
Includes bibliographical references and index.
ISBN 978-0-8142-1215-8 (cloth : alk. paper) — ISBN 978-0-8142-9316-4 (cd)
1. English literature—Early modern, 1500–1700—History and criticism. 2. People with
disabilities in literature. I. Hobgood, Allison P., 1977– II. Wood, David Houston.
PR423.R43 2013
820.9'3527—dc23
2012048536

Cover design by MaryAnn Smith
Text design by Juliet Williams
Type set in Adobe Garamond Pro
Printed by Thomson-Shore, Inc.

9 8 7 6 5 4 3 2 1

CONTENTS

ILLUSTRATIONS

ACKNOWLEDGMENTS

I WISH TO thank foremost my coeditor, Allison Hobgood, who took this volume so seriously since we dreamed it up some years ago. Thanks, too, to Susan Crutchfield and Simi Linton, to Sandy Crooms at The Ohio State University Press, and especially to our contributors, whose work I have found endlessly pioneering, fascinating, and insightful. I also want to name Lindsey Row-Heyveld and Sara van den Berg as crucial sounding boards for our introductory material during the seminars and special topic sessions that Allison and I cochaired during the completion of this volume at the 2009 Shakespeare Association of America in Washington, DC; the 2009 Modern Language Association in Philadelphia; and the 2011 Renaissance Society of America in Montreal. Our introduction profits in part from material published as "Shakespeare and Disability" in the *Blackwell Literature Compass* 8.5 (May 2011). Closer to home, I completed this work with the help of release time and funds granted to me by Dean Michael Broadway at Northern Michigan University, and it is to him and my English department chair, Ray Ventre, that I owe great thanks. To my wife, Vicki, and our kids, Maddie, Henry, and Nate, of course, I owe all. I dedicate this volume to the memory of Tyler Rigg (1972–96) and to the Tyler Rigg Foundation, through which his memory lives.

DHW

THANKS MOST OF ALL to my collaborator and friend, David Wood, whose energy, insights, and generosity made this undertaking tremendously pleasurable throughout. I am forever grateful also to Rosemarie Garland-Thomson for her mentor-friendship and support of this project even before I could conceive of it fully myself. Special thanks goes to the volume's senior editor, Sandy Crooms, copyediting coordinator, Maggie Diehl, and anonymous readers at The Ohio State University Press; to our contributors whose diligent efforts made this work come to life; to members of the 2009 Shakespeare Association of America meeting in Washington, DC, where David and I first envisioned this collection; and to wonderful colleagues at Willamette University, Emory University, and Spelman College who engaged my ideas and words about early modern disability studies over their long evolution and growth. Thanks especially to Sara van den Berg for her expertise and assurance, Lindsey Row-Heyveld for her humbling knowledge about the field and incredible collegiality, and Ann Fox for her conversation and confidence. Rebecca Olson is the best reader and champion I know, and I thank her immensely for that. I likewise am indebted to all the "other mothers" whose day-to-day care and love for my daughters sustained them while I pursued this endeavor. And to my family (especially Fred Schnell), as always, I owe so much: I appreciate most your love, patience, listening, and laughter along the way.

APH

Ethical Staring

Disabling the English Renaissance

ALLISON P. HOBGOOD AND
DAVID HOUSTON WOOD

This is a book about difference, but more importantly, about how we stare at difference. As disability scholar Rosemarie Garland-Thomson remarks, "we don't usually stare at people we know, but instead when unfamiliar people take us by surprise."[1] *Recovering Disability in Early Modern England* encourages us to stare at the extraordinary and to honor the surprise, discomfort, and bewilderment that come with noting the unfamiliar. Our book does not condone detached gazing but instead insists upon productive looking. The essays that follow play to our human penchant for "obsessive ocularity,"[2] asking readers to grapple with non-normative bodies and minds as well as the radically different social, historical, and literary contexts in which those bodies and minds were assigned and helped make meaning. This encounter with embodied difference and with a past that embodies that difference enables a reimagining of what we think we know about disability in an early modern context.

Toward this end, Garland-Thomson's seminal rehabilitation of the staring encounter as a "conduit to knowledge" and "an opportunity to recognize one another in new ways"[3] functions as a key logic shaping this collection. Following Garland-Thomson, we propose early modern disability studies, as exemplified by the essays assembled here, as a means for more ethical staring practices and hence robust and transformative scholarship. "Productive interactions"[4] with literary history and the representations produced therein require, in other words, new ways of looking. In its efforts to recover disability in early modern England, our collection suggests that we have not been staring hard or well enough at representations of disability right beneath our noses and, moreover, that the encounters we have had with those representations—the ways we stared upon finally recognizing them—should better reflect efforts toward ethical beholding. This *generous* stare at history, literature, and disability representation should, to borrow again from Garland-Thomson, "be understood as a potential act of be-holding, of holding the being of another particular individual in the eye of the beholder."[5]

Certain social, cultural, and intellectual prohibitions, akin to those that police our daily staring practices, have made it difficult for early modernists to identify disability in their midst and, even more so, to acknowledge it as worthy of scholarly pursuit. *Recovering Disability in Early Modern England,* as it cements early modern disability studies as a field of inquiry, calls attention to what Sharon Snyder and David Mitchell have described as "the myriad ways that traditional fields have been willing to study their topic from a distance without embracing the ideas of disabled persons concerning their own predicament."[6] This collection invites readers to reflect on their own relationship to disability both now and in the English Renaissance and prods us to stare differently at disability, disability histories, and disability representations. It mandates that we stop refusing to look or that we, equally problematically, cease gawking unilaterally at the extraordinary; instead, it proposes engagement in a reciprocal interaction in which disability, disability histories, and disability representations stare back. This reciprocity and mutual recognition may cause unease in readers, but such is the price, and ultimate advantage, of ethical staring encounters.

As they practice ethical staring, these essays unapologetically make visible "urgent efforts to make the unknown known, to render legible something that seems at first glance incomprehensible."[7] They also, as good staring should, "[offer] an occasion to rethink the status quo," presenting and corroborating Garland-Thomson's insistence that "who we are can shift into focus by staring at who we think we are not."[8] This volume thus confirms that, as she puts it, "things happen when people stare."[9] In the case of *Recovering Disability in Early Modern England,* a proper beholding of the early modern English past in which we look ethically and with fresh eyes reveals a new disability history, a new early modern scholarship, and a new commitment to "redress the exclusion of disability and disabled people from our critical discourses, our scholarly imaginations, and our classrooms."[10]

Disability Studies

In nearly all its iterations, our world is a place of compulsory able-bodiedness that insidiously excludes, stigmatizes, and devalues difference.[11] Disability studies and its attention to the non-normative uncloak this compulsory demand for ability and strive, as Snyder and Mitchell explain, "to operationalize some maneuverability for bodies deemed excessive, insufficient, or inappropriate on the basis of their impairments (actual or perceived)."[12] Disability studies also reveals how these "insufficient" bodies and persons, paradoxically, are made less visible the more they demand notice, or, as Tobin Siebers offers, "according to the logic of compulsory able-bodiedness, the more visible the disability, the greater the chance that the disabled person will be repressed from public view and forgotten."[13] As this collection uncovers narratives and representations of early modern disability, it first illuminates how normativity requires and rewards the repression or forgetting of disability difference. Second, the volume's recovery work explores the potency of reading disability representation as a theoretical, practical, and political strategy for dismantling this ableist silence. Again, Siebers explains:

> Narratives about disability identity are theoretical because they posit a different experience that clashes with how social existence is usually constructed and recorded. They are practical because they often contain solutions to problems experienced by disabled and nondisabled people alike. They are political because they offer a basis for identity politics, allowing people with different disabilities to tell a story about their common cause.[14]

Identifying and constructing new disability narratives in the English Renaissance unites the personal, political, and theoretical to unpack, and often to undermine, current cultural imaginations of disability. Together, the essays assembled here employ disability theory to read literary representations of non-normativity and, in doing so, expose ableist hegemony so as to resist and subvert its dominance.

With its interest in revealing the contingent and constructed nature of "normal," disability studies appeals to professionals beyond the fields of medicine, rehabilitation, special education, social services, and civil rights. More pointedly, disability studies cultivates a wide-ranging audience in large part because of its interdisciplinary, intersectional, and strategically open theoretical nature. Historian Catherine Kudlick defines disability studies as "an interdisciplinary field dating from the mid-1980s that invites scholars to think about disability not as an isolated, individual medical pathology but instead as a key defining social category on par with race, class, and gender."[15] As her definition makes clear, disability studies is invested in approaching disability "as a social category rather than as an individual characteristic"[16] and theorizes difference through a complex, multivalent sense of what constitutes disability identity. The 1990 Americans with Disabilities Act (ADA), as well as its more recent amendments, leaves much room for interpreting disability and deliberately works against too narrowly defining the term: "The term 'disability' means, with respect to an individual: (A) a physical or mental impairment that substantially limits one or more of the major life activities of such individual; (B) a record of such an impairment; or (C) being regarded as having such an impairment."[17] While the ADA's definition certainly addresses the "individual," the looseness of its prescriptive categories (note the flexible language of "limit" and "regard," for example) allows for broader theorizing about the nature of individual experience as it is situated in particular historical moments and cultural imaginaries.[18]

Since its inception, disability studies has theorized difference in a number of ways. As Simi Linton explains, "disability studies takes for its subject matter not simply the variations that exist in human behavior, appearance, functioning, sensory acuity, and cognitive processing but, more crucially, the meaning we make of those variations."[19] The field has defined and explained this meaning-making by responding, first, to a "medical model" of disability. This model, while instrumental in preventing disease and enabling human vitality, has been heavily critiqued for its pathologizing of difference. Under the medical model, individual impairment remains a personal matter that reduces disabled people to objects of medical scrutiny. It also assumes that disability needs to be "cured" and that pitiable, impaired "sufferers" crave the "health" and normativity that medicine might provide them.

Constructivist models of disability have resisted this pathologizing of difference by refusing to mark disability—and its associated impairments—biomedically. These models instead understand disability, and disabled people, as a sociopolitical category defined by common experience. Constructivist models are emblematic of New Disability Studies, whose goal, according to Garland-Thomson, is to "transfigure disability within the cultural imagination."[20] "This new critical perspective," she outlines, "conceptualizes disability as a representational system rather than a medical problem, a discursive construction rather than a personal misfortune or a bodily flaw, and a subject appropriate for wide-ranging cultural analysis within the humanities instead of an applied field within medicine, rehabilitation, or social work."[21] Perhaps even more importantly, New Disability Studies makes visible the myriad ways that embodied difference "is part of a historically constructed discourse . . . [and] social process that intimately involves everyone who has a body and lives in the world of the senses."[22]

Two of the most dominant critical perspectives in New Disability Studies are the social and cultural models of disability.[23] As medieval disability scholar Joshua Eyler explains, these constructivist models "acknowledge both the specific, individual realities of people with disabilities and also the role played by society in constructing disability by imposing definitions of normativity and ability onto the social world, which consequently limits access, in all its forms, for people with physical and mental differences."[24] The social model determinedly separates "impairment" from "disability," suggesting that impairment connotes corporeal difference that becomes disability only when social obstruction denies access or accommodation for that difference. Lennard Davis clarifies this distinction: "Impairment is the physical fact of lacking an arm or a leg. Disability is the social process that turns an impairment into a negative by creating barriers to access."[25]

Contrastingly, the cultural model—sometimes described as the material model—reunites impairment and disability to "theorize [the] interactional space between embodiment and social ideology."[26] This model attends to the ways lived particularity interacts with environment, and it especially understands the meanings and consequences of disability as determined by embodiment's interface with cultural narratives, language, and representations. Materiality itself is a social process,[27] in other words, such that cultural narratives and representations of disability have the power to shape corporeal experience even as those narratives themselves are being shaped by the material realities of non-normative bodies and minds. This model responds to a certain dis-embodiment inherent in the social model by expanding "the social construction of reality toward a material-discursive understanding of phenomena and matter."[28] The cultural model instead emphasizes the reciprocity between body and culture, between lived corporeal difference and social perception of that lived difference. It destigmatizes disability while still preserving individual, lived experience; as Eyler notes, it "allows us to take into account the entire spectrum of experience for people with disabilities and does not force us to focus on constructed perceptions of disability at the expense of real, bodily phenomena."[29]

As one might imagine, social and cultural models of disability are not the only concepts theorized in disability studies. Modern American literature and disability scholar Michael Davidson, for example, conceives in his work of a "disability aesthetics."[30] Interested in the formal nature of artistic works, he uses disability theory to articulate how disability shapes artistry and artistic production. For Davidson, the materiality of art depends on the materiality of the—often exceptional—body. His scholarship focuses on the "spectral body of the other that disability brings to the fore, reminding us of the contingent, interdependent nature of bodies and their situated relationship to physical ideals."[31] Davidson's disability aesthetics foregrounds, in other words, "the extent to which the body becomes thinkable when its totality can no longer be taken for granted, when the social meanings attached to sensory and cognitive values cannot be assumed."[32] Following Davidson, who interrogates the crucial sense of defamiliarization and aesthetic distinctiveness embodied within, and prompted by, art, disability, and disability art, Tobin Siebers specifically theorizes the representation of disability in modern art to "return aesthetics forcefully to . . . the body and its affective sphere" and, moreover, to make "obvious" the relationship of aesthetic history to "the influence of disability."[33] For Siebers, "disability aesthetics refuses to recognize the representation of the healthy body—and its definition of harmony, integrity, and beauty—as the sole determination of the aesthetic"; this refusal forces reckoning with new perspectives and bodies that "test presuppositions dear to the history of aesthetics."[34]

Like these two scholars, Lennard Davis argues for a conception—and utility—of disability that moves beyond the social and cultural models. He argues, in *Bending over Backwards: Disability, Dismodernism, and Other Difficult Positions,* for disability as the quintessential postmodern subject position. For Davis, all humans are "wounded" and disability is, therefore, the norm: "impairment is the rule, and normalcy is the fantasy."[35] Furthermore, Davis understands disability as a provocatively unstable category that transcends identity politics.[36] Insofar as "disability" lacks internal coherence—people can fall in and out of disability (and disability identification) at various points in their lives, for example—it functions as hard evidence of the general instability of "identity politics" in postmodernity. The main problem with an identity group model, according to Davis, is its exclusivity, and disability's inherent lack of fixity instead promotes a radical inclusivity that "create[s] a new category based on the partial, incomplete subject whose realization is not autonomy and independence but dependency and interdependence."[37] For Davis, experiencing the body's limitations provokes a usefully different universal, and this new "normal" "argues for a commonality of bodies within the notion of difference" and hence "create[s] a dismodernist approach to disability as a neoidentity."[38]

Disability Histories

Responding in part to Paul Longmore's call for "careful studies of disability-specific histories and contemporary experiences as the foundation for rigorous analysis of disability as a common category,"[39] *Recovering Disability in Early Modern England* attempts to perform in early modern English studies what David Mitchell and Sharon Snyder have described as "a new historicism of disability representations."[40] Agreeing that the disabled body is indeed a "cultural artifact produced by material, discursive, and aesthetic practices that interpret bodily variation,"[41] this book examines those variations as well as the various practices that constituted those "differences." Representations of non-normativity in the Renaissance serve for us as viable mechanisms for recreating, interpreting, and understanding a historically remote cultural imagination of disability. More specifically, this collection recovers disability in the English Renaissance by exploring the link between representation and embodiment. The essays in this volume undo the impulse to read early modern disability as predominately metaphorical, for example, and instead insist, as Sally Chivers and Nicole Markotić do, that "how experience is represented textually and how that representation is projected onto and via audiences are both central aspects of the experience itself. That is, the *representation* of disability does not exist separate from disability itself."[42] Early modern representations of disability not only function toward metaphorical ends, in other words, but rather offer insights into the material, lived experiences of disabled individuals in the distant past.

As we have argued previously in a special issue of the open-access, online journal *Disability Studies Quarterly*, the notion of early modern disability is not anachronistic because human variation, though conceived of and responded to diversely, has always existed.[43] Careful excavation of this variation via representations from the early modern period requires sensitivity to how, as Lois Bragg clarifies, disability has been sequentially redefined over time[44] and hence how disability "looks" and "means" differently in sixteenth- and seventeenth-century England. "Disabled" was indeed an operational identity category in the English Renaissance, though it continues to be misidentified, or at the very least underexplored, in early modern scholarship. Many useful and important, though discursively and theoretically inflexible works, insist on inertly conceptualizing the marvelous, monstrous, and deformed, for instance, to describe early modern bodily difference. *Recovering Disability in Early Modern England* resists limiting early modern disability as such. It encourages scholars who have been pursuing a kind of disability analysis, but overlooking the field's rich theoretical paradigm, to explore the incisive ways disability methodologies might productively inform their work. In doing so, our book promotes an early modern disability studies that transcends static readings of disability in its premodern iterations— via stark categories such as "monster" or "fool," for example—by recognizing how such iterations both explicitly and implicitly function in the theoretical context of contemporary disability studies.

To be clear, we are not advocating a wholesale appropriation of "modern" disability and its attendant language and ideas onto the Renaissance. Certainly, as Margaret Winzer points out, "the concept of exceptionality throughout history has not been static."[45] We should, in other words, carefully contextualize even the notion of "extraordinariness" with which we began this introductory essay, acknowledging that the material conditions of everyday life in the early modern period support the assumption that impairments, especially physical ones, "were noticeably more prominent than they are today."[46] Daily realities such as unchecked illness, unsanitary conditions, the perils of pregnancy and childbirth, and rampant war made the presence and visibility of disabled individuals in the Middle Ages and Renaissance more likely and hence, in certain ways, less exceptional. In his searching account of the history of western cultural responses to disability, Henri-Jacques Stiker clarifies that in medieval Europe, for instance, "normality was a hodgepodge, and no one was concerned with segregation, for it was natural that there should be malformations. . . . There was an acceptance, at times awkward, at times brutal, at times compassionate, a kind of indifferent, fatalistic integration."[47] However, insofar as disabled individuals most often were "integrated" into medieval communities of the poor and indigent and, eventually, within early modern internment facilities for the "mad" and "incurable," even less "exceptional" human variations in pre- and early modern societies came to be constructed, contained, and policed in very particular—and often notably disabling—ways.

We agree, that is, with Joshua Eyler on two counts: first, that early modernists, like medievalists, have too often relied on "easy stereotypes and one-dimensional paradigms as explanatory mechanisms" of disability;[48] and second, that an unthoughtful mapping of disability onto an early modern context is not necessarily a way out of this conundrum. Eyler suggests, and we concur, that we must innovate new models of disability studies that are historically specific and less broadly constructivist.[49] A historically oriented disability studies must, to echo Eyler, "scrutiniz[e] the very terms in which we talk about the subject in order to determine the degree to which such terms are relevant."[50] This sort of ethical staring at disability representation has already begun in medieval studies, a field to which early modernists might look for models of new disability history-making and intradiscipline dialogue.

Jeffrey Jerome Cohen's *Of Giants: Sex, Monsters, and the Middle Ages*, for example, initiates a critical reassessment of "'subjectivity' as something that occurs only in, through, and upon bodies, and only in somatic terms; and 'embodiment' as a corporeal process suspended in a psychical and social matrix."[51] Cohen, we would argue, evidences an overt interest in disability matters; for instance, he discusses, in language that anticipates Garland-Thomson's *Staring*, the "visual and epistemological impossibility" of "comprehend[ing] simultaneously both the body of the giant and the human body as complex, totalized wholes."[52] *Of Giants* never mentions disability, however, but rather strictly aligns itself with a psychoanalytically informed cultural theory. While we are not insisting that Cohen's book serve a disability purpose, we do want to draw attention to the fruitful conversation that occurs when this scholarship is augmented by a book such as David M. Turner and Kevin Stagg's *Social Histories of Disability and Deformity*. In an effort to elaborate the relationship between disability, deformity, and defect, Turner and Stagg's volume contextualizes "monstrosity" from within an early modern disability discourse. The chapters in *Social Histories* "set out to provide a more complex understanding of processes of devaluation associated with human anomaly in past societies" by exposing how "in the early modern period the concept of disability was subsumed under other categories, notably deformity and monstrosity."[53]

As in Turner and Stagg's work, the ever-burgeoning field of medieval disability studies has fully embraced Lennard Davis's sense that the disabled body "is never a single thing so much as a series of attitudes toward it."[54] Scholars such as Lois Bragg, Joshua Eyler, Irina Metzler, Tory Vandeventer Pearman, and Edward Wheatley especially have worked to excavate, historicize, and understand those competing attitudes.[55] Valuably, these scholars productively disagree about the nature of disability in the medieval period as well as the discursive and methodological uses of contemporary disability studies in their field. For instance, Eyler and Metzler debate best practices around how medievalists should rely upon constructivist models of disability. In *Disability in Medieval Europe: Thinking about Physical Impairment during the High Middle Ages*, Metzler employs a social model, starkly differentiating "impairment" from "disability" in order to make more visible the ways that physical difference is constructed as disability through social obstructions that deny access to non-normative bodies. Contrastingly, Eyler's *Disability in the Middle Ages: Rehabilitations, Reconsiderations, Reverberations* advocates for a cultural model of disability that acknowledges and unites embodiment and corporeal difference. For Eyler, an ideal disability model is more broadly encompassing insofar as it fuses bodily experience and social perception.

Renaissance scholars should look to this compelling work in the medieval period as we forge our own early modern disability studies. As Metzler suggests, and the essays in this volume perform, our goal is not merely to "catalogue evidence of different impairments or 'disabilities' . . . , but to try and explain their meanings within a specific cultural context."[56] Ideally, this new scholarship initiates an ethical staring encounter both across time and between disciplines. Renaissance scholarship should not single-mindedly benefit from disability studies, that is, but rather each discipline should generously behold the other. *Recovering Disability in Early Modern England* is a book that holds appeal for both early modernists and contemporary disability scholars as it not only reveals the utility of disability studies to early modern scholarship but also advocates a thesis we have asserted elsewhere: "that Renaissance cultural representations of non-standard bodies might provide new models for theorizing disability that are simultaneously more inclusive and specific than those currently available."[57]

Like Kim F. Hall in the epilogue to her groundbreaking study *Things of Darkness: Economies of Race and Gender in Early Modern England,* we worry that current tendencies to deem the study of Renaissance disability somehow anachronistic or to "impose absolute historical boundaries between early modern and contemporary constructions" of normativity provide us the unfortunate "luxury of *not* thinking" about such matters.[58] More precisely, these tendencies maintain and encourage ableist privilege especially in early modern studies as they dismissively mute—purportedly in the name of ahistoricity—socially responsible dialogue about anti-ableist politics and disability advocacy in both our work and classrooms. Forging alliances between disability and early modern studies, then, makes a number of important sparks fly, and it does so in a reciprocal manner across both disciplines. For example, new historicist impulses in Renaissance scholarship can shake up the now seemingly unspoken assumption in disability studies that the late eighteenth and nineteenth centuries introduced "the systematized, divided structure of normal and abnormal bodies whose various disabilities are to be institutionalized, treated, and made into a semiology of metonymic meanings."[59] Likewise, recent emphasis in early modern studies on gendered and raced bodies and their distinct corporeal materialities will enhance conversations in disability scholarship about how to attend more carefully to the deeply embodied nature of impairment. Conversely, employing disability studies contemporizes theoretically the processes of deep historicization engaged by Renaissance literary scholars and, perhaps more crucially, politicizes work that might otherwise seem to function predominately as an apolitical reconstruction of the past and its modes of representation.

Early Modern Disability Histories

Our "Disabled Shakespeares" collection, published in *Disability Studies Quarterly,* set out to explore the unexamined ubiquity of Shakespearean disability representations. Those essays variously investigate the ways Shakespearean drama engages disability both on its own terms (via keen, new critical reading strategies, for example) and by squaring such non-normative psychophysiological representations within the sociopolitico-theological climates that furnished disabled selves with a range of cultural associations. Certainly, Shakespeare's literary interest in staging disability begins early in his career, with numerous mutilated bodies in *Titus Andronicus* and the congenital deformity of Richard Gloucester in the first *Henriad,* and ranges through to his career's end in the psychosomatic breakdown of Leontes in *The Winter's Tale* and the extraordinary representation of the "savage and deformed native of the island," Caliban, in *The Tempest.*[60] Between these bookends, Shakespeare's creative output encompasses a broad range of disabled selfhoods: it moves across a spectrum from bodily to metaphysical disfigurement, ranging from instances of blindness to limping, from alcoholism to excessive fat, from infertility to war wounds, from cognitive impairments to epilepsy, from senility to "madness," and from feigned disability to actual. Our extension in this collection beyond Shakespeare into other early modern English disability representations similarly illustrates the cultural inheritance that pervasively defines ableist discourses and corporeal "norms" against disability and non-normativity. *Recovering Disability in Early Modern England* thus takes as its impetus the ubiquity of early modern disability representations across the literary record, in canonical and noncanonical works alike.

Shakespeare's consistent literary exploration of stigmatized, disabled otherness is, accordingly, not a singular fixation unique to his own characterological obsessions and literary output. Far from it: the humoral medical paradigm so important to Renaissance conceptions of the body, for example, sheds important light as we define early modern disability discourses. Early modern selfhood, in this somatic sense, can be construed as a historicized exploration of corporeal variation and difference that highlights the ubiquity of disability in sixteenth- and seventeenth-century England. After all, early modern theories of health and illness hinged upon the psychosomatic construct of embodied selfhood espoused by humoral theory, which flowered in early modern England out of classical origins.[61] It comes as no surprise to anyone interested in Renaissance literature and culture, of course, that illness, disease, and deformity serve as hallmark representations of the self during the period. But it is important to acknowledge that the fundamental concept of material embodiment as understood within humoral theory, in the relative mixture of the four principal humors (choler, sanguinity, melancholy, and phlegm), is implicitly based upon aberration, imperfection, and thus *corporeal difference:* excesses or deficiencies of these humoral components, early modern medical theorists insist, manifestly explain the very concepts of health and illness.[62]

The normative states of flux and volatility that characterize early modern selfhood within humoral theory, further, center upon their involvement with a range of environmental stimuli—such as relative caloric and moisture registers—especially worthy of consideration in a disability context. Indeed, the very porousness by which humoral selves were conceived grants them what can best be understood as a receding horizon of normalcy. While the salubrious goal of individual health was an apparently rare humoral equipoise, such moments of humoral stasis were belied by the ostensible norms of humoral imbalance. The ubiquity of such imbalances, however, should not shield us from the stigmatizing otherness they facilitated, as Ben Jonson's grotesque humoral types reveal. At the same time, though, the dynamic, transformative representations of humoral selves in works by Shakespeare, among others, indicate the shifting and even volatile stuff of which the early modern self was composed. In this sense, early modern categories of disability must be perceived as far more labile than we today presume them to be.

Indeed, the diurnal and seasonal regimens prescribed by late medieval and early modern physicians—that of "purging" choler through bleeding, for example—indicate that before the discovery of the circulation of the blood by Englishman William Harvey was published in 1628 (Latin) and 1649 (English), and the gradual implementation of such observation-driven science over the latter half of the seventeenth and eighteenth centuries, the interactive flux of self and environment that constitutes early modern selfhood helps define embodied disability in the period. As Gail Kern Paster and John Sutton have shown, the transformation from humoral conceptions of the self to Cartesian modes of subjectivity, while far from immediate, was remarkable. With this shift, early modern theories of personhood changed from perceiving the self as humorally porous, and thus essentially unitary both in its integration of mind and body and its interaction with the environment, to an estranged concept of the self that stressed both its mind-body duality and its essential isolation from environmental situatedness.

This profound early modern shift in defining precisely what a self *is* becomes crucial to any understanding of early modern disability discourses. What Paster presents as the "semi-permeable irrigated container"[63] of the humoral self yields to the Cartesian self John Sutton describes as "a static, solid container, only barely breached, in principle autonomous from culture and environment, tampered with only by diseases and experts."[64] Writing on the verge of this tectonic transformation from humoral to Enlightenment philosophies of mind, early modern English authors portray stigmatized illness, disease, and deformity—in a word, disability—by conceiving of it in ways that can simultaneously appear either entirely alien to current Western (that is, Cartesian) ways of thinking or, on the contrary, as utterly and even painfully familiar. Just as Erving Goffman and Lerita Coleman acknowledge that different cultures stigmatize differently, so too does humoral theory, as employed by English Renaissance physicians and artists, display hierarchies of value that stigmatize differences, both inward and outward.[65]

Humoral theory thus offers one useful lens through which we might begin to engage the three rival methodologies most closely associated with disability studies. Each methodology, we would argue, responds differently to the material fabrics of embodiment as they are couched within humoral theory and other early modern philosophies of the self. For example, the first methodology, the medical model, quite literally medicalizes the humoral self as susceptible to various sorts of aberration and non-normativity—and such potentially stigmatizing medicalization can then serve as the narrative catalysts Mitchell and Snyder identify as narrative prostheses, or spurs to narrative. As they define the notion, stories frequently set forth disability as an aberration for which a narrative subsequently seeks to account by examining its origins and manifestation within the work. Ultimately, Mitchell and Snyder suggest, disability must be either rehabilitated or expunged: this "cure or kill" phenomenon thus medicalizes disability as it serves as an essentialist discourse that treats variation as pathology.[66]

As we suggest above, two constructivist models have arisen within disability scholarship in reaction to this medical model: the social and the cultural. The social, particularly as it is taken up in our collection, identifies psychophysiological impairments (often tied to humoral aberrations) and suggests that those differences manifest within an early modern English cultural environment whose systemic barriers transformed impairment into disability. The rival constructivist model, the cultural, is represented as well in this volume and critiques the social model by accounting more deliberately for corporeality and embodiment, fusing lived materiality with social ideology and marking the ways disabled bodies and minds both shaped and were shaped by their cultural environments. Subtending all three of these models as we present them here is the diminishment of disability framed merely as metaphor and, consequently, an escalating interest in early modern disability representations as embodied, early modern verisimilitude.

But against this burgeoning investment in such ostensible materialism, the tug of metaphor remains keen. Particularly in the theological realm, early modern disability depictions often present an explicitly figurative link whereby character disfigurements and impairments function, put simply, as penalties for sin.[67] This metaphorically driven discourse of disability is one Edward Wheatley has termed, using medieval examples, the "religious model" of disability, and it is traceable in medieval writers who Wheatley suggests generally script "exemplary texts featuring characters with disabilities [that] do not engage in what readers would call 'characterization' of them; [such characters] remain flat and emblematic, the site where God's work can be made manifest."[68] Wheatley proceeds to link, provocatively, medieval views on religion to modern medical views,[69] situating the two as adjuncts to the medical model of disability. Wheatley thus identifies "resemblances between [the] discursive power of religion in the Middle Ages and that of medicine in the modern world. At its most restrictive, medicine tends to view a disability as an absence of full health that requires a cure; similarly, medieval Christianity often constructed disability as a spiritually pathological site of absence of the divine."[70] Where modern medicine, he continues, "holds out the possibility of cures through development in research[,] medieval Christianity held out the possibility of cure through freedom from sin and increased personal faith"; thus, in both schemas, "there is a tacit implication that somehow the disabled person is to blame for resisting a cure."[71]

While the religious model certainly offers a useful groundwork for engaging premodern disability representations, Joshua Eyler rightly observes that medieval Christianity was surely far more multifaceted than this top-down approach allows.[72] The tidiness of Wheatley's religious model—similar to Metzler's medieval social model, which, we would argue, too neatly demarcates "impairment" from "disability"—requires nuance and dynamism, especially as we approach the Renaissance era. We share in terms of our own historical focus, that is, Eyler's call for disability "models that examine many different kinds of texts in an effort to determine how, precisely, medieval people viewed disability and how they rectified their religious views with the reality of corporeal difference."[73] Such a pursuit, as it examines disability representations well beyond post-Reformation England, involves engaging a period of great cultural transition in which the turn from Roman Catholic to Protestant ideologies—in all its fits and starts—produced a sea change in attitudes toward disability.

Lindsey Row-Heyveld's work notably takes up this radical shift and illuminates how an investigation of sixteenth- and seventeenth-century England requires that we complicate current medieval disability scholarship somewhat. More precisely, Row-Heyveld's work reveals that Wheatley and Metzler's assessments of medieval disability serve as but pieces of a decidedly more complex disability story in England ranging from the Middle Ages to the Reformation. "Disability in the Middle Ages was characterized by its important role in a system of spiritual exchange in which the non-standard body served as a conduit for God," explains Row-Heyveld; "this exchange granted people with non-normative bodies a level of subjectivity and spiritual agency that their early modern counterparts did not experience."[74] She clarifies:

> In part due to the example of Francis of Assisi and the rise of the Franciscans in the thirteenth century, disabled people regularly engaged in a mutually beneficial exchange with the normative population. Able-bodied Christians gave them alms . . . and, in return, experienced an encounter with the divine facilitated by the disabled person. . . . In this capacity, people with physical impairments—commonly and ironically called "the limbs of God"—provided a necessary service to society. . . . This type of charity was not a one-sided act but a mutual exchange—salvation for alms, alms for salvation—with disability as the crux on which this commerce balanced.[75]

While medieval theological doctrine initially integrated disabled individuals into a mutually beneficial exchange with able-bodied people, Protestant doctrinal focus upon human inner depravity and secularizing theological systems of charity led to a remarkable hierarchical disempowerment of disabled individuals over the course of the sixteenth and seventeenth centuries. As in so many other ways, that is, the English Reformation crucially transformed categories of sensory, somatic, and mental non-normativity. As Row-Heyveld has suggested, after the Reformation in England,

> Prayers could no longer be purchased formally . . . and, therefore, disabled persons had no services to offer in exchange for the aid given to them. Without this tradition of spiritual commerce to frame an important mutuality between able-bodied and disabled Christians, their relationship quickly became solely hierarchical. . . . The goods and services that had

been traded in exchange for prayers or affirmations of salvation now simply became charity.[76]

The cultural legacy we share regarding disability and disabled selves, in other words, has been preconditioned in part by these extraordinary shifts from premodern taxonomies of psychophysiological variation that facilitated mutuality toward an early modern, unilateral power hierarchy in which "persons with disabilities became objects to be acted upon rather than individuals to be interacted with."[77] The essays in this collection, both implicitly and explicitly, confirm how the English Reformation foreclosed a more multivalent legacy of medieval Christian attitudes to disability and incited new challenges and complexities around disability—and the agency of disabled individuals—in the early modern era.

Disabling the English Renaissance

As they unsettle standard narratives about the English Renaissance and early modern subjectivities, the essays in *Recovering Disability in Early Modern England* speak to one another across time, genre, methodology, and discipline. Sara van den Berg's "Dwarf Aesthetics in Spenser's *Faerie Queene* and the Early Modern Court" opens the volume by calling attention to often overlooked dwarf bodies in the Renaissance. Specifically, van den Berg examines the ways that Spenser's fictional dwarfs compare with the lives of real dwarfs in the courts of early modern Europe. Spenser's poem, in van den Berg's account, "itself is a kind of court, where dwarfs play significant roles as characters and narrators" and hence, as a group, "chart the development of Spenser's authorial narrator and the moral complexity of his allegorical fiction." Like van den Berg, Emily Bowles rereads the stigmatized early modern body through an exploration of Restoration writer Aphra Behn's fascination with the intersection of sexuality and disability. Drawing on Aristotelian and Galenic models of human sexuality, organs, and gendered traits, Bowles shows how Behn literalizes the relationship between defect and femaleness by satirizing contemporary social and scientific discourses that showcase "her awareness of the limitations that her contemporaries' understanding of gender, sex, and sexuality placed on women's bodies via representation of the slippages between desirability and disability."

Interested in how cultural narratives of disability influenced early modern literary form, David M. Turner, Lindsey Row-Heyveld, and Rachel E. Hile all reimagine traditional literary genres from non-normative perspectives. Turner examines English jest books and the ways disability humor "shaped meanings of embodied difference." He argues that humor had the potential to "interrogate conventional wisdom about bodily norms," and he redefines comic narratives of the sixteenth and seventeenth centuries as both evidencing and sculpting the English cultural imagination of disability and the social experiences of early modern disabled individuals. Similarly, Row-Heyveld reconceives genre but, in this case, with a focus upon the English stage. Her essay offers a new study of madness as disability as it reconsiders the role of "insanity" within the revenge tragedy tradition. She suggests that madness has an explicit narrative function in revenge plays, "making the morally ambiguous revenge tradition palatable for early modern audiences" and hence "facilitating the consumption of its ethically compromised but emotionally cathartic plot for audiences trained to condemn but hungry for vigilante justice." Rachel E. Hile likewise examines genre and audience response but in the context of Spenserian readership. "Disabling Allegories in Edmund Spenser's *Faerie Queene*" illuminates how Spenser's narrative mechanisms, allegory specifically, deploy disability. Arguing that reader response determines metaphorical meaning, Hile identifies the narrative ways Spenser calls on "his audience's shared biases and preconceptions related to bodily differences" in order to achieve "desired moral interpretations." According to Hile, Spenser's impaired allegorical figures conjure disgust and rejection, leading readers to moral conclusions not through intellectual reasoning but emotional impulse.

In contrast, Simone Chess, Lauren Coker, and Marcela Kostihová focus squarely upon the materiality of bodily difference in the Renaissance. Chess's essay, "Performing Blindness: Representing Disability in Early Modern Popular Performance and Print," examines early modern interest and investment in medical knowledge and in lived experiences of the blind. Chess uncovers literary instances in which the metaphorical trappings of visual impairment fade in order to foreground blindness as an embodied physical condition that engages material, early modern disability concerns. Chess reads sixteenth- and seventeenth-century scientific texts, cheap-print ballads, and broadsides in order to explore "how examining these representations of blindness on the stage and in print (and, alongside them, representations of the adaptive technologies used by early modern blind individuals) can unsettle the relationship between seeing and knowing, disability and agency, blindness as metaphor and as experiential." Similarly interested in embodied experience, Lauren Coker reads "disability drag" in Ben Jonson's *Volpone* to stress how the metatheatrical staging of disability showcases the possibility of corporeal deceit via the disconnect between Volpone's decision to appear ailing while acknowledging his able-bodiedness to the audience. Coker argues that this metatheatrical imposture of disability accentuates Volpone's manipulation of social practices and institutions intended for the early modern ailing poor and likewise "undercuts the perception of disability as a material and lived bodily condition." Although the metatheatricality of Jonson's play reinforces social models of disability, Coker concludes that its deployment of disability drag provokes questions about embodiment and the "il/legitimacy" of disability that affect people of all social strata.

Marcela Kostihová, in "Richard Recast: Renaissance Disability in a Postcommunist Culture," discusses the disability context of a recent, and "wildly popular," staging of Shakespeare's *Richard III* in the postcommunist Czech Republic. Kostihová pursues the ways in which a "particular case of disabling the Renaissance may feed off of—and feed into—contemporary political tensions surrounding the normative discourses of humanity, masculinity, and citizenship." As Kostihová explains, the major draw of the Czech production rested on the interpretation of Richard's famed "deformity" in casting disabled actor Jan Potměšil, a veteran of the 1989 Velvet Revolution, in the leading role. Kostihová observes the ways that Potměšil's performance "blurred the boundaries between the actor and character by foregrounding the actor's past in all promotional and evaluative materials, frequently as the defining feature of the production and of the entire collective." Kostihová outlines the cultural implications of fusing Richard's ambiguous "natural deformity" with Potměšil's accidental disability acquired in the process of political activism, suggesting that "this production's version of Renaissance disability, in its multivalent ambiguity, uneasily captures a postcommunist transitionality wherein (corpo)realities are in flux, the future multiple and uncertain, and the narratives of the past uncomfortably unsettled."

In essays by Mardy Philippian, Jr., and Nancy J. Hirschmann, finally, we close by returning to narratives of the past to reconsider construction of the "individual" in Renaissance society. Philippian's work engages the Book of Common Prayer as a "therapeutic" instance of textual accessibility in early modern England. He calls attention to a "methodological logocentrism" in the study of literary history, examining this devotional text as "a behavioral script that ushered those of atypical cognitive development into corporate religious and social life." More specifically, he argues that the Book of Common Prayer functioned in early modern England as an inclusive "textual apparatus" and "communicative mode" that uniquely made accessible to both disabled and nondisabled parishioners an emerging post-Reformation theological system of beliefs and practices. Nancy J. Hirschmann's "Freedom and (Dis)Ability in Early Modern Political Thought" likewise explores the individual within the social body but through an analysis of Enlightenment conceptions of freedom in Thomas Hobbes and John Locke. Hirschmann employs a disability perspective to reveal how early modern political philosophy defines freedom by depending on "a particular body with particular physical and mental capacities and orientations, a particular set of assumptions about what constitutes a human being, and a particular set of social relations that exclude disabled individuals from the role of political citizen." She articulates, in other words, how for Hobbes and Locke "what the disabled body or mind can or cannot do shapes the parameters of what freedom can mean." Aptly, Hirschmann's work brings our volume's historicism into the twenty-first century as it illuminates how these inherently ableist Enlightenment conceptions of freedom determine even our postmodern ideas about freedom and political citizenship.

Notes

1. Rosemarie Garland-Thomson, *Staring: How We Look* (Oxford: Oxford University Press, 2009), 3.
2. Ibid., 13.
3. Ibid., 15.
4. Ibid., 4.
5. Ibid., 194.
6. Sharon Snyder and David T. Mitchell, "Afterword—Regulated Bodies: Disability Studies and the Controlling Professions," in *Social Histories of Disability and Deformity*, ed. David M. Turner and Kevin Stagg (New York: Routledge, 2006), 179.
7. Garland-Thomson, *Staring*, 15.
8. Ibid., 6.
9. Ibid., 4.
10. Rosemarie Garland-Thomson, "Introduction: Integrating Disability into Teaching and Scholarship," in *Disability Studies: Enabling the Humanities*, ed. Sharon Snyder, Brenda Brueggemann, and Rosemarie Garland-Thomson (New York: Modern Language Association of America, 2002), 3.
11. See Robert McRuer, "Compulsory Able-Bodiedness and Queer/Disabled Existence," in Snyder et al., *Disability Studies*, 88–99.
12. Snyder and Mitchell, "Regulated Bodies," 179.
13. Tobin Siebers, "Disability as Masquerade," *Literature and Medicine* 23, no. 1 (2004): 6.
14. Ibid., 8.
15. Catherine J. Kudlick, "Disability History: Why We Need Another 'Other,'" *American Historical Review* 108, no. 3 (2003): 764.
16. Ibid., 765.
17. See the U.S. Department of Justice, Americans with Disabilities Act of 1990: www.usdoj.gov/crt/ada/pubs/ada.txt.

18. Rosemarie Garland-Thomson (*Staring*, 1–2) clarifies how "disability encompasses physical, sensory, and mental impairments; illnesses; congenital and acquired differences thought of as disfigurements or deformities; psychological disabilities; stamina limitations due to disease or its treatment; developmental differences; and visible anomalies such as birthmarks, scarring, and the marks of aging," which include "the naturally occurring or acquired bodily variations that accrue as we move through history and across cultures."

19. Simi Linton, *Claiming Disability: Knowledge and Identity* (New York: New York University Press, 1998), 2.

20. Rosemarie Garland-Thomson, "Beauty and the Freak," in *Points of Contact: Disability, Art, and Culture,* ed. S. Crutchfield and M. Epstein (Ann Arbor: University of Michigan Press, 2000), 181.

21. Ibid.

22. Lennard J. Davis, *Enforcing Normalcy: Disability, Deafness, and the Body* (London: Verso, 1995), 2.

23. For further interdisciplinary and cross-continental conversation about disability models and representations, see the work of British scholars such as Colin Barnes, Len Barton, David Bolt, Mike Oliver, and Tom Shakespeare.

24. Joshua Eyler, *Disability in the Middle Ages: Rehabilitations, Reconsiderations, Reverberations* (Burlington, VT: Ashgate, 2010), 4.

25. Lennard J. Davis, *Bending over Backwards: Disability, Dismodernism, and Other Difficult Positions* (New York: New York University Press, 2002), 12.

26. Sharon Snyder and David T. Mitchell, *Cultural Locations of Disability* (Chicago: University of Chicago Press, 2006), 7.

27. Ibid.

28. Rosemarie Garland-Thomson, "Misfits: A Feminist Materialist Disability Concept," *Hypatia* 26, no. 3 (Summer 2011): 593.

29. Eyler, *Disability,* 6.

30. Michael Davidson, *Concerto for the Left Hand: Disability and the Defamiliar Body* (Ann Arbor: University of Michigan Press, 2008), 1.

31. Ibid., 4.

32. Ibid.

33. Tobin Siebers, *Disability Aesthetics* (Ann Arbor: University of Michigan Press, 2010), 2 and 3, respectively. In *My Body Politic: A Memoir* (Ann Arbor: University of Michigan Press, 2006), Simi Linton mentions a number of such disability artists, including, for example, Homer Avila (194–212).

34. Siebers, *Disability Aesthetics,* 3.

35. Davis, *Bending,* 31. In a world where humanist desires for completion and independence are outmoded modern goals, explains Davis, "the dismodernist subject is in fact disabled, only completed by technology and interventions" (30).

36. Ibid., 23. Davis's work responds to Jim Swan's realization that "the accumulated stories of embodied subjects and voiced bodies cannot fail to problematize such [disability] categories and motivate a search for better ways to conceptualize disability"; see "Disabilities, Bodies, Voices" in Snyder et al., *Disability Studies,* 286.

37. Davis, *Bending,* 30.

38. Ibid., 31, 26.

39. Paul K. Longmore, *Why I Burned My Book and Other Essays on Disability* (Philadelphia: Temple University Press, 2003), 11.

40. David T. Mitchell and Sharon L. Snyder, *Narrative Prosthesis: Disability and the Dependencies of Discourse* (Ann Arbor: University of Michigan Press, 2001), 25.

41. Garland-Thomson, "Beauty and the Freak," 181.

42. Sally Chivers and Nicole Markotić, eds., *The Problem Body: Projecting Disability on Film* (Columbus: The Ohio State University Press, 2010), 4.

43. Allison Hobgood and David Houston Wood, Introduction, "Disabled Shakespeares," *Disability Studies Quarterly* 29, no. 4 (Fall 2009): n.p. http://dsq-sds.org/article/view/991/1183.

44. Lois Bragg, *Oedipus Borealis: The Aberrant Body in Old Icelandic Myth and Saga* (Madison, NJ: Fairleigh Dickinson University Press, 2004), 167.

45. Margaret Winzer, "Disability and Society before the Eighteenth Century," in *Disability Studies Reader*, ed. Lennard J. Davis, 1st edition (New York: Routledge, 1997), 80.

46. Ibid., 76.

47. Henri-Jacques Stiker, *A History of Disability* (Ann Arbor: University of Michigan Press, 1999), 65. See also Edward Wheatley, *Stumbling Blocks before the Blind: Medieval Constructions of a Disability* (Ann Arbor: University of Michigan Press, 2010), chap. 1, esp. 7–8.

48. Eyler, *Disability*, 2.

49. Ibid.

50. Ibid., 7.

51. Jeffrey Jerome Cohen, *Of Giants: Sex, Monsters, and the Middle Ages* (Minneapolis: University of Minnesota Press, 1999), xvii.

52. Ibid., xiii.

53. Turner and Stagg, *Social Histories*, 4.

54. Davis, *Bending*, 22.

55. In an early modern context and for a historiography of intellectual disability, see also C. F. Goodey, *A History of Intelligence and 'Intellectual Disability': The Shaping of Psychology in Early Modern Europe* (Farnham, Surrey; Burlington, VT: Ashgate, 2011).

56. Irina Metzler, *Disability in Medieval Europe: Thinking About Physical Impairment during the High Middle Ages, c. 1100–1400* (London: Routledge, 2006), 9.

57. Hobgood and Wood, "Introduction," *DSQ* (see n. 43).

58. Kim F. Hall, *Things of Darkness: Economies of Race and Gender in Early Modern England* (Ithaca, NY: Cornell University Press, 1995), 255.

59. Davis, *Bending*, 66.

60. See "Names of the Actors" for *The Tempest* in *The Norton Shakespeare*, ed. Stephen Greenblatt, Walter Cohen, Jean E. Howard, Katharine Eisaman Maus, and Andrew Gurr, 1st ed. (New York: W. W. Norton, 1997).

61. For primary sources engaging this topic, see, for example, medical texts by Philip Barrough, Timothy Bright, Robert Burton, and Thomas Wright.

62. The resurgent interest in early modern embodiment owes more to Gail Kern Paster's *The Body Embarrassed: Drama and the Disciplines of Shame in Early Modern England* (Ithaca, NY: Cornell University Press, 1993) than can be adequately stressed. Her *Humoring the Body: Emotions and the Shakespearean Stage* (Chicago: University of

Chicago Press, 2004) and *Reading the Early Modern Passions: Essays in the Cultural History of Emotion* (Philadelphia: University of Pennsylvania Press, 2004), coedited with Katherine Rowe and Mary Floyd-Wilson, are equally significant studies for the ways in which they situate the complexities involved in engaging early modern humoral selfhood. Mark Breitenberg, too, in *Anxious Masculinity in Early Modern England* (Cambridge: Cambridge University Press, 1996) and Michael Schoenfeldt, *Bodies and Selves in Early Modern England: Physiology and Inwardness in Spenser, Shakespeare, Herbert, and Milton* (New York: Cambridge University Press, 1999), present materialist readings of embodied selfhood that provide a crucial groundwork for the kinds of analyses that early modern disability studies will find indispensable in engaging early modern texts.

63. Paster, *Body Embarrassed*, 8.

64. John Sutton, *Philosophy and Memory Traces: Descartes to Connectionism* (Cambridge: Cambridge University Press, 1998), 41.

65. See Erving Goffman, "Selections from *Stigma*," and Lerita Coleman, "Stigma: an Enigma Demystified," in Davis, *Disability Studies Reader*, 203–15 and 216–31, respectively. Stigmatized humoral constitutions can be traced in the arc of Falstaff's shift from a jolly, ruddy, and sanguine disposition in *1 Henry IV*, to a melancholy, cold, and anemic one in *2 Henry IV*; Shakespeare provides a more immediate example in Hotspur's comical rage, identified as his "woman's mood" (1.3.237), against King Henry IV, at the beginning of *1 Henry IV*.

66. See Mitchell and Snyder, *Narrative Prosthesis*.

67. For more on this link in a contemporary context, see Nancy L. Eiesland, *The Disabled God: Toward a Liberatory Theology of Disability* (Nashville: Abingdon Press, 1994), 69–75.

68. Wheatley, *Stumbling Blocks*, 25.

69. According to Wheatley, "repeatedly in medieval literature, art, and religious teaching," in the religious model "impairment . . . functioned in ways largely structured by Jesus's miracles. . . . Indeed, proof that a potential saint had performed miracles while alive was integral to the canonization process, and paramount among those was the cure of impairments." Ibid., 11.

70. Ibid.

71. Ibid.

72. Eyler, *Disability*, 7.

73. Ibid.

74. See Lindsey Row-Heyveld, "'The Lying'st Knave in Christendom': The Development of Disability in the False Miracle of Saint Albans," *Disability Studies Quarterly* 29, no. 4 (2009): n.p. http://www.dsq-sds.org/article/view/994/1178.

75. Ibid.

76. Ibid.

77. Ibid.

CHAPTER 1

Dwarf Aesthetics in Spenser's *Faerie Queene* and the Early Modern Court

SARA VAN DEN BERG

n "An Execration upon Vulcan," Ben Jonson dismissed "Dames and Dwarfes" along with "the whole summe / Of errant Knighthood."[1] He was describing the romance tradition since Malory's *Morte d'Arthur*, but he might well have included Spenser's *Faerie Queene*, an epic narrative of questing knights and alluring ladies, four of whom are accompanied by dwarfs. Most of the dwarfs in romances play minor roles as gatekeepers, attendants, and messengers. Spenser, however, gives them more important roles as allegorical figures who contribute to the layered meanings of the poem. In this meaningfulness, Spenser's dwarfs are comparable to those in actual courts of early modern Europe. The dwarf could carry political, religious, psychological, and aesthetic meaning, serving as a surrogate for the ruler, the subject, the self, and perhaps the artist.[2] These meanings constitute a "dwarf aesthetics" that was adapted and expanded in literature and art. Spenser's poem itself is a kind of court, where the dwarfs play a significant role as characters and as narrators. Many speakers offer interpolated narratives throughout *The Faerie Queene*, but the dwarf narrators as a group chart

This essay is part of a book in progress about representations of the dwarf body from the early modern era to the present. I am grateful to members of the Spenser Society session at MLA in 2010 and the Early Modern Research Group at Washington University for their encouragement and provocative questions.

the development of Spenser's authorial narrator and the moral complexity of his allegorical fiction.[3]

It is not entirely clear why dwarfs were such a prominent feature of the early modern European court. Yet there they are, "marvelous monsters," unexamined and enigmatic.[4] Of the many different types of dwarfism then and now, the two most common are pituitary dwarfism, in which the body is perfectly proportioned, and achondroplasia, in which the body is marked by a normal-sized torso and shortened arms and legs. The many portraits of early modern court dwarfs indicate that all types were valued as members of an aristocratic entourage.[5] The only common denominator was their small size. It is the exceptional size of the dwarf body in relation to others that will be the main determinant of its meaning.

To decode the meaning of the dwarf body, we can begin with the more general problem of the human body as a cultural signifier. Mary Douglas argues that the human body is both a complex structure and "a source of symbols for other complex structures."[6] More recent critics have focused attention on the body in earlier eras—perhaps in order to understand our own cultural preoccupation with the body. Since Leonard Barkan's pioneering account of early modern symbolic readings of the ideal body, there has been an outpouring of cultural studies of early modern bodies—gendered, mutilated, deformed, monstrous.[7] Rosemarie Garland-Thomson, turning from the ideal body to its opposite, argues that both extremes pose a cultural problem: "By its very presence, the exceptional body seems to compel explanation, inspire representation, and incite regulation."[8] The term "deformity" was used in the early modern era to keep the focus on divergence from ideal form, whether from birth or from injury; "disability," the term in use today, emphasizes bodily performance rather than form. Disability theorists focus on the specific enigma of the disabled body[9] and have appropriated the methodology of cultural studies in part to redeem disabled people from the monolithic construct of Disability. To achieve that goal, disability studies scholars show how the disabled body is socially constructed as abnormal, and how the dichotomy of normal/abnormal constrains and regulates difference. In the history of disability, the struggle has always been to expose the social construction of disability and to oppose the medical reification of the disabled body.

Dwarfs, because they can often function normally, both are and are not disabled. Early modern medical texts, for example, barely mention dwarfs in the catalogue of monstrous deformities.[10] As a result, the dwarf body is and is not subject to the social construction of deformity in the early modern era or of disability today. In some cases, dwarfs are limited only by their size;

in myth and literature, they often demonstrate remarkable agility, strength, and speed. The perspective of disability studies, however, remains especially useful to any discussion of the cultural meaning of the dwarf body. Dwarfs occupy a liminal position at the intersection of self and other, human and monster. Because of their liminal position, Leslie Fiedler called dwarfs "the most favored, the most successful, the most conspicuous and articulate" of human freaks, "but by the same token, the most feared and reviled."[11] Dwarfs, moreover, serve as an instrument of social construction. They may be regulated as individual people, but as symbolic figures they may also be a means of regulating others, even the most powerful. Indeed, dwarfs are the only human group to have become a common verb to evaluate literal or figurative size: something large or important is said to "dwarf" something else. Even then, agency is given to the larger entity that constructs the other as "dwarfed."

In early modern courts, it was not just the dwarf body that was socially constructed but also the symbolic meaning of that body. The court dwarf gained symbolic meaning in an era when the discourse of power emphasized the royal body. As a frequent companion to authority, yet entirely lacking authority, the dwarf signifies and critiques the power of others.[12] The dwarf could also provide religious, psychological, and aesthetic meaning, serving as a surrogate for and critique of the subject, the self, and the artist as well as the ruler. These meanings constitute a "dwarf aesthetic"—playful and contradictory, decorative and enigmatic, pure and transgressive, powerless and powerful—that challenged humanist ideals of perspective, proportion, and stable form in art and in politics. In this aesthetic, there is a surprising realignment of the ordinary link between size and value. Small size can contradict and critique accepted values, forcing on others a point of view that can diminish their stature to that of a dwarf.[13]

That aesthetic is embodied in the dwarfs of the early modern court. Court dwarfs were at once prominent and invisible, public and private. Some were trusted officials and attendants; a dwarf's position at court depended entirely on the favor of the ruler, whose attitude might veer from respect to contempt, affection to condescension, intimacy to indifference. More often the court dwarf functioned as a resident entertainer, free to offer cynical commentary or bawdy jokes. Licensed to mock, the dwarf was often the object of mockery as well. Frequently an attendant to noble children, the dwarf was often seen as a kind of child, but as a companion for a ruler the dwarf could also seem a kind of human pet, more associated with leisure than with labor, whose presence testified to the luxury and magnificence of the court.[14] In social terms, the dwarf served as a commodity fetish, a luxurious accessory whose value lay precisely in being exempt from productive labor. The court dwarf was an ornament, and the combination of small size and intricate detail was often part of the dwarf's value. For example, in the course of preparing a major portrait of the Countess of Arundel, Rubens drew an elaborate sketch of her dwarf, including extensive notes about his luxurious clothing.[15]

The miniature body of the dwarf also had a more disturbing appeal. Dwarfs were disturbing in their difference and may have been brought to court in part to deflect the threat of difference by converting it into entertainment. Susan Stewart argues that a miniature body, like a miniature book, "presents a diminutive, and thereby manipulable, version of experience, a version which is domesticated and protected from contamination. It marks the pure body."[16] However, the dwarf could represent danger as well as purity.[17] In psychological terms, the dwarf body could represent, and thereby deflect, a range of sexual fears, from asexuality to insatiable appetite. Other kinds of fear—of vulnerability, of deficiency, of rejection—are also emblemized and allayed by the presence of the court dwarf. Patricia Fumerton contends that the miniature was not just an ornament but because of its size functioned as a sign of inwardness, intimacy, and the "private" or "true" self.[18] The dwarf as a living miniature became one sign of the possibility of secrecy, privacy, and intimacy in the public world of the early modern court.[19]

As a material object on display, the dwarf body fascinated early modern artists.[20] The dwarf challenged everything they knew about how to represent the human body. In social terms, court dwarfs were rather like the artists who painted them: outsiders, yet with privileged access to power.[21] In depicting a dwarf, in some sense artists depicted themselves. Dwarfs were especially prominent and numerous in the Spanish court, perhaps the most codified and ritualized of all European courts.[22] Velázquez famously paired himself and court dwarfs in *Las Meninas,* and he painted portraits of court dwarfs, most memorably Don Sebastián de Morra, whose body is structured by squares and circles, abstract geometry defining and confining its form (see figure 1).[23] Yet he must be read not only as an object but also as a subject with personal anxieties and burdens, whose intense and haunting gaze insists he can never be contained, defined, or known.

There are very few instances in early modern literature or life when a dwarf speaks of his own experience. One of those fictive moments comes in Jonson's *Volpone* when Nano describes himself as "little and wittie, / And euery thing, as it is little, is prettie." Acknowledging that dwarfs were often compared to monkeys, he suggests that both are enjoyed "for pleasing

Figure 1. Don Sebastián de Morra, c. 1643–44 (oil on canvas) by Diego Rodríguez de Silva y Velázquez (1599–1660), Prado, Madrid, Spain/The Bridgeman Art Library

imitation / Of greater mens action, in a ridiculous fashion." Dwarfs, more-over, are inexpensive: "Beside, this feat body of mine doth not craue / Halfe the meat, drinke, and cloth, one of your bulkes will have." Finally, he sets up the dichotomy of body and intellect: "Admit your fool's face be the mother of laughter, / Yet, for his brain, it must always come after" (3.3.9–18).[24] Jonson's Nano concludes his collection of advantages by admitting that his comical appearance will always be the first thing people notice, but at the same time he slyly suggests that his wit, nonetheless, will "come after."

A personal statement by an actual dwarf would not appear until 1754, when William Hay began his autobiographical essay with this declaration:

> It is offensive for a Man to speak much of himself. . . . Bodily Deformity is visible to every Eye; but the Effects of it are known to very few; inti-mately known to none but those, who feel them; and they generally are not inclined to reveal them. . . . I do not pretend to be so ingenious as *Montaigne,* but it is in my power to be as ingenuous. I may with the same *Naivete* remove the Veil from my mental as well as personal Imperfections; and expose them naked to the World. And when I have thus anatomized my self, I hope my Heart will be found sound and untainted, and my Intentions honest and sincere.[25]

Like Nano, Hay acknowledges the impact of his body on others. His pur-pose, however, is far from comic. Hay speaks as one person to others, focus-ing on the internal self that joins him to humanity rather than the external deformity that sets him apart. Yet he admits he had been "ashamed of my person" and experienced "Uneasiness in my younger days."[26]

Something of that anxiety is evident in Van Dyck's portrait of Jeffrey Hudson with his mistress, Queen Henrietta Maria (see figure 2). The queen is flanked by a draped table holding her crown (her public life) and Hudson holding a monkey on a velvet leash (her private life). By placing her hand on the monkey, the queen adopts the conventional gesture of condescension, but by placing her hand on the monkey rather than on Hudson she protects him from social diminution. They share the pet. However, the rose-colored velvet leash binds the monkey to the dwarf, who wears a suit of the same rose velvet, so that both are in some sense her pets.[27] By anxiously looking up at the queen, Hudson indicates that he cannot take her favor for granted. A dwarf's position at court depended entirely on the ruler, whose attitude might veer from respect to contempt, affection to condescension, intimacy to indifference. So, too, the artist was a figure of luxury, whose survival depended on his aesthetic labor and his patrons' favor. The artist, like the

Figure 2. Sir Anthony van Dyck, Queen Henrietta Maria with Sir Jeffrey Hudson, 1633, Samuel H. Kress Collection. Image courtesy of the National Gallery of Art, Washington, DC

court dwarf, existed on the border that marks the limits of power, and the only way to thrive on that border was to define and challenge it in art.

Whether in portraits or in literature, the court dwarf could be read as a moral political text. *The new-yeeres gift* (1636), an elegant miniature book, was written for Jeffrey Hudson by "Microphilus" (Lover of little things).[28] A tiny engraving of Hudson adorns the book, with this epigraph: "Gaze on with wonder, and discerne with me / The abstract of the worlds Epitome." The author begins in a mock-heroic vein, making every bad joke on size imaginable. The book, we are told, is "penned in short-hand" and proves that "Little Things are better then [*sic*] Great." The text ranges from semantic and logical jokes about size to Brownian baroque: "Is not a Microcosme better than a Macrocosm, the little-world, Man, than the Great world, Earth? Nay Man the lesser world is lord OF the Greater."[29] If Jeffrey is the microcosm, he is also a figure of Europe: "We know there are foure parts of the World, and among them Europe the least; yet, in fertility of grounds, variety of people and kingdoms, and in the most flourishing wits of most learned men, it surpasses the Greatest."[30] The author describes the court dwarf as "natures humble pulpit," a means to preach to "High-aspiring Mortals."[31] Hudson, he declares, serves as a model for king and subject. To the king, Hudson stands as a "theological" reminder: "O King, remember how thou art little."[32] To the subject, the dwarf acts as a "politicall" reminder that "those who desire to approach neere Princes ought not to be ambitious of any Greatnesse in themselves."[33]

Jeffrey Hudson frequently danced in the court masques that overtly marked the border between the state and its fictions, enacting the threat of disorder and the fantasy of order. The antimasque always featured figures of disorder: country bumpkins, fantastic animals, demons. Hudson's dwarf body consigned him to disorderly roles in the antimasque rather than in the stately visions that conclude these regal fictions.[34] Only in D'Avenant's *Salmacida Spolia,* the last great Caroline masque (1640), did Jeffrey Hudson appear twice, first in the antimasque of disorder, then in the final scene as an attendant, seated at the feet of the king and queen as part of the royal vision of order.[35] Perhaps the inclusion of the dwarf signifies the reconciliation of disorder and order in the court's idealizing fiction of itself. Or, conversely, it could mean a disruption or corruption of that vision of order, signifying the risk that would culminate in civil war, the execution of Charles I, and the exile of the queen and her court, including Hudson himself.

If the king had two bodies—the natural and the political—the dwarf mediated between them as a kind of "third term" and defined their difference. The king could contrast the dwarf's weakness to his own regal power, and at the same time he could see the dwarf's body as a sign of his own natural weakness. Ato Quayson has persuasively argued that this capacity for different interpretations prevents the comforting narrative of redeeming disability and instead elicits "aesthetic nervousness," a "subliminal unease" that makes meaning complex, uncertain, and questioning.[36] By their license to mock and by their own transgressive bodies, court dwarfs challenged the dichotomy of the monarch's being. Marjorie Garber developed the concept of the "third term" to explore how transvestites destabilize the common dichotomy of gender.[37] As a "third term," the dwarf did not simply participate in the system of meanings at court but challenged it. The "third term" puts in question both the one-to-one power relationship of monarch and subject and the very idea of oneness: of identity, self-sufficiency, and self-knowledge. As a transgressive subject who claimed the identity that society often denied, the dwarf challenged the limits of a culture that at once privileged and controlled identity. Ato Quayson again complicates this reading by arguing that the disabled body can be uninterpretable, a hermeneutic impasse that may define others but resist interpretation itself.[38] That resistance is inseparable from the dwarf's trauma of being. The dwarf always inhabits a Bakhtinian grotesque body, threatening, containable only in carnival or court.[39] For the dwarf, the grotesque body is not a willed or chosen representation but ineluctable fact. The court served as a "contact zone" for dwarfs, seeming to convert to an asset the physical grotesquerie that gave them access.[40]

Living on the border twixt earnest and game, between silence and transgressive speech, between human and animal, the dwarf marks the border between safety and danger, between power and vulnerability. Spenser's dwarfs would have been read by his audience in relation to what they knew about the meaningfulness of court dwarfs as these various cultural and moral signs. We can read them as figures of a social and moral aesthetic that takes the measure of the poet as well as society. Each of the four dwarfs in Spenser's *Faerie Queene* is at some point a narrator (like so many characters in the poem), and as narrators they provide a distinctive reflection on the author. The four dwarfs in Spenser's *Faerie Queene* function as attendants and messengers, even a jailer, and all of them serve noble ladies. As Ronald Horton notes in the *Spenser Encyclopedia,* two serve virtuous ladies (Una and Florimell), while two serve wicked ladies (Poeana and Briana). These dwarfs have been read as an allegorical representation of reason, usually at its lowest level of "common sense," occasionally as "the flesh," and once as "comic realism."[41] However, since the rest of *The Faerie Queene* has rewarded many different types of interpretation, any single reading offers only a partial explanation of the dwarfs' role and meaning. All four dwarfs are narrators, either in words or as signs. Together, they constitute a kind of meditation on narrative—as linkage and separation, record and promise, abbreviation and expansion, truth and deception—and on Spenser himself.[42]

The four court dwarfs in *The Faerie Queene* are private companions to court ladies. Una's dwarf appears early in book 1, lagging behind his lady, seeming "lasie" for "being euer last" (1.1.6). He is not a privileged ornament but a personal servant, "wearied" with carrying Una's bag of "needments" (1.1.6). Later, serving Redcrosse, he carries the knight's "needless" spear and armor "missing most at need" (1.1.11). Neither lazy nor weary, but "carefull" and "wary," the dwarf warns Redcrosse to avoid the Cave of Error and, later, the House of Pride. The dwarf's bond with Una, however, remains unbroken. When Redcrosse and the dwarf flee the Cave of Error together, leaving Una behind, she "Lookt for her knight, that far away was fled, / And for her Dwarfe, that wont to wait each houre; / Then gan she waile and weepe, to see that woefull stowre" (1.2.7). Her feelings for the dwarf are clearly reciprocated. When he brings Una the woeful news that Redcrosse has been defeated and imprisoned by Orgoglio, the dwarf is as devastated as she:

> The messenger of so vnhappie newes
> Would faine haue dyde: dead was his hart within,
> Yet outwardly some little comfort shewes:
> At last recouering hart, he does begin
> To rub her temples, and to chaufe her chin,
> And euery tender part does tosse and turne:
> So hardly he the flitted life does win
> Vnto her natiue prison to retourne. (1.7.21)

The physical and psychological bond between the dwarf and Una heightens the force of the narrative. Although he cannot initially show her much care, by trying to help her he brings his own "dead" heart back to life as well. The "needless" signs he carried in his hands (armor, spear) are less important than the much-needed wordless work of his hands, as he brings Una comfort and shares her grief.

As a caring narrator who agrees to tell "the whole discourse" that led to her plight, the dwarf worries about the effect as well as the accuracy of his story. He counteracts the impact of his words by the intimacy of his touch. Ironically, the dwarf (who is imprisoned in his own body) is a kind of jailer who persuades Una's soul, her "flitted life," to return to her body, its "natiue prison." But as a jailer, the dwarf is an anti-Orgoglio, who acts sympathetically in the interest of his lady's earthly life. He can be read as a sign of physical life and its value, as he cares for her being in this world.

Later in the poem, the dwarf is the opposite of a jailer. In his most extensive speech, he warns Redcrosse to flee the House of Pride, "For on a day his wary Dwarfe had spide, / Where in a dungeon deepe huge numbers lay / Of caytiue wretched thralls, that wayled night and day" (1.5.45). In a complicated narrative move, Spenser presents as his own the dwarf's narrative of what he had seen and why Redcrosse must flee. These stanzas merge the narrator and Una's dwarf, who by now is described as "his" dwarf, attending Redcrosse. The experience of Redcrosse tests and verifies the narrative of the dwarf. Fleeing the House of Pride by a back way, Redcrosse must climb over "A dunghill of dead carkases" (1.5.53). The dwarf told his tale to Redcrosse, as Spenser tells the reader. But what may seem allegorical for the reader becomes for Redcrosse all too material, a "dreadful spectacle" of dead bodies.

After Redcrosse is defeated by Orgoglio, the dwarf mournfully carries the knight's "ruefull moniments of heauinesse"—"his forlorne weed, / His mightie armour, missing most at need; / His siluer shield now idle maisterlesse; / His poynant speare, that many made to bleed" (1.7.19). The narrative of his thoughts endows each item with a poignant detail, a memory untold. As silent signs, they "tell his great distress"—that of Redcrosse and of the dwarf. For Una, no words are necessary. The dwarf and his burden are "the signes, that deadly tidings spake," and "She fell to ground for sorrowfull regret" (1.7.20). Although she reads the "signs" of Redcrosse's armor, she nonetheless wants to know "the wofull Tragedie, the which these reliques sad present vnto mine eie" (1.7.24). The dwarf's condensed version nonetheless provides the "whole discourse": a plain chronological abstract that gives the essence of each crisis. Una's response shows her patience, sorrow, and love for Redcrosse (27). The dwarf leads her, and she follows "All as the Dwarfe the way to her assynd" (28). In the final line of canto 7, Una and Arthur both trust him: "So forth they went, the Dwarfe guiding them ever right" (1.7.52).

The dwarf's actions and his narratives constitute links in the "Goodly golden chaine" that becomes a figure for human community and for the poem:

> O Goodly golden chaine, wherewith yfere
> The vertues linked are in louely wize:
> And noble minds of yore allyed were,

> In braue poursuit of cheualrous emprise,
> That none did others safety despize,
> Nor aid enuy to him, in need that stands,
> But friendly each did others prayse deuize
> How to aduaunce with fauourable hands,
> As this good Prince redeemed the Redcrosse knight from bands. (1.9.1)

The chain of concord emblemizes the linked virtues detailed in the poem, and the linked narratives of Una, Arthur, the dwarf, and Spenser himself. The chain of community, opposed to the "bands" that imprisoned Redcrosse, provides freedom rather than confinement. In that community the dwarf is an assistant: carrying whatever is needed, offering comfort and guidance, and telling the truth. Given these attributes, he is a figure of the reliable narrator—perhaps of Spenser himself.

Florimell's dwarf, who seeks her throughout several books of the epic, can be read as a figure of the poet's quest as well. Like Una's dwarf, Florimell's dwarf serves a virtuous but threatened lady. Unlike Una's dwarf, he is first seen separated from her, searching fruitlessly for her. Arthur, in pursuit of his own "worthiest" love, meets the dwarf and hears his story:

> He met a Dwarfe, that seemed terrifyde
> With some late peril, which he hardly past,
> Or other accident, which him aghast;
> Of whom he asked, whence he lately came,
> And whither now he trauelled so fast:
> For sore he swat, and running through that same
> Thicke forest, was bescratched, and both his feet nigh lame. (3.5.3)

Arthur believes him, if only because the dwarf's "bescratched" lame body physically confirms what he says. Only his loyalty and his story are strong. Although the dwarf and Arthur join forces for a time, Florimell is not the object of Arthur's quest so he soon goes off on his own.

Later, in book 5, Artegall will meet Florimell's dwarf and force him to stop his pursuit in order to relate his "store" of "sundry newes . . . But chiefely of the fairest Florimell, / How she was found againe and spousde to Marinell." (5.2.2). Only then is this dwarf named:

> For this was Dony, Florimels owne Dwarfe,
> Whom hauing lost (as ye haue heard whyleare)
> And finding in the way the scattred scarfe,
> The fortune of her life long time did feare. (5.2.3)

This passage provides another instance of Spenser merging with the dwarf narrator: Dony repeats what "ye" (we) have been told and gives us the outcome. Dony speaks for and with Spenser.

Dony is the only dwarf in the poem who has a name—perhaps derived from Donizello (squire or page), Adonio (a knight in the *Orlando Furioso*), or Donald (Gaelic for "ruler"). If the name derives from Adonio or Donald, then Dony would be a mocking diminutive name. However, a mocking name would not suit his role, which is entirely positive. Reading the name as an affectionate rather than mocking nickname for Donald would suit the political allegory of Florimell as a figure of Ireland, who needs to be rescued by and for England.[43] The most likely possibility seems to be that "Dony" derives from the Latin or French word for "gift," because dwarfs were often presented to a lord or lady as a gift. Moreover, as a narrator, Dony gives Artegall a gift, conveying to him the story we had already received from Spenser. In this case, our experience as readers validates the dwarf's narrative.

The other two dwarfs in the poem—Poeana's dwarf in book 4 and Briana's dwarf in book 6—serve wicked ladies and are themselves deceptive or dangerous narrators. One is a jailer, the other a messenger. Each of them serves as a negative counterpoint to the first two dwarfs in narratives that Paul Suttie describes as ambivalent and "unsettling."[44] These are narrators who withhold rather than give, who deceive rather than tell the truth, who separate rather than join the knights and those they seek.

In the tale of Poeana, Spenser explores the contest of love and friendship. Poeana, the daughter of the giant Corflambo, is described as given "to vaine delight, / And eke too loose of life, and eke of love too light" (4.8.49). Her name, derived from the Greek for "pain," suits her when we first see her, "complayning of her cruell Paramoure." Her dwarf gets caught in the tangle of relationships that Reed Dasenbrock has termed the "doubling and transference and acting out" of Petrarchan love in the narrative of book 4.[45] Amyas, the Squire of Low Degree, was captured by Poeana, who was enthralled by him. His friend Placidas, pretending to be a prisoner of love, changes places with Amyas and kidnaps the dwarf. Dasenbrock, the only critic who even mentions this episode, is not sure what it means, but speculates that it may simply be "a gesture of independence" by Placidas. What is most visually striking is the confusion of Placidas and the dwarf. The Squire, we are told,

. . . came galloping as he would flie;
Bearing a little Dwarfe before his steed
That all the way full loud for aide did crie,
That seem'd his shrikes would rend the brasen skie. (4.8.38)

Caught between Arthur and Corflambo, "Both Squire and dwarfe did tumble downe / Vnto the earth, and lay long while in senselesse swowne" (4.8.42). Only then does the dwarf's allegiance come clear, as he "right sorie seem'd and sad, / And howld aloud to see his Lord there slaine, / And rent his haire and scratcht his face for paine" (4.8.46). If his shrieks "rend" the sky, tearing apart the fabric of Nature, he tears his own hair, wounding his own body as a sign of his inner pain.

Whatever sympathy we have for him is short-lived. The dwarf, we learn, served the lady Poeana as "her dearling base," functioning as the jailer

> To whom the keyes of euery prison dore
> By her committed be, of speciall grace,
> And at his will may whom he list restore,
> And whom he list reserue, to be afflicted more. (4.8.54)

This dwarf serves not only as the lady's confidant but as her erotic agent, the representation and representative of her desire. This makes explicit another common assumption that the court dwarf could be a figure of sexual license.[46] He also has a limited but real power of his own, to "restore" prisoners to her favor or "reserue" them for continued affliction according to his own desire. The dwarf may be a figure of the poet in that both of them can reserve or release other characters at will. However, when Arthur compels him "To open vnto him the prison dore, / And forth to bring those thralls, which there he held" (4.9.8), the dwarf's voice is reduced to an impotent shriek. He has no other narrative power. The dwarf, moreover, does not share in the resolution of the story. Poeana's name shifts to Paeana, derived from the Greek word for "joy," when Arthur arranges her marriage to Placidus. She is last seen as a happily married woman, who has "reformd her waies, / That all men much admyrde her change, and spake her praise."[47] The dwarf, no longer by her side, has disappeared from the narrative.

In book 6, the Legend of Courtesy, the narrator fears courtesy has become "nought but forgerie," no longer gold but brass (6.Proem.5). Sir Calidore, the knight of courtesy, proves just as problematic. Critics debate whether he should be dismissed as "the glib epitome of false courtesy" or admired as "one of Spenser's finest heroes."[48] James Nohrnberg sees Calidore as "a kind of poet of conduct, but he is also a hypocrite."[49] Sir Calidore, true ladies' man, learns of Briana, who violates courtesy and hospitality. Her dwarf is implicated in that corruption. After Calidore slays her household (violating courtesy in the name of courtesy), she derisively labels him a "Cowherd" and sends her dwarf to bring back her lover, giving him "a ring of gould, / A priuy token" (6.1.29). The dwarf travels all night and returns in the morning with Crudor's answer, his "basenet" (part of his armor) "as a faithfull band" matching her ring (6.1.31). Calidore kills Crudor and converts Briana to virtue, but the dwarf disappears from the story. He is not redeemed into courtesy but remains forever a go-between, who facilitates disorder and discourtesy. He may carry a ring of gold, but his message is dross.

The pairing of "Dames and Dwarfes" can bring together reader and narrator in a caring bond or a prison of falsehood and self-serving violence: "For who can descry the cunning traine [of falsehood]?" (1.7.1). In an allegory as complex as Spenser's *Faerie Queene,* the poet's "aesthetic nervousness" is manifest in the radical linking of the authorial narrator to the dwarf narrators. As we have seen, at times the narratives of Una's dwarf and Florimell's dwarf are indistinguishable from those of the poetic narrator. The actions of the last two dwarfs in *The Faerie Queene* are far less attractive. They serve vicious ladies and are corrupted in that service.[50] They may thereby mirror what has been described as Spenser's increasing disillusionment with his epic project. It is also possible to consider Spenser not as disillusioned but as more complex and critical in his vision of court, poem, and self, offering narratives at once affirmative and ambivalent. As Paul Suttie argues, the later books of the poem increasingly admit that there is no "stable point" outside the narrative from which all ethical quests can be judged.[51] Instead, the narrator is always within his text, his interpretation interpreted through a reading of other narrators in the poem.

A disability perspective can offer new insight into Spenser's narrator and, perhaps, into Spenser himself. Like the dwarfs, Spenser's narrator was in service, carrying the burden of "needments" for his characters. In the Proem to the *Faerie Queene,* Spenser even describes himself as a kind of dwarf, his art disabled: "Me, all too meane, the sacred Muse areeds / To blazon broad amongst her learned throng," despite "my feeble eyne," "my thoughts too humble and too vile," and "mine afflicted stile" (1.7–8, 4.5–8). It is even tempting to read the opening words, "Lo I the man," as a kind of punning demand that we attend to the low stature of the poet who dares to celebrate the "Great Lady of the greatest Isle." In the Proem to book 6, the narrator's steps are "weary," his travels "tedious," and his spirit "dulled." By echoing the description of Una's dwarf, Spenser distances himself from the dwarfs who served Poeana and Briana as jailer and go-between. Instead, he has proved himself careful and wary, able to guide us ever right, so that we too may be "rauisht with rare thoughts delight" (6.Proem.1).

As an artist, the author marks the border, standing between art and life, between truth and fiction. Moreover, despite the risk of being confined by the social and moral framework of narrative, the author—like the court dwarf—is ultimately free to play, to recreate himself, to create new fictions, to deceive new audiences. The dwarf as narrator provides what Harry Berger has termed "micro-events"[52] of the self-interpretive activity that links authors and their audiences. The dwarfs in Spenser's epic vanish as their stories end, even as the poet finally escapes from his fictions and cannot be contained by them. At the same time, in some sense even great writers are ultimately dwarfed by their own art. They are, finally, its servant.

Notes

1. Ben Jonson, "An Execration upon Vulcan," *Vnder-wood* XLIII.66–67, in *Works*, ed. C. H. Herford and Percy and Evelyn Simpson, vol. 8 (Oxford: Clarendon Press, 1947), 205.

2. The religious meaning of the dwarf body will not be discussed in this essay, other than to note the biblical list of those prohibited from serving as priests: "a blind man, or a lame, or he that hath a flat nose, or anything superfluous, or a man that is brokenfooted, or brokenhanded, or crook-backt, or a dwarf" (Leviticus 20.18–20). The dwarf in Malory's *Morte d'Arthur* who has "a grete mouth and a flat nose" is the only dwarf in English romances who is physically described. Although there were some representations of dwarfs as morally diminished, dwarfs were not portrayed as villains until the nineteenth century (in works by Scott, Dickens, Poe, and Wilde). That thread of representation, which often focused on "Renaissance" dwarfs, traced their villainy to social mistreatment and continues in such twentieth-century works as Pär Lagerkvist's *The Dwarf.* Many of these representations are mentioned by Betty Adelson in *The Lives of Dwarfs: Their Journey from Public Curiosity toward Social Liberation* (New Brunswick, NJ: Rutgers University Press, 2005). This important compendium offers a somewhat simplified reading of the history of representation, but I am indebted to her for the information she provides.

3. The dwarfs have been discussed as a group only by Ronald Horton, who reads them as perspectives on reason, yet they would have had a much greater symbolic capacity for Spenser and his readers; see his entry "Dwarfs," in *The Spenser Encyclopedia,* ed. A. C. Hamilton (New York: Routledge, 1991), 230. Unlike the dwarfs in Spenser's epic, dwarfs in English romances are much less interesting. They are merely accessories, attendants, messengers, and watchmen who are never "characterized" or named. They almost never speak.

4. Dwarfs were common in Celtic fairy lore, where they often had magical powers. See W. Y. Evans-Wentz, *The Fairy-Faith in Celtic Countries* [1911], intro. Carl McCollman (Franklin Lakes, NJ: New Page Books, 2004). Paul Acker argues that dwarfs in Icelandic literature are reclusive and wise, and live in isolation; "Dwarf-Lore in Alvissmal," in *The Poetic Edda,* ed. Paul Acker and Carolyne Larrington (New York: Routledge, 2002), 213–28. The many dwarfs in Malory's *Morte d'Arthur* are for the most part attendants to knights and ladies and do not have magical powers. The etymology of "dwarf" is linked to magic, not to reduced size, but by the time of Malory

the word merely denoted a person of small stature. I prefer to use "dwarfs" as the plural, rather than "dwarves," which was coined by J. R. R. Tolkien to describe the distinctive race analogous to "elves." See Michael D. C. Drout, *J. R. R. Tolkien Encyclopedia: Scholarship and Critical Assessment* (London: Routledge, 2006), 134–35. On court dwarfs as "marvelous monsters," see Joanna Woods-Marsden, "A Vision of Dwarfs," in *Dreams and Visions: Presenting the Past*, ed. Nancy Van Deusen (Leiden: Brill, 2010), 325–37.

5. Many of these paintings are reproduced in Alfred Enderle, Dietrich Meyerhofer, and Gerd Unverfehrt, eds., *Small People—Great Art: Restricted Growth from an Artistic and Medical Viewpoint* (Bremen: Artcolor Verlag, 1994).

6. Mary Douglas, *Purity and Danger: An Analysis of Concepts of Pollution and Taboo* (New York: Routledge and Kegan Paul, 1966), 142.

7. Leonard Barkan, *Nature's Work of Art: The Human Body as Image of the World* (New Haven, CT: Yale University Press, 1975). Foundational critical studies of the early modern body as symbolic form include Jonathan Sawday, *The Body Emblazoned: Dissection and the Human Body in Renaissance Culture* (New York: Routledge, 1995), and Katharine Park and Lorraine Daston, *Wonders and the Order of Nature, 1150–1750* (New York: Zone Books, 1998).

8. Rosemarie Garland-Thomson, "Introduction: From Wonder to Error—A Genealogy of Freak Discourse in Modernity," in *Freakery: Cultural Spectacles of the Extraordinary Body* (New York: New York University Press, 1996), 1.

9. See Victor Turner, *Dramas, Fields, and Metaphors: Symbolic Action in Human Society* (Ithaca, NY: Cornell University Press, 1974).

10. See Ambroise Paré, *On Monsters and Marvels,* ed. and trans. Janis L. Palliser (Chicago: University of Chicago Press, 1982).

11. Leslie Fiedler, *Freaks* (New York: Simon and Schuster, 1978), 90.

12. Michel Foucault, "Truth and Power," in *Power/Knowledge: Selected Interviews and Other Writings, 1972–1977,* ed. Colin Gordon (New York: Pantheon Books, 1980), 109–34. On royal power and symbolism, see Clifford Geertz, "Centers, Kings, and Charisma: Reflections on the Symbolics of Power," in *Rites of Power: Symbolism, Ritual, and Politics since the Middle Ages,* ed. Sean Wilentz (Philadelphia: University of Pennsylvania Press, 1985), 13–40.

13. "Dwarf aesthetics" is a term derived from, but independent of, "disability aesthetics." The latter term was formulated by Davidson in *Concerto for the Left Hand* and developed by Siebers in *Disability Aesthetics.* Davidson demonstrates how disability shapes the work of artists. Siebers argues that what is "modern" in art was perceived since National Socialism as disability, and that disability must finally be redeemed as a social and an aesthetic value. I would argue, in formulating dwarf aesthetics, that the dwarf as the object of representation shapes the artist's representation, the artist's sense of self, and the response of the audience. When a dwarf is represented, the artist and the audience not only gaze upon the dwarf but may also share the dwarf's gaze. This aesthetic can be developed when the dwarf is one component of what is represented, as in *The Faerie Queene,* and has implications for the nature of representation itself. I am grateful to Katherine Eggert for an initial conversation about these issues. Garland-Thomson comments on the verb "dwarf" to instance scale as a value in *Staring,* 162.

14. Yi-Fu Tuan, *Dominance and Affection: The Making of Pets* (New Haven, CT: Yale University Press, 1984), 153–61.

15. Enderle et al., *Small People,* 180–83.

16. Susan Stewart, *On Longing: Narratives of the Miniature, the Gigantic, the Souvenir, the Collection* (Baltimore: Johns Hopkins University Press, 1984), 69.

17. Douglas, *Purity and Danger,* 140–42.

18. Patricia Fumerton, "'Secret' Arts: Elizabethan Miniatures and Sonnets," *Representations* 15 (Summer 1986), 57–97.

19. Julian Yates echoes Patricia Fumerton's reading of portrait miniatures as a world of secret, intimate, private shared display in *Error, Misuse, Failure: Object Lessons from the English Renaissance* (Minneapolis: University of Minnesota Press, 2003), 37. The portrait miniature reduces the painted subject to a dwarf, and the minute details of the image demand attention.

20. Representative works of art are reproduced and discussed in Enderle et al., *Small People,* 1994.

21. On the transgressive body in early modern culture, see Peter Stallybrass and Allon White, *The Politics and Poetics of Transgression* (Ithaca, NY: Cornell University Press, 1986). On the containment of difference and danger, see Stephen Greenblatt, "Invisible Bullets," in *Shakespearean Negotiations: The Circulation of Social Energy in Renaissance England* (Oxford: Clarendon Press, 1988), 21–65.

22. J. Moreno Villa provides a catalogue of Spanish court dwarfs in *Locos, enanos, negros y niños palaciegos* (Mexico: La Casa de España en Mexico, Editorial Presencia, 1939). Barbara Otto surveys dwarfs in other court cultures in *Fools Are Everywhere* (Chicago: University of Chicago Press, 2001); see also Adelson, 3–17.

23. Enderle et al., *Small People,* 180–83. See also Michel Foucault, *The Order of Things: An Archaeology of the Human Sciences* (New York: Vintage, 1970); Jonathan Brown, *Velázquez: The Technique of Genius* (New Haven, CT: Yale University Press, 1998); and Stephen Orso, *Velázquez, "Los Borrachos," and Painting at the Court of Philip IV* (Cambridge: Cambridge University Press, 1993). More than one dwarf became an artist. Dick Gibson, a dwarf in the court of Charles I, became famous for his miniature portraits of the English aristocracy. His daughter, also a dwarf, followed in that career. See John Murdoch and V. J. Murrell, "The Monogramist DG: Dwarf Gibson and His Patrons," *Burlington Magazine* 123, no. 938 (May 1981): 282–91. "Mr. Logan," another royal court dwarf, became a popular artist at Tunbridge Wells in the eighteenth century. His best-known work was a drawing that featured Samuel Richardson, Dr. Johnson, Beau Nash, David Garrick, Elizabeth Chudleigh, and William Pitt at leisure; see Lewis Melville, *Society at Royal Tunbridge Wells in the Eighteenth Century—and After* (London: Eveleigh Nash, 1912), 100–101.

24. Jonson, *Works,* vol. 5, 70.

25. William Hay, *Deformity: An Essay,* ed. Kathleen James-Cavan (Victoria, BC: University of Victoria, 2004), 24.

26. Ibid., 25.

27. Yi-Fu Tuan, in discussing Van Dyck's portrait of Queen Henrietta Maria and Jeffrey Hudson in *Dominance and Affection,* notes that the queen places her hand on the head of the monkey rather than on the dwarf. He argues that this conventional gesture was "inconsistent" with the identification of monkeys and dwarfs as pets (157), but I would argue that the court dwarf retained human status even when he was linked to nonhuman pets.

28. Microphilus [Master Slater], *The new-yeeres gift, presented at court, from the lady*

Parvula to the Lord Minimus (commonly called Little Jefferie) Her Majesties servant, with a letter as it was penned in short-hand: wherein is proved little things are better then [sic] *great* (London, 1636). My discussion of this text builds on information provided in Nicholas Page, *Lord Minimus: The Extraordinary Life of Britain's Smallest Man* (London: HarperCollins, 2001). Page does not comment on the jokes or the symbolic meanings of the court dwarf.

29. *The new-yeeres gift,* 5–6.

30. Ibid., 75–76.

31. Ibid., 99.

32. Ibid., 103–4.

33. Ibid., 104–5.

34. See also Mark Franko, "Political Erotics of Burlesque Ballet, 1624–1627," in *Dance as Text: Ideologies of the Baroque Body* (Cambridge: Cambridge University Press, 1993), 65–107.

35. William D'Avenant, *Salmacida Spolia,* in English Verse Drama Full-Text Database (Cambridge: Chadwycke-Healey, 1994).

36. Ato Quayson, *Aesthetic Nervousness: Disability and the Crisis of Representation* (New York: Columbia University Press, 2007), 14, 261. Quayson offers an alternative to Mitchell and Snyder's influential argument, in *Narrative Prosthesis,* that narrative interpretation as prosthesis restores the disabled body to normalcy.

37. Marjorie Garber, *Vested Interests: Cross-dressing and Cultural Anxiety* (New York: Routledge, 1991), 9–11.

38. On the disabled body as hermeneutic impasse, see Quayson, *Aesthetic Nervousness.*

39. See Stallybrass and White, *Politics.*

40. Mary Louise Pratt introduced the term "contact zone" to describe the encounter of different cultures; see her influential essay "Arts of the Contact Zone," in *Profession 91* (New York: MLA, 1991), 33–40. I have appropriated the term to describe any socially defined space where disabled and able-bodied people encounter each other. Note also that the conversion I outline above was at best problematic. Laughter at a dwarf's expense was common and continued well after the early modern era. See Simon Dickie, *Cruelty and Laughter: Forgotten Comic Literature and the Unsentimental Eighteenth Century* (Chicago: University of Chicago Press, 2011), 47–72.

41. Edmund Spenser, *The Faerie Queene,* ed. A. C. Hamilton; text ed. Hiroshi Yamashita and Toshiyuki Suzuki. Revised 2nd edition. Harlow, UK: Pearson Education, 2001. All subsequent references are to this edition and appear within the text.

42. On the proliferation of narrators in *The Faerie Queene,* see Merrilee Cunningham, "The Interpolated Tale in Spenser's *Faerie Queene* Book I," *South Central Bulletin* 43, no. 4 (1983): 99–104.

43. Pauline Henley identified Florimell with Ireland in *Spenser in Ireland* (1928; repr. New York: Russell and Russell, 1969), 137–38. Her reading was defended and developed by Isabel E. Rathbone, "The Political Allegory of the Florimell-Marinell Story," *English Literary History* 12, no. 4 (1945): 279–89.

44. Paul Suttie, *Self-interpretation in 'The Faerie Queene'* (London: D. W. Brewer, 2006), 183.

45. Reed Way Dasenbrock, "Escaping the Squires' Double Bind in Books III and IV of *The Faerie Queene.*" *Studies in English Literature* 26, no. 1 (Winter 1986), 35.

46. The sexuality of the court dwarf is emphasized in a famous episode in Ariosto's *Orlando Furioso* (book 28), which Sir John Harrington translated into English. He was banned from court until he had translated the entire work, which he completed in 1592.

47. Hamilton, *Spenser Encyclopedia,* 192.

48. Jacqueline Miller, "The Courtly Figure: Spenser's Anatomy of Allegory," *Studies in English Literature* 31 (1991): 55.

49. James Nohrnberg, *The Analogy of 'The Faerie Queene'* (Princeton, NJ: Princeton University Press, 1976), 668.

50. Hamilton, *Spenser Encyclopedia,* 498–500. For the argument that Spenser is not disillusioned, see Jeffrey B. Morris, "To (Re)Fashion a Gentleman: Raleigh's Disgrace in Spenser's Legend of Courtesy," *Studies in Philology* 94, no. 1 (1997): 38–58.

51. Suttie, *Self-interpretation,* 212.

52. Harry Berger, Jr., "Displacing Autophobia in *The Faerie Queene,*" *English Literary Renaissance* 28 (March 1998): 163–82.

CHAPTER 2

Maternal Culpability in Fetal Defects

Aphra Behn's Satiric Interrogations of Medical Models

EMILY BOWLES

The abrupt and jarring proximity of desirability and so-called birth defects fascinated Aphra Behn and her circle. Dwarfs, giants, mute women, deaf women, disfigured women, and men and women with birthmarks, scars, and smallpox populate their writings and often take on central positions in the networks of sexuality and power circulating throughout the plays, poems, and prose narratives that were popular during the Restoration. Two prose narratives posthumously attributed to Behn foreground this crucial linkage of sexuality and disability. In "The Unfortunate Bride: Or, The Blind Lady a Beauty" and "The Dumb Virgin: Or, The Force of Imagination," Behn depicts women of extraordinary beauty that is contiguous to their disabilities.[1] Celesia in "The Unfortunate Bride" is "blind to all [her] riches, having been born without the use of sight, though in all other respects charming to a wonder," and Maria in "The Dumb Virgin" is "the most beautiful daughter" despite being "naturally and unfortunately dumb," the perfect counterpoint to her "distorted" and "bent" sister Belvideera.[2] The women's bodies engender desire despite and because of their failure to conform to standards of normalcy. Celesia falls in love with her cousin's lover Frankwit and marries him after Belvira dies in a freak accident; Maria and Belvideera compete with each other for a mysterious man who rapes Maria before it is revealed that he is their long-lost brother. Desire culminates in

43

and on the bodies of the visually and vocally impaired heroines, the blind and mute rather than the able-bodied Belvira or the disfigured Belvideera.

For Behn, desire circulates between able and disabled bodies in a way that draws attention to the seventeenth-century medical community's broader sense that women's bodies simply replicated male bodies in a defective, different form. During the late seventeenth and early eighteenth centuries, the continuum of what we now label gender, sex, and sexuality hinged on the notion that "sexual difference should be constructed as defect,"[3] a point not too far removed from Judith Butler's critique of sex as a "regulatory ideal whose materialization is compelled."[4] Aristotelian and Galenic models of human sex organs layered gendered traits on women's bodies, thereby organizing, regulating, and forcibly constructing the genitals. In *On the Usefulness of Parts of the Body,* Galen explains: "All the parts, then, that men have, women have too, the difference between them lying in only one thing . . . namely that in women the parts are within the body, whereas in men they are outside."[5] The womb was concealed, dark, duplicitous, confusing, weak, and invisible—all words that became inscribed on the body in order to reify broader patterns or associations between women and dishonesty; "a woman's anatomy is physically the imperfect inversion of a man's."[6] Felicity Nussbaum interprets medical depictions of women's sex organs as fitting neatly into misogynistic structures because they identify "women's flaws" as "natural and intrinsic to their sexual difference."[7] Behn's literalization of the relationship between defect and femaleness in "The Unfortunate Bride" and "The Dumb Virgin" draws attention to several interconnected components of the disabled female body in Restoration culture. Central to these texts is the question of who creates defect or disability. Does medical discourse make women into defective creatures, interpellating them into and as the identities prescribed by its language, or do physicians simply describe actual bodies?

Judith Butler's concept of corporeal signification offers a model for understanding the shifting relation between cultural scripts and embodiment. For Butler, the body is always beyond the boundary that demarcates its material surface. She explains in *Bodies That Matter* that bodies are "a kind of materialization governed by regulatory norms," and she suggests that much effort has been put into the false naturalization of categories and qualities that "fix the site" of the body.[8] The following analysis of "The Dumb Virgin" is based in part on Butler's ideas about the materiality of the body and its refusal to be disciplined, for the women in this novel (the mother and her two disabled daughters) are produced by the discourses assigned to both their exterior surfaces and interior organs. Behn selects heroines whose defects and disabilities simultaneously reinforce and undermine codes of gendered, sexualized, and corporeal correctness; she uses her disability narrative to satirize the social and scientific discourses that make some women more available and more desirable than others. Behn begins her critique of the discursive constitution of the sex-gender system with a hyperbolic, satiric invocation of the double-braided myths of seventeenth-century motherhood. She showcases her awareness of the limitations that her contemporaries' understanding of gender, sex, and sexuality placed on women's bodies via representation of the slippages between desirability and disability, and she crafts Belvideera and Maria as self-abnegations of their own forms. They are archetypes and exemplars of female sexuality because of the non-normative bodies that destroy their semantic and corporeal stylizations. The body morphologies that Behn sets up in "The Dumb Virgin" disrupt the systems that value and devalue them, but ultimately the female characters cannot exist outside of the language, prejudices, and inscriptions that demarcate and define their bodies as other, as different.

THE TREMENDOUS POPULARITY of Dorothy Leigh's *The Mothers Blessing* (1616) and Elizabeth Jocelin's *The Mothers Legacie* (1624) underscore the cultural value placed on motherhood during the seventeenth century. They also show how precarious a state motherhood was. The best mothers were often dead ones, as these posthumously published texts demonstrate. In most of Behn's writings, mothers are dead (usually having died in childbirth), or they suffer abortive births. The mother in "The Dumb Virgin" died in childbirth after having given birth first to Belvideera and subsequently to Maria. Yet her failure to take on a socially and medically sanctioned role as wife and mother is the central component of "The Dumb Virgin."

Advice books for women centered on matrimonial and maternal obligations, and seventeenth-century women were encouraged to think of their identities as contingent to these social roles. The mother in "The Dumb Virgin" is defined solely by her failed adherence to these expectations. She was "a beautiful and virtuous Lady, who had rendered [her husband Rinaldo] the happy Father of a Son" (341), but her desire for something beyond the scope of her domestic framework produces a series of corporeal failures that are replicated on and written onto her daughters' bodies. In the second paragraph of the narrative, "*Rinaldo*'s Lady" (the only name conferred on her in the text) "begg'd her Husbands [*sic*] permission to view" an "Island in the *Adriatick* Sea, about twenty leagues" from their home in Venice.[9] The virtuous lady has transformed, in this interval, into a desiring creature; she entreats her husband, "repeating her request" until he yields, "his love not permitting him the least shew of command" (341).

As is often the case in her writing, Behn shows a subtler inversion of gender binaries in relation to power. The male lover refuses to *command* his desiring beloved. Behn often draws on the tension between male political power and female sexual power. In *Love-Letters between a Nobleman and His Sister* (1684–87) and *Oroonoko* (1688), for instance, she shows women who transgress and attempt to acquire some degree of political agency only to take on singularly sexualized roles, and in her poem *The Disappointment* (1684), she develops a critique on the usual accordance of power and sexuality in pastoral and premature ejaculation poetry by spotlighting a woman whose sexual desires go unmet because of her male lover's impotence. By doing so, she wryly demonstrates that feminine sexual submissiveness is a falsely naturalized category. With Rinaldo's Lady, Behn constructs a satiric representation of the model by which female desire must remain controlled in order to reproduce normalcy.[10]

Behn alternates between aligning Rinaldo's Lady with her male companion, "a faithful Servant call'd *Gasper*" (342), and setting her up as a foil to the male characters, different and defective in her feelings, her needs, and her mind. Behn implicates Gasper in upholding a private/public split that ultimately leads to the downfall of his private or domestic world.[11] Yet she repeatedly invokes the cultural prescriptions that make this Rinaldo's Lady's fault. Rinaldo's Lady realizes she has lost everything:

> the heaviest load of misfortunes lay on *Rinaldo's* Lady, besides the loss of her liberty, the danger of her honour, the separation from her dear Husband, the care of her dear Infant wrought rueful distractions; she caught her Child in her arms, and with tears exorted thro fear and affection, she deplored the misfortune of her babe, the pretty Innocent smiling in the embraces of its Mother, shew'd that Innocence cou'd deride the persecution of fortune; at length she delivered the infant into the hands of *Gasper*, begging him to use all endeavours in its preservation, by owing it for his, when they fell into the hands of the enemy. (342)

Rinaldo's Lady recognizes that her desire to transgress or exceed the boundaries prescribed to her of wife and mother—her desire to leave her domestic space—has broken down the fictions of conjugal and maternal identity; she delivers her child into Gasper's hands (a word choice that suggests a rewriting of childbirth, redelivering her child so that he is reborn outside of her womb and her world).

Behn depicts Rinaldo's Lady as having a feminine, defective mind,[12] stating that "to a weak mind, that danger works still the strongest that's most in view; but when the Pyrate, who by this time had fetch'd them within shot, began to Fire; she seem'd pleas'd that her Infant was out of that hazard, tho exposed to a greater" (343). Rinaldo's Lady is impressionable, pliant, and (in Michel Foucault's sense of the term) docile.[13] Her "weak mind" can only ascertain its material and corporeal surroundings; it cannot project or think beyond that circumference, yet it is Rinaldo's Lady's yearning for more than this that produces, first, her desire to leave Venice and then her powerful imagination, which engenders her daughters' disabled bodies.

After she gives up her son, the force of her imagination impinges on what would have been understood as her obligation to maintain what Laura Gowing describes as the "ecosystem which determined their future child's health."[14] Her pregnancy is predicated on extreme emotion, for she learns that Gasper died and her son was lost: "her grief at the recital of this tragick story, had almost transported her to madness" (343–44). The *recital* of the *story* is what spirals Rinaldo's Lady toward madness, not an event, an action, or a body. In this way, Behn upholds the misogynistic system by which women are implicated in all fetal defects while critiquing the fact that this system contains and creates gender and power asymmetries. By repeating and reinscribing it, she also refuses and satirizes it. She shows that feminine defects of mind are written onto the bodies of children, a maneuver that replicates medical discourse while suggesting that women have a powerful ability to control what their bodies produce. The narratives that they believe are literally written onto the children contained in their womb (a metaphor that was popular with early modern booksellers and writers, many of whom compared publishing a book to giving birth). Belvideera and Maria embody Rinaldo's Lady's story—it is written on their bodies through their mother's form.

The storied nature of feminine defect is, in a sense, Rinaldo's Lady's failing but also her supposed natural state, which she imposes on her daughters by replicating, proliferating, and writing her defects onto their bodies. Belvideera's disfigurement is set up as the result of her imagination (so like a novel or a work of fiction and fancy): "upon its appearance their sorrows were redoubled, 'twas a Daughter, its limbs were distorted, its back bent, and tho the face was the freest from deformity, yet had it no beauty to recompense the dis-symmetry of the other parts" (344). Even though she is immediately called "a Daughter," this initial description of Belvideera insistently degenders her, which is true later in the plot when Belvideera's distorted, bent, and deformed body confounds Dangerfield. He attempts to read her body morphology at a masquerade but finds it does not correlate to any rules of embodiment that he has learned: "*Sir,* (said he) *if you are a man, know that I am one, and will not bear impertinence; but, if you are a Lady, Madam, as I hope in Heavens you are not, I must inform you, that I am under a vow, not to converse with any Female tonight*" (346).

Belvideera's birth literally produces Maria's disability. This is true in Behn's satiric invocation of medical discourse, for she attributes Maria's muteness to Rinaldo's Lady's sadness:

> the Mother grew very melancholy, rarely speaking, and not to be comforted by any diversion. She conceiv'd again, but no hopes of better fortune cou'd decrease her grief, which growing within her burden, eased her of both at once, for she died in Child-Birth, and left the most beautiful Daughter to the World that ever adorn'd *Venice,* but naturally and unfortunately dumb; which defect the learn'd attributed to the silence and melancholy of the Mother, as the deformity of the other was to the extravagance of her frights. (344)

The "learn'd," Behn's ironic tone here suggests, are not exactly subtle in their ways of thinking about the female mind or the female body. Here Behn clearly demarcates Rinaldo's Lady's mind, her pregnancies, and her daughters as the defamiliarized bodies of satire, and herself, a first-person but detached narrator, as a Menippean satirist bent on critiquing medical discourse in order to argue for the need for a new way of identifying difference.

THE DEFECTIVE WOMEN are the consequences of the mother's failure to follow prescribed rules concerning the control of her imagination and her emotions or—again borrowing from Gowing—her resistance to the perceptions about maternal responsibility that were designed to "control women's bodies and undermine women's autonomy."[15] Rinaldo's Lady felt too much for the loss of her son while pregnant with Belvideera, and she was too silent and melancholic during her third pregnancy. Along these lines, her identity as a mother functions as a part of a polymorphous body morphology. Her body is read by her husband/lover while simultaneously being read *onto* the body of her unborn child. The potential for women to engender disability begins with their sexuality and ends with maternity. As Gowing has suggested, "physical disabilities" could be read as having "sexual implications";[16] women's bodies were thought capable of deforming or disabling men's bodies through excessive, aggressive, or otherwise non-normative sexuality. At the same time, their bodies were the cultural signs of biological difference. Behn's fictions repeatedly yield up a sense of disjuncture between the apotheosis of motherhood and the socially proliferating reality that the female body was always already marked as defective and monstrous, as a faulty male body. The Galenic and Aristotelian medical discourses created women as close to monsters, thereby designating them as abject and other—a necessary tactic for excluding women from equal treatment with men in nonbiological sectors, and one that was arbitrary, linguistic, and falsely naturalized.[17]

Terming disabled bodies monstrous was typical during the seventeenth century, as the following excerpt from Jane Sharp's *The Midwives Book* (1671) makes clear:

> As for Monsters of all sorts to be formed in the womb all nations can bring some examples; Worms, Toades, Mice, Serpents, Gordonius saith, are common in Lumbardy, and so are those they call Soole kints in the Low Countries, which are certainly caused by the heat of their stones and menstrual blood to work upon in women that have had company with men; and these are sometimes alive with the infant, and when the Child is brought forth these stay behind, and the woman is sometimes thought to be with Child again; as I knew one there my self, which was after her childbirth delivered of two like Serpents, and both run away into the Burg wall as the women supposed, but it was at least three moneths after she was delivered of a Child, and they came forth without any loss of blood, for there was no after burden. Again in time of Copulation, Imagination ofttimes also produceth Monstrous births, when women look too much on strange objects.[18]

Sharp's emphasis here on *imagination* is specifically the site and subject of Behn's critique—she even gives "The Dumb Virgin" the subtitle "The Force of Imagination." Imagination should produce fiction, not real bodies, Behn suggests. Yet midwives and physicians continue to set up female imagination as a crucial and detrimental component of sexual difference, as in this 1740 tract on female sexuality, in which an anonymous physician explains, "That Excess of Love cannot be particularly ascribed to the same Heat, but to the Inconstancy of their Imagination, or rather to the Providence of Nature, that has made them to serve us for Playtoys after our more serious Occupations."[19]

Monstrosity was often literally assigned to sex organs. In *The Midwives Book,* monstrosity is aligned with a body's refusal to correspond to expectations:

Amongst false conceptions all monstrous births may be reckoned, for a monster saith Aristotle is an error of nature failing of the end she works for, by some corrupted principle; sometimes this happens when the sex is imperfect, that you cannot know a boy from a girl; they call these Hermaphrodites: there is but one kind of Women Hermaphrodites, when a thing like a Yard stands in the place of the Clitoris above the top of the genital, and bears out in the bottom of the share-bone; sometimes in boys there is seen a small privy part of the woman above the root of the Yard, and in girls a Yard is seen at the Lesk or in the Peritoneum. But three ways a boy may be of doubtful sex.[20]

Sharp's construction of "monstrous births" as the result of female excesses (such as the imagination) or actions (looking at unpleasant objects) is not unique to her writing; she has consolidated much classical and current medical knowledge in *The Midwives Book* in order to make it accessible. As Caroline Bicks and Elaine Hobby have both argued, Sharp performs a unique and decidedly woman-oriented task when she publishes *The Midwives Book* by ensuring that knowledge of women's bodies is available to them and to the male and female midwives who were responsible for their reproductive health. But she reports on and even reinscribes many of the biases comprising the system of medical knowledge that was available to her, thereby inscribing bodies with the limitations placed on them by discourse and replicating the process of insisting on falsely naturalized binaries of monstrous and normal, of male and female.[21]

As mentioned above, Belvideera's deformity aligns her with monstrosity and, in Dangerfield's reading of her, with androgyny or mixed-sex identity. At the same time, Belvideera and Maria uphold a complex system of sexual exchange in the narrative. Both women's bodies fascinate Dangerfield, and his response to them becomes part of Behn's larger and more systematic critique of the ways these women have been situated as other or different. First they are women, essentially reducible to the construction of the female body as an inversion of or defective variation on the male body. Sexual difference is their most essential categorical inversion, and the one that corresponds to the largest organizing binary. Then they are inversions of each other. One is externally "distorted," the other "Beautiful"; one is witty, the other dumb. Their proximity to one another produces and exacerbates their sexual desirability, for just as sexual difference within a heterosexual matrix demands difference, so too does the privileging beauty over wit or vice versa, for Dangerfield vacillates between these women: "his love was divided between the beauty of one Lady, and wit of another, either of which he loved passionately, yet nothing cou'd satisfy him, but the possibility of enjoying both" (349). Crucially Behn does not "unwittingly replicate . . . the idea of woman as a defect of nature";[22] instead she satirizes it and sets up an economy in which women are in fact more highly valued for their defects, until these defects are pushed to their most intense and dramatic point. Their bodies underline how female desirability is always underscored by a "continuum of female disorder and 'normal' feminine practice" rather than a disruption or divergence between the disordered and normal body.[23]

EXISTING OUTSIDE of the spectrum of bodies understood as normal, Belvideera and Maria develop beauties that expand their defects rather than correct them. After their mother's death, Belvideera and Maria receive their father's full support and attention: "their defects not lessening his inclination but stirring up his endeavours in supplying the defaults of Nature by the industry of Art" (344). This tension between nature and art, defaults and industry, function as the underlying pattern for the remainder of "The Dumb Virgin," and Behn explores their relationship in order to heighten her readers' awareness of how highly inscriptive "defaults of Nature" are, even when they are culturally set up as essential, unchangeable, and natural.

Belvideera's desire for intellectual mastery suggests an attempt to balance her corporeal defects with mental perfections:

> The eldest called *Belvideera,* was indefatigably addicted to study, which she had improv'd so far, that by the sixteenth year of her age, she understood all the *European* Languages, and cou'd speak most of 'em, but was particularly pleas'd with the *English,* which gave me the happiness of many hours conversation with her; and I may ingenuously declare, 'twas the most pleasant I ever enjoy'd, for besides a piercing wit, and depth of understanding peculiar to herself, she delivered her sentiments with that easiness and grace of speech, that it charm'd all her hearers. (344)

Belvideera's study results in a vast knowledge of languages and sociability, piercing wit, and charm. Her knowledge helps her enter into society rather than making her ostracized from it, in some ways making her character, like Angellica Bianca in *The Rover,* exhibit allegorical features of Behn's ideas about female authorship.

Translation was one of Behn's most marketable and sociable of skills; her deft turns of phrase, her confidence, her originality, and her knowledge helped her become as key a player in male intellectual culture as she was in the commercial world of the stage. Her facility with French and her engaging Latin paraphrases earned her the praise and friendship of John Dryden and Nahum Tate.[24] In her translation of book 6 of Abraham Cowley's *Of Plants* (1689),[25] she sets out one of her most direct entreaties for fame and respect in a section set off with the phrase "The Translatress in her own Person speaks":

> I by a double right thy Bounties claim,
> Both from my Sex, and in *Apollo*'s Name:
> Let me with *Sappho* and *Orinda* be
> Oh ever sacred Nymph, adorn'd by thee;
> And give my Verses Immortality. (325)

Belvideera demonstrates a similarly acute power over language, but her unpublished, spoken discourse requires mediation in order to outlast her. Behn's narrator, like her narrator in *Oroonoko,* must confer immortality on her.

Maria's voicelessness directly opposes Belvideera's conversational skill and Behn's published writing. Mute, Maria seems most clearly to conform to the expectations seventeenth-century society placed on beautiful, marriageable women. She is docile and silent. However, her corporeally encoded and enforced silence leads her to learn or perhaps even create an alternate discourse:

> she had improv'd her silent conversation with her Sister so far, that she was understood by her, as if she spoke, and I remember this Lady was the first I saw use the significant way of discourse by the Fingers; I dare not say 'twas she invented it (tho it probably might have been an invention of these ingenious Sisters) but I am positive none before her ever brought it to that perfection. ("Dumb Virgin" 345)

Because she is unwilling to allow her disability to remove her from discourse, she develops a system for "silent conversation with her sister" that becomes crucial to their bond and to Belvideera's ability to confer Maria's meaning to outsiders. Because she is thought to know Maria's otherwise unintelligible meanings, she has the power to represent her to others. She engineers Dangerfield's first interpretations of her, she applies meanings that she wants to the syntax of Maria's body, and she gives Maria reasons to envy "her Sister the advantage of Speech" (348).

The sisters complement each other on some very basic levels—they are the ugly and the beautiful, the witty conversationalist and the mute woman, the mind and the body. Set in binaries, they prove inseparable. Dangerfield loves them both. Belvideera's "Tongue claim'd an equal share in his heart with *Maria*'s eyes" (347). Their pathologies are subordinated to their perfections; their desirability comes from the traits that have been amplified because of their disabilities. The text reaches its climax when Maria's body becomes the focus of Dangerfield's gaze. He sees her in her nightgown and finds himself "like *Venus* caught in *Vulcan*'s net, but 'twas the Spectator, not she was captivated" (351). Vision becomes a destabilizing power, like Rinaldo's Lady's imagination. Dangerfield sees what he desires, and he rapes Maria. Here all of the points of Behn's satire converge, for she brings together the traits most valued in women by patriarchal society (silence, beauty, passivity, and visual/corporeal availability) under the male gaze. After her rape, Maria learns that Dangerfield is her brother. He kills himself, and Maria speaks: "the working force of her anguish racking at once all the passages of her breast, by a violent impulse broke the ligament that doubled in her tongue, and she burst out with this exclamation; *Oh! Incest, Incest*" (359). The word "force" refers to the subtitle of the text, "The Force of Imagination," and Behn draws together the dead mother and her now-dead daughter with their shared balancing of this clause—Rinaldo's Lady is *Imagination;* Maria, *Force.*

HAVE FEMALE DEFECT and difference produced this tragic end, or does Behn accord blame to the systems that codify and produce female bodies as defective? The medical discourses that invented Rinaldo's Lady's "Monstrous births" (for Behn does see these as invented rather than described by medical discourse) and the sociosexual discourses that valorize the compensatory fictions produced on Belvideera's and Maria's bodies are part of the same set of practices, and the narrative offers a way of understanding how much of disability, female sexuality, and femininity is a product of the imagination.

Although Behn offers some real material details about the nature of disability, its causes, and its "correctability," "The Dumb Virgin" is most instructive in its modification of and response to the marginalization of disabled, defective bodies. Belvideera's physical deformity takes on some stereotypical features typical of Behn's antiheroines, for she is presented as duplicitous and bent internally in ways that match her exterior form. At the same time, she takes on the highest level of intellectual perfection in the text. Maria's beauty and her voicelessness, on the other hand, mark her as conforming to patterns of sexual value that she disrupts by learning sign language, engaging in conversation with her sister, and finally making herself unwittingly but corporeally available to Dangerfield.

With the attention that she pays to the construction of disability by seventeenth-century texts, Behn gives readers a clear sense of how disability was constructed by doctors, midwives, and even aesthetic theorists during the period while simultaneously highlighting the gendering of defects. The very literal and specific attention Behn plays to disability in this narrative has larger implications for the study of her writing, for she experiments with narrative tactics, allegories of authorship, theories of translation, and characterization that are contained in her more canonical works. Furthermore, her incorporation of medical discourse in these texts—especially Galenic theories and material about pregnancy and childbirth from books such as Sharp's *The Midwives Book*—shows the dialogue that exists between her writing and documents about female biology and disability. Putting Behn's writing into conversation with Sharp's, as well as with other texts about the body and its reproduction, helps demonstrate the many sites of Behn's satire and her attempt to reproduce through her fiction a space for the interrogation of discourses that rendered women as other, different, and defective.

Notes

1. I refer to these generically complex prose narratives as novels here because, first, they receive that label on their title page in the original sense of newness or novelty. Additionally, Behn employs literary and stylistic conventions of the novel, especially in her experimentation with narrative voice, intertextuality, and dialogue in these texts.

2. Aphra Behn, "The Dumb Virgin: Or, The Force of Imagination" and "The Unfortunate Bride: Or, The Blind Lady a Beauty," in *The Works of Aphra Behn*, vol. 3, edited by Janet Todd (London: William Pickering, 1995), 327 and 344, respectively. Subsequent references to these works will be to this edition and will appear within the text.

3. Felicity Nussbaum, "Dumb Virgins, Blind Ladies, and Eunuchs: Fictions of Defect," in *Defects: Engendering the Modern Body*, ed. Helen Deutsch and Felicity Nussbaum (Ann Arbor: University of Michigan Press, 2000), 31. I follow Deutsch and Nussbaum in retaining the word "defect" as period-specific terminology "with eighteenth-century currency" (Nussbaum, "Dumb Virgins," 35).

4. Judith Butler, *Bodies That Matter: On the Discursive Limits of Sex* (New York: Routledge, 1993), 1.

5. Galen, *On the Usefulness of the Parts of the Body*, trans. Margaret Tallmadge May (Ithaca, NY: Cornell University Press, 1968), 628.

6. Martha A. Brožyna, *Gender and Sexuality in the Middle Ages: A Medieval Source Documents Reader* (Jefferson, NC: McFarland, 2005), 141.

7. Nussbaum, "Dumb Virgins," 32.

8. Butler, *Bodies That Matter*, 16.

9. Although (and because) it is awkward to refer to her as "Rinaldo's Lady," I have

chosen to use this name throughout my paper to highlight the contingency of her identity, her namelessness, and her subordination.

10. Elizabeth V. Young provides a compelling overview of Behn's status as a satirist in "De-Gendering Genre: Aphra Behn and the Tradition of English Verse Satire," *Philological Quarterly* 81 (2002): 185–205. This study provides a much-needed corollary to broader, male-dominated trends in satire and helps showcase the ways in which seventeenth-century satire was constantly subverting the categories that were in the process of being codified by John Dryden and others in literary theory.

11. The narrative ends with incestuous sex between Rinaldo's son and Maria, followed by the death of Maria and her brother.

12. Although I refer to "Behn" as the author and ostensibly the narrator of this text, I want to emphasize that it is her fictional narrative persona rather than Behn's actual, historical self that enters into this text. As in *Love-Letters between a Nobleman and His Sister, Oroonoko, The Fair Jilt,* and other prose narratives, Behn's narrator enters into this story in passages like these: "this Lady was the first I saw"; "the two Sisters sent presently for me"; and "I was pleas'd to find so great an example of English bravery" (Nussbaum, "Dumb Virgin," 345). At the same time, the narrator is not an autobiographical self but instead a fictional character in the text who takes on the role of the Menippean satirist, not lampooning or using invective but offering modulated critiques of the system her heroines inhabit. When I use "Behn" rather than "Behn's narrator" throughout this study, it is for simplicity rather than to flatten or ignore this important point.

13. That is, her body is represented as a site of coercions that manipulate "its elements, its gestures, its behaviors"; see Michel Foucault, *Discipline and Punish* (New York: Vintage, 1979), 138.

14. Laura Gowing, *Common Bodies: Women, Touch and Power in Seventeenth-century England* (New Haven, CT: Yale University Press, 2003), 122.

15. Ibid..

16. Ibid., 115.

17. Rosi Braidotti has suggested that "woman as a sign of difference is monstrous," which is precisely how deformity and disability were set up in seventeenth-century discourse; see "Mothers, Monsters, and Machines," in *Writing on the Body,* ed. Katie Conboy, Nadia Medina, and Sarah Stanbury (New York: Columbia University Press, 1997), 65. Felicity Nussbaum argues that Sarah Scott crafts an alignment of deformity with womanhood in *Millenium Hall* (1762) and that women's observations of harems, as in Mary Wortley Montagu's *Turkish Embassy Letters* (1762), inscribe the body of the Other woman with signs of alterity, difference, and even monstrosity; see *Torrid Zones: Maternity, Sexuality, and Empire in Eighteenth-Century English Narratives* (Baltimore: Johns Hopkins University Press, 1995). Thus, according to Sara Mendelson and Patricia Crawford, "the female body was one of the most significant sites where contemporary medical theorists wrote the text of women's otherness, weakness, inferiority, and passivity"; see *Women in Early Modern England* (New York: Oxford University Press, 1998), 18.

18. Jane Sharp, *The Midwives Book* (London, 1671), 11–12. Available through the Brown Women Writers Project: http://www.wwp.brown.edu.

19. Quoted in Vivien Jones, ed., *Women in the Eighteenth Century: Constructions of Femininity* (New York: Routledge, 1990), 82.

20. Sharp, *Midwives Book,* 115.

21. See Caroline Bicks, "Stones Like Women's Paps: Revising Gender in Jane Sharp's *Midwives Book*," *Journal for Early Modern Cultural Studies* 7, no. 2 (2007): 1–27; Elaine Hobby, "'To God Alone Be All Praise and Glory' or 'Serving Mine Own Sex First'?: Nicholas Culpepper, Jane Sharp, and the Restoration Midwifery Manual," in *The Female Wits: Women and Gender in Restoration Literature and Culture* (Huelva, Spain: Universidad de Huelva, 2006), 249–63; and "'The Head of This Countefeit Yard Is Called Tertigo' or, 'It Is Not Hard Words That Perform the Work': Recovering Early-Modern Women's Writing." *Women's Writing, 1550–1750* (Bundoora, Australia: Meridian, 2001), 13–23.

22. Nussbaum, "Dumb Virgins," 38.

23. Susan Bordo, "The Body and the Reproduction of Femininity," in Conboy et al., 93.

24. Dryden and Tate's praise of Behn's translations always inscribes them in her femaleness, her femininity, and her gendered education.

25. Abraham Cowley, *Of Plants*, translated by Aphra Behn, in *Works*, vol. 1, 311–53. The translation is part of a larger, multiauthor compilation of translations of Cowley's works "by several hands." In his preface to the text, Nahum Tate notes that Behn's translation, with its personalized elements like the passage above, "o'er tops all the others" (quoted in editor's notes to *Of Plants*, 343).

CHAPTER 3

Disability Humor and the Meanings of Impairment in Early Modern England

DAVID M. TURNER

Among the jokes in *A Hundred Merry Tales* (1526), often regarded as one of the first native English jest books, was a story that described an encounter between a courtier and a carter. In the paradoxical style made fashionable by Renaissance humanists, the courtier "in derision praised the carter's back, legs, and other members of his body marvellously," meticulously ridiculing every aspect of the man's deformed frame. After enduring this humiliation, the carter told the courtier that there was "another property" of his body that he had failed to notice. Looking "aside over his shoulder upon the courtier," the carter told him, "Lo, Sir, this is my property, I have a wall eye [squint] in my head," a sensory imperfection that in fact gave him a clear-eyed view of the character defects of others, "for I never look over my shoulder this wise but I lightly espy a knave."[1]

Humor provides an intriguing insight into representations of disability in the early modern period. The treatment of disability as a source of laughter is one way in which scholars have demarcated attitudes toward disabled people in premodern societies from those of "enlightened" modernity. Mockery of ugliness, disfigurement, or deformity is often taken as evidence of the "unkindness" with which physical difference was treated in preindustrial societies.[2] However, this kind of comic production has received relatively little analysis in its own right.[3] Focusing on physical and sensory deviations from the normative, this chapter uses a variety of prose jest books produced in sixteenth- and seventeenth-century England to explore how disability humor shaped meanings of embodied difference. Although jokes have historically worked to denigrate disabled people by exaggerating their "otherness," the ludicrous possibilities of joking situations gave humor the potential to interrogate conventional wisdom about bodily norms. In the early modern period, as we shall see, comic narratives might invoke disability in a variety of contexts, to explore issues around the causes of disability and the social experiences of disabled people, as well as to explore a wider range of concerns, including gender and authority.

Existing scholarship paints a largely negative portrait of the treatment of disability in early modern popular culture. Since ancient times, deformity had occupied a central place in theories of laughter.[4] Thomas Hoby's 1561 translation of Baldassare Castiglione's *Book of the Courtier* explained that "laughing matters arise of . . . a certain deformitie or ill favourdnesse, because a man laugheth onlie at those matters that are disagreeing in themselves."[5] In the seventeenth century, Thomas Hobbes famously extended this connection in his description of laughter as "sudden glory" caused "by the apprehension of some deformed thing in another by comparison whereof" people "suddenly applaud themselves."[6] Although "deformity" was intended to be interpreted broadly, drawing on Aristotle's definition of the "ugly" as an exaggerated version of the self, and referring as much to follies of character and vices as it did to physical anomaly, there can be no doubt that "deformed" or disabled bodies were ripe for comic exploitation. Deformity's association with sin and corruption made the impaired body a powerful image in lampoons, satires, and defamatory verses, perhaps most famously those produced in the aftermath of the death of Robert Cecil in 1612, in which the former Lord Chancellor's "crooked" back came to symbolize a range of faults, from political corruption to adultery.[7] As a corollary, historians and literary scholars have pointed to the ways in which the deaf, blind, "crippled," aged, and "ugly" were routinely presented as figures of derision in the period's popular culture. For example, in his study of mid-eighteenth-century jest books Simon Dickie argues that disabled people were "standing jokes . . . almost automatic figures of fun"; running contrary to the humanitarian forces of the Enlightenment, which increasingly cast disabled people as objects of pity and sympathy. Laughter at such jokes may have served as a "safety valve," as a means of discharging the fears of the able-bodied about physical degeneration, while simultaneously asserting their superiority over the "otherness" of "deformed" and impaired people.[8]

There can be no doubt that in the early modern period (as today) jests could be cruel toward disabled people. But this derisive treatment needs to be examined more closely and put into context. Although Roger Lund has shown how certain nonstandard bodies, especially "crooked" forms, especially lent themselves to mockery in the eighteenth century thanks to their offense to aesthetic sensibilities, there has been little attempt to assess the similarities and differences in the comic portrayal of different types of physical and sensory disability in the early modern period as a whole.[9] Consequently, existing scholarship tends to view jokes involving disabled characters in a rather uniform way, as automatically raising the same kind of mocking laughter. As Dickie suggests, a good deal may be learned by exploring the discursive strategies by which certain physical signs—a withered leg, a crooked back—were represented in a comic way.[10] Furthermore, recent work on eighteenth-century humor regards cruel jokes at the expense of nonstandard bodies as a remnant of older comic forms that survived the "civilizing process" of the Enlightenment.[11]

Yet the portrayal of disability in jest books of the sixteenth and seventeenth centuries—and its social and cultural context—remains relatively unexplored. Renaissance handbooks of "civility" were just as concerned with the propriety of laughing at physical difference as their Enlightenment counterparts. Authors of sixteenth- and seventeenth-century guides to gentlemanly conduct frequently condemned the incivility of jesting that mocked others in company or put them ill at ease.[12] According to della Casa's *Galateo,* "they that scoffe at any man, that is Deformed, ill shapen, leane, little, or a Dwarfe" were "unworthy to beare the name of an honest gentleman."[13] As the joke that began this chapter illustrates, the mockery of physical difference was not entirely unquestioned in jest books themselves. Ultimately in that story the tables are turned, the humble carter has the last laugh, using his visual impairment to deliver a killer line that stops his arrogant social superior in his tracks. The moral was clear: "By this tale a man may see that he that used to deride and mock other folks is sometimes himself more derided and mocked."[14] As this chapter will show, although jest books frequently ignored warnings against using deformity or other forms of bodily anomaly as a pretext for laughter, it is by no means evident that all disabled figures were "automatic figures of fun." Rather than exploring jests purely in terms of their function, the emphasis of this analysis is on the various ways in which authors tried to make disability or deformity funny, and what these narratives tell us about disability discourse in the early modern period.

However, jest books present problems of interpretation. Repeating, adapting, and often plagiarizing material from other collections or foreign and historical sources, jest books are problematic sources for examining "attitudes" toward disability in early modern England since it is often difficult to ascertain whose "attitudes" they were reflecting, or indeed how they were read. Indeed, some of the common themes of this literature, such as the cruel gulling of blind people or the stereotype of the greedy or false disabled mendicant, have their antecedents in medieval ballads, farces, and fabliaux.[15] Late sixteenth- and early seventeenth-century jest books ranged in style from relatively short biographical accounts of trickster figures printed in black letter type to lengthier collections of jokes and epigrams that, judging from the sophistication of some of their allusions, may have envisioned an educated middling or elite audience.[16] As Dickie concedes, the popularity of derisive treatments of the old, "deformed," and disabled in eighteenth-century jest books may have been due to the fact that the comic world of the jest provided a license to laugh at subjects no longer deemed acceptable in polite society. The enjoyment of a comic story was different from taunting a "cripple" or blind beggar in the street.[17] Rather than viewing jests as straightforward reflections of societal "attitudes," or of social practices concerning disability, it may be more helpful to see them as participants in a debate about different meanings of disability, as attempts to provide a framework through which to interpret bodily differences by exploring the ludicrous possibilities of the body's excesses and deficits.

THE BODY'S manifold opportunities for evoking laughter are well documented in Anthony Copley's *Wits, Fits and Fancies: Or, a Generall and Serious Collection of the Sententious Speeches, Answers, Jests and Behaviour of all Sortes of Estate, from the Throne to the Cottage* (1614), which provides a useful starting point for this discussion. The comedy of corporeality was represented by jests about "Face and Skarres," beards, noses, extremes of bodily size and appearance, "of Fat and Grosse" and "of Leanes" and "of Talness and Littlenes," of "blindness," and also "crookedness and lameness." Although "crookedness" and "lameness" might proceed from a variety of causes and have different effects, they were yoked together by the author of this and other jest books. They were categorized as markers of physical difference akin to other extremities of excess or deficit such as fatness, thinness, tallness, or shortness, rather than as "disabilities" that conferred a special identity on their bearer. First and foremost, the "crooked" or "lame" body provided an opportunity for authors of jests to prove their verbal creativity through the production of puns and word play.[18] Contrasts between normative "straight" or "upright" bodies and deviant "crooked" ones were particularly common. In one jest, the Duke of Medina Celi, "having a crooked back'd lady to his wife," asked a jester for his opinion on his "stately new hall at Madredejos," to which he replied that it was indeed "a stately hall . . . and . . . tall, yet cannot . . . your Lady stand upright therein." In another story, a "crookback'd plaintiff" at law asked the judge in his case to "see him right" (which also meant to straighten); the judge replied, "Wel may I heare you, but right I cannot doe ye." In a variation on this theme, "One quarrelling with a lame man, threatned that he would set his foot straight ere he had don[e]." The "lame" man answered, "In so doing I will accompt you my friend" for restoring his body to a normative state.[19]

As a hybrid of the familiar and the strange, the disabled body was a fertile topic for witty wordplay, extended metaphor, and comic resemblances. In *Wits, Fits and Fancies,* "One seeing a very misshapen and crooked person in the streete said, that he had a Camell to his nurse."[20] Dwarfs were sometimes referred to as "apes," and other deformed or crooked people as "monkeys."[21] Such analogies marked out deformity as stigma, a spoiled identity that threatened to contaminate the integrity of the species itself.[22] The notion that a "crooked" body might be formed in the maternal nurturing of a human by a camel placed this reading of the nonstandard body in the context of species pollution, at a time when animal cross-breeding was a recognized phenomenon.[23] In this way, "dwarfs" and the "crooked" seemed to question the status of humanity. Misshapen bodies also resembled the devil.[24] The Norfolk gentleman Sir Nicholas Le Strange recorded in his manuscript jest book a tale of a Cambridge "Scholler that had very deformed leggs and Feete," who, when he revealed his feet to a shoemaker, caused the artisan to startle "as if the Divell had offerd him his cloven foote."[25]

This blurring of boundaries between human and animal, and the role of the supernatural, drew on ideas familiar from early modern accounts of monstrous births.[26] However, other jests drew analogies between "crooked" or impaired bodies and mundane, everyday objects. A hunched back was likened to a person carrying a load; a blind eye was described as a shuttered window.[27] The joke in which the straight lines of architecture were contrasted with the house's "crooked" occupier who could not "stand upright" within it served to describe the "deformed" body as lacking in order, form, and symmetry, an "error" of creation or manufacture rather than a prodigious wonder. In another example, "One seeing a man of excellent learning, crooked and deformed in body, said, Lord, what a *poor Cottage doth yonder good wit inhabit.*"[28] By drawing a distinction between the man's qualities of mind and the "deformed" body he "inhabited," the jest presented a challenge to thinking about bodily anomaly that viewed deformity as an index of the mind. As Bacon pointed out in his essay "Of Deformity," in spite of there being a natural "consent between the body and the mind," "deformed" people might, "if they be of spirit," prove to be "excellent persons," as Aesop,

Socrates, and other historical notables proved.[29] Thus, while some jests might exploit familiar connections between the "deformed" and the "monstrous," others might use different analogies to suggest that such associations were not inevitable.

While the treatment of the non-normative in jests shared common features, different types of impairment were the occasion for different types of comic scenario. The ways in which deaf people might mishear others and provide inappropriate responses in conversation provided much amusement, particularly by showing the permeable boundaries between civility and rudeness. *A Banquet of Jeasts* (1630) described how a young gentleman had, in order to make his dinner companions "merry," made a mock toast to his deaf "hostesse," drinking to her "and all her friends," namely, "the Bawdes and Whores in *Turnebull Street*," to which the woman returned thanks, "I know you remember your Mother, your Aunt, and those good Gentlewomen your sisters."[30] Sir Nicholas Le Strange recorded several variations on this theme, perhaps with the aim of using them to delight guests at his own table. In one, which he attributed to his father, Thomas Getting had "dranke to an old woman here one Christmas, and instead of a Drinking salutation, sayd, kisse mine arse Besse," to which she "being very Deafe, and suspecting no ill, answered, I thanke you hartily Thomas; and Dorothy too I pray (which was Thomas Getting's wife)." In another (supplied by his mother), Sir Henry Sidney was said to have toasted an old, deaf woman with the phrase "Ile be your bedfellow this night," to which she replied, "I thanke your good Worshipp, with all my Hart, Sir you know what's good for an old Woman."[31]

The bawdiness of these jokes, and their focus on the impairments of elderly, deaf women in particular, show ways in which jests might employ disability to reinforce the dominant misogyny of early modern humor. The sexuality of elderly and disabled individuals was considered transgressive, and laughter at jokes of this kind may have served to restore normative values that classified desire as the prerogative of the young and physically whole. In jests about sex, marriage, and cuckoldry hierarchies of disablement were mapped onto hierarchies of domestic authority, in the process revealing how the meanings of impairment might be distinctly gendered.[32] It was a familiar adage that a deaf husband, unable to hear his wife's scolding, and a blind wife, unable to see her husband's faults, made for a "peaceable life in marriage."[33] Other disabilities were presented as assisting in women's subjection. A young gentleman being asked "what he meant to marry so deafe a Gentlewoman" replied, "Because I hop'd she was also dumbe."[34]

Yet, while it was suggested (albeit ironically) that deaf men might enjoy relatively peaceful marriages, in many cases physical or sensory disability was seen to compromise men's authority. In the domestic economy of early modern England men's disability might lead to a renegotiation of household roles and division of labor, giving their wives greater responsibility in the running of homes and businesses, and in controlling resources.[35] According to Lindsey Row-Heyveld, the perception of disability as "effeminizing" grew in the late sixteenth century as pre-Reformation notions of disability as a spiritually ennobling condition, and the spiritual practice whereby the disabled poor might sell prayers or affirmations of salvation, were swept away by religious reformers and harsher regimes of social welfare that cast many disabled people as passive objects of charity.[36] Patriarchal authority rested on a fundamental assumption of able-bodiedness. As Alexandra Shepard has shown, men in early modern England did not benefit equally from the "patriarchal dividend," and cuckold jokes regularly underscored male anxieties about the ways in which their authority might be diminished through their own bodily shortcomings or deficits by casting wronged husbands as infirm or disabled.[37] Sexual impotence, a common cause of wifely infidelity in early modern cuckold jokes, was itself described as a physical impairment or "defect," a handicap that compromised men's ability to control their wives.[38] The stereotypical victim of cuckolding, the elderly man married to a young woman, had his horning "justified" by reference to his physical infirmities.

For example, the seventeenth-century ballad *The Cuckold's Calamity, Or the Old Usurer Plunder'd out of his Gold by His Young Wife,* has the husband lament, "Oh! She took me for my gold, tho' I'm goughty, lame and old."[39] The susceptibility of blind husbands to cuckolding was a theme found in medieval texts such as Chaucer's *Merchant's Tale,* and early modern jests similarly reflected on the dangers of visual impairment to men's sexual honor.[40] *Wits, Fits and Fancies* related a tale of "an honest man that had but one eie and a queane to his wife" who was in bed with a "knave" one evening when he returned home. Hearing her husband's voice, the woman hid her lover and bade her husband enter the bedchamber, telling him that she had had a dream in which his sight had been restored. In order to see whether it was true, she placed her hand over his "seeing eie," asking him whether he could "discern any thing with the other," providing the cover that allowed her lover to escape.[41]

The juxtaposition of different types of impairment was another common theme in jest books.[42] This was partly a reflection of the incongruity that many early modern jests used to achieve their comic effect: if disabled characters might be considered objects of mockery in their own right, then the yoking together of "opposite" types of bodily difference such as blindness and lameness, or people of small stature with the exceedingly tall, might enhance the comic spectacle. But juxtaposition also emphasized the incompleteness of disabled bodies that prevented disabled characters from being fully accepted as persons in their own right. In jest books and other writings the contrast between sensory and physical disabilities provides a means of exploring the qualities of mind and body. William Basse's *Helpe to Discourse* (1619), which mixed jests with questions and answers on more serious topics, used a story about a blind man and a "cripple" to answer the questions of whether the soul or the body "have the greater hand in sinne, and why for the sinne of the one they should be together jointly punished." The owner of an orchard, it related, had two keepers, "one of the which is lame, and the other blinde." The "cripple" spotted some golden apples hanging on a tree and desired for himself, but not being able to take them, lacking "legges to beare him to them," he asked his blind companion for help. Having established that the blind man "would not sticke [i.e., hesitate] to pull the apples if [he] had but . . . eyes to see them," they hatched a scheme to take the fruit. Riding on the blind man's shoulders, the "cripple" was able to snatch the apples, which the two men ate. Upon discovery of the theft, the master of the orchard "punisheth both with one equall punishment as they had both deserved." Thus the story gave the example that the "wise Governour exempt neither body nor soule, because they both lend their furtherance to sinne."[43] The incompleteness and physical or sensory deficits of the two men provided serviceable metaphors for the body and soul and for showing their interdependence. Aphra Behn similarly made the contrast between physical and sensory disability central to her novel *The Dumb Virgin* (1700), which focused on the rivalry between two disabled sisters—the witty yet "deformed" Belvideera and the beautiful yet mute Maria—for the handsome suitor Dangerfield. Whereas the young women's contrasting disabilities gave Behn the opportunity to compare the appeal of the qualities of mind against the beauties of the body, the plot's tragic and sensational denouement in which Maria gives in to the sexual advances of Dangerfield only to discover that he is her long-lost brother, followed by the deaths of all but Belvideera who is left a miserable recluse, sent out a message once again of the dangerous desires of disabled people.[44]

The juxtaposition of disabled characters in jest books might have taken further inspiration from the alliances between paupers of all kinds—including disabled beggars—that occurred in early modern England. The mutual dependence of blind and physically disabled beggars was noted elsewhere in early modern English culture and society. In 1706, for example, indigent companions Henry Banford, "a Blind Man," and William Jones, "a Lame Man," were indicted at the Old Bailey for highway robbery.[45] Jest books were interested in the stresses of daily life, and they contributed to a growing body of writing in the late sixteenth and early seventeenth centuries concerning encounters with the disabled poor. Although begging was not the sole lens through which authors of jest books approached disability, the mendicancy of the blind and "crippled," and interactions between beggars and "respectable" pedestrians, provided a context for the discussion of disability in this literature. If authors of conduct literature questioned the "scornful" treatment of the unfortunate in jests, concerns about the veracity of impairments displayed by disabled beggars—which in turn raised questions about the "truth" of all bodily infirmities—appeared to justify some of the cruelest humor at the expense of the impaired. Suspicions about the disabled poor had been present in the Middle Ages, but, according to Row-Heyveld, concerns about imposture intensified during the Reformation. The declining belief in the holiness of poverty and allied notion of disability as a spiritually ennobling condition, which we discussed earlier, together with the exposure of sham disabled mendicants in cony-catching pamphlets, and Tudor welfare legislation that criminalized those "sturdy beggars" who shunned work, served to focus attention on the criminality and imposture of the disabled poor.[46]

In *The Booke of Bulls* (1636), two men "passing the street in a serious discourse" are interrupted by a "dumb man" who "begg'd of them after his mute manner." Furious at this interruption, one of the men threatened to "kick him" to send him on his way. "O fie," said his companion, "will you kicke a dumbe man? Is hee dumb, repli'd he, why did he not tell me so then?"[47] *Oxford Jests* (1671) related how "one losing one of his arms in the Wars" was refused alms by a passerby who said, "I'll give you nothing, you are no Gentleman, you cannot shew your arms."[48] Demanding that the dumb beggar speak or the maimed soldier "shew arms" reflected a pervasive suspicion about the truth of impairment and the honesty of the disabled poor. The cruelty of these jokes also reflected the violence (threatened or real) used by the authorities to unmask or punish fraudulent disabled beggars. In Shakespeare's *2 Henry VI,* the feigned lameness of the pilgrim at St. Albans, who appears before the king in act 2, scene 1, is revealed when he runs away to escape the beadle's whip. The powers invested in the authorities, such as magistrates and the officers of London's Bridewell, to physically search those who were believed to be counterfeiting disabilities or concealing other bodily secrets, together with the whipping that was prescribed as punishment for vagrants in successive poor law statutes from the late fifteenth century onward, meant that the threat of violence or forced exposure was a constant risk for the disabled poor of early modern England.[49]

But if anxieties about begging and imposture appeared to justify the cruel streak of early modern humor that seems indicative of a "Hobbesian" desire to denigrate the weakness of disabled people, it is also clear that writers used the abject position of disability or deformity to challenge conventional relationships of power or authority. Disabled bodies, like the "grotesque body" Bakhtin described in his study of Rabelais, were an unruly presence on the pages of jest books—as on the streets of early modern London—serving to challenge the orderly standards of the increasingly idealized "classical body" by highlighting the vulnerable corporeality of everyone.[50] Similarly, Naomi Baker has shown that the ugly or deformed body in its "insistent and uncontrolled corporeality" presented a threat to emerging early modern forms of identity predicated on self-regulation and transcendence of the body.[51] Aforementioned jests in which the civilities of the dining table were mocked by the exploitation of the impediments of deaf guests were one way in which disability might provide a vehicle for satirizing these developing social conventions. Beyond this, the disorderliness of the disabled body, its inability to play by the rules or to follow the script of "normal" expectations, gave impaired characters in jest books the opportunity to challenge authority and turn the tables on those who would mock the afflicted.

For example, the inability of blind people to read others by their deportment or through cultural trappings of status such as dress gave them opportunities, in the world of the jest, to speak truth to power. One jest repeated in seventeenth-century collections concerned a group of courtiers crossing the New Bridge in Paris where they "espied a blind Man with the balls of his eyes so faire that they suspected hee was a counterfeit." In order to prove this, a duke "being basely borne" told the company he would prove the imposture since "if hee can see hee must needs know mee, he daily sitting here, and I daily passing by, and being a man of eminency." The nobleman then went up to the beggar "and pulled him by the nose, whereat the beggar roar'd out, and call'd him bastardly rogue." Thus, said the duke, "he sees perfectly, he could never have known mee so well else," but in fact "the man indeed was blind, and this onely a vicious speech often in his mouth."[52] While placing the encounter in the context of familiar concerns about imposture—which appeared to justify the tweaking of the man's nose—the aptness of the beggar's swearing meant that it is the pretensions of the elite that end up being exposed in their true colors. Ultimately the counterfeit is the duke who lacks noble blood by birth, rather than the disabled beggar.

Another example of this kind of humor in which disability mocked the pretensions of those in authority is recorded by Le Strange in an anecdote concerning a "lame fellow at Ipswich" who, being demanded by Bishop Matthew Wren "Why he did not bow at the name of Jesus," replied, "Why my Lord, [. . .] one knee does bowe but the other will not." Being asked why not, the man replied, "why because 'tis stiffe and lame."[53] The simple inability of the "lame" body to do what it was commanded encapsulated the difficulties facing Wren in enforcing Laudian church reforms in the Diocese of Norwich during the mid-1630s.[54] Elsewhere, those who inquired too impertinently into the causes of disability, who patronized the afflicted or acted with incivility toward them, were given short shrift. For instance, in a jest that appeared in *Tales and Quick Answers* (c. 1535) a man who refused to kiss a maid on the grounds that her nose was too long is told by the woman, who "waxing shamefast and angry in her mind (for with his scoff he a little touched her)," that he may kiss her where "I have nary a nose" (i.e., her buttocks).[55] The jest registered the feelings of the victims of such cruel and unchivalrous behavior and, in the woman's sharp-witted repartee, showed how a well-judged response might provide a means by which those with nonstandard bodies might revenge themselves on their abusers, in the process restoring their self-worth. In a similar example, a "tall personable man offered to accompany a dwarfe in the streete, saying that the people would the less gaze and wonder at his miserable littlenesse," to which the "dwarf" answered in riposte, "Rather they will wonder at my folly, to see me leade an Asse along by me, and not ride."[56] By the eighteenth century, the "merry cripple" was becoming a more notable feature of jest books and other writings on disability, as stoical good humor, smart repartee, and the ability to be "merry" about one's own disabilities or deformities, became accepted as an important means of coping with the stigma of physical difference and for making disabled people acceptable to nondisabled society.[57]

JOKES ABOUT the "crippled," blind, deaf, and "crooked" were a regular feature of jest books of the early modern period. Work on eighteenth-century jest books suggests that this material was ubiquitous, but it is just as important to put this kind of humor into its context, too. In the sixteenth and seventeenth centuries, jests that specifically dealt with impairment, or involved disabled characters, amounted to a small proportion of the total number of jests in this period. Indeed, some well-known late sixteenth- and early seventeenth-century collections contained no jokes at all about disability. It was not until later in the seventeenth century when jest books became lengthier and published in greater volume that jests involving disabled characters became a common feature of this literature. For example, the 1630 edition of Archie Armstrong's *A Banquet of Jeasts* contained only one jest concerning what we might recognize as a "disability"—the joke about the deaf hostess discussed earlier—although it did contain four jests about large or missing noses.[58] The expanded version of the text published in 1660, however, contained five jests about physical or sensory impairments.[59] Pressure to include more material may have led to an increase of jests concerning anomalous bodies. Furthermore, the "anti-civility" of Restoration rakes and libertines may have led to an increased interest in more "cruel" jokes at the expense of the unfortunate.[60] The "frolicks" of the Earl of Rochester and his cronies included violent and humiliating treatment of disabled people—a form of wit satirized in Thomas Otway's play *Friendship in Fashion* (1678) in which the rake Malagene seeks to demonstrate that he is a man of "parts" by boasting of how in one of his "merry witty fits," he had taunted a lame beggar who asked him for assistance by tripping up "both his wooden Legs."[61] However, even in the later seventeenth century only a small proportion of jest book material was concerned overtly with disability or deformity. Only fifteen of the 583 jests in William Hicks's *Oxford Jests* (1671) concerned deformity, "crippled" or maimed bodies, sensory impairments, and speech defects.[62] As such, the notion that disabled characters were "standing jokes" in early modern jest books needs careful qualification.[63]

Nevertheless, for scholars seeking to uncover the meanings of disability in premodern society, jest books provide important material that provides insight into discourses of disability in Renaissance England. Jokes did not simply mock disabled characters; instead, the exaggerated, topsy-turvy world of the jest provided license for authors of jests to reflect on the nature of disability as stigma (via anxieties about pollution of the species), the relationship between qualities of the mind and the "defects" of the body, social concerns about the dangers of the disabled poor, and the gendered identity of disabled people, especially men. While a short essay such as this is unable to do justice to the full variety of these jests, several important themes emerge. There can be no doubt that there was a strong element of exploitation in early modern jest books in which the deformed body might provide an opportunity for the nondisabled to triumph over the "otherness" of impaired individuals. Disabled characters in jest books had the veracity of their afflictions challenged or mocked, were subjected to violence whether threatened or actually inflicted, or provided vehicles for the nondisabled to prove their verbal dexterity via ingenious word play and extended metaphors that highlighted their nonhuman attributes or appearances, subjecting them to what Tom Shakespeare describes as a "normalizing verbal barrage."[64] Material from jest books provides reinforcement for Row-Heyveld's argument that representations of disability were becoming increasingly negative in England after the Reformation, as changes in religious practice and social welfare combined to devalue disabled persons, intensifying fears of imposture and criminality while simultaneously representing disabled men in particular as "impotent" and effeminized.

However, paying closer attention to the structure of this material allows us to shed light on the multiple meanings of impairment in this period. Although "deformed" bodies might be described in grotesque terms, jests did not merely view disability through the lens of the monstrous or the exotic. References to impairment being a punishment from God, or of outward deformity being a reflection of inner moral failings—made popular by Shakespeare's portrayal of Richard III or ballads concerning "monstrous" births—were not often made explicit in this material. Authors of this material were more concerned, like others of the time, with the question of whether impairment was real or faked, rather than its spiritual dimensions. Moreover, whereas jests provided an outlet for exploring anxieties raised by encounters with the disabled poor on the streets of the early modern city, disabled characters were sometimes given the opportunity to fight back and turn the tables on those who sought to denigrate them. Disabled characters were not only victims but also trickster figures who challenged the status quo, and the unruliness of the disabled body might provide a powerful tool for satirizing social conventions.[65] Disability humor, like the experience of disability itself, resists straightforward categorization.

Notes

1. P. M. Zall, *A Hundred Merry Tales and Other Jestbooks of the Fifteenth and Sixteenth Centuries* (Lincoln: University of Nebraska Press, 1963), 112. On the paradoxical praise of deformity see Naomi Baker, "'To make love to a Deformity': Praising Ugliness in Early Modern England," *Renaissance Studies* 22, no. 1 (2007): 86–109.

2. Stuart M. Tave, *The Amiable Humorist: A Study in the Comic Theory and Criticism of the Eighteenth and Early Nineteenth Centuries* (Chicago: University of Chicago Press, 1960), 51.

3. Keith Thomas, "The Place of Laughter in Tudor and Stuart England," *Times Literary Supplement,* 21 January 1977, 77–81; Simon Dickie, "Hilarity and Pitilessness in the Mid-Eighteenth Century: English Jestbook Humor," *Eighteenth-Century Studies* 37, no. 1 (2003): 1–22; Simon Dickie, *Cruelty and Laughter: Forgotten Comic Literature*

and the Unsentimental Eighteenth Century (Chicago and London: University of Chicago Press, 2011), chap. 2; Roger Lund, "Laughing at Cripples: Ridicule, Deformity and the Argument from Design," *Eighteenth-Century Studies* 39, no. 1 (2005): 91–114.

4. Robert Garland, *The Eye of the Beholder: Deformity and Disability in the Graeco-Roman World* (London: Duckworth, 1995), 74.

5. Baldassare Castiglione, *The Courtyer of Count Baldessar Castilio divided into Foure Books,* trans. Thomas Hoby (London, 1561), sig. Si.

6. Thomas Hobbes, *Leviathan* (1651), ed. Richard Tuck (Cambridge: Cambridge University Press, 1991), 43.

7. Pauline Croft, "The Reputation of Robert Cecil: Libels, Political Opinion and Popular Awareness in the Early Seventeenth Century," *Transactions of the Royal Historical Society,* 6th ser., I (1991): 43–69.

8. Dickie, "Hilarity and Pitilessness," 14, 16.

9. Lund, "Laughing at Cripples.", 94-95.

10. Dickie, "Hilarity and Pitilessness," 17.

11. Ibid., 4.

12. Anna Bryson, *From Courtesy to Civility: Changing Codes of Conduct in Early Modern England* (New York: Oxford University Press, 1998), 237–38.

13. Giovanni della Casa, *Galateo of Maister John Della Casa,* trans. Robert Peterson (London, 1576), 63.

14. Zall, *Hundred Merry Tales,* 112.

15. Wheatley, *Stumbling Blocks,* chap. 4.

16. F. P. Wilson, "The English Jestbooks of the Sixteenth and Early Seventeenth Centuries," *Huntington Library Quarterly* 2, no. 2 (1938): 121–58; Derek Brewer, "Prose Jest-Books Mainly in the Sixteenth to Eighteenth Centuries in England," in Jan Bremmer and Herman Roodenburg (eds.), *A Cultural History of Humor: From Antiquity to the Present Day* (Cambridge: Polity, 1997), 90–111.

17. Dickie, "Hilarity and Pitilessness," 11.

18. Baker, "Praising Ugliness," 87.

19. [Edward Copley], *Wits, Fits, and Fancies* (London, 1614), 185–86.

20. Ibid., 186.

21. William Hicks, *Oxford Jests, Refined and Enlarged* (London, 1671), 80, 171.

22. Erving Goffman, *Stigma: Notes on the Management of Spoiled Identity* (Englewood Cliffs, NJ: Prentice-Hall, 1963).

23. Erica Fudge, "Monstrous Acts: Bestiality in Early Modern England," *History Today* 50, no. 8 (2000): 22.

24. Copley, *Wits,* 186.

25. Nicholas Le Strange, *Merry Passages and Jeasts: A Manuscript Jestbook of Sir Nicholas Le Strange (1603–1655),* ed. H. F. Lippincott (Salzburg: Institut für Englische Sprache und Literatur, Universität Salzburg, 1974), 65.

26. Katherine Park and Lorraine Daston, "Unnatural Conceptions: The Study of Monsters in Sixteenth- and Seventeenth-Century France and England," *Past and Present* 92 (1981): 20–55.

27. Copley, *Wits,* 186.

28. *Poor Robin's Jests: Or, the Compleat Jester* (London, 1672), 84.

29. Francis Bacon, "Of Deformity," in *The Essays,* ed. John Pitcher (Harmondsworth, UK: Penguin Books, 1985), 192.

30. [Archie Armstrong], *A Banquet of Jeasts; Or Charge of Cheare* (London, 1630), 58.

31. Le Strange, *Merry Passages and Jeasts,* 18; see also 148.

32. See also Baker, "Praising Ugliness."

33. Copley, *Wits,* 88.

34. Ibid., 90; see also Zall, *Hundred Merry Tales,* 119–21.

35. David M. Turner, *Disability in Eighteenth-Century England: Imagining Physical Impairment* (New York and London: Routledge, 2012), 133–34.

36. Row-Heyveld, "'The Lying'st Knave in Christendom'" (see introduction, n. 73).

37. Alexandra Shepard, *Meanings of Manhood in Early Modern England* (Oxford: Oxford University Press, 2003).

38. For example, William Hicks, *Coffee-House Jests* (London, 1677), 88–89. See also Elizabeth A. Foyster, *Manhood in Early Modern England: Honour, Sex and Marriage* (London: Longman, 1999), 68.

39. *The Cuckold's Calamity, Or the Old Usurer Plunder'd out of his Gold by His Young Wife,* Pepys Ballads 5.256 (n.d.), http://ebba.english.ucsb.edu/ballad/22091/image. I am grateful to Catherine Horler for this reference.

40. Wheatley, *Stumbling Blocks,* 144–49.

41. Copley, *Wits,* 98. For an earlier version, see Zall, *Hundred Merry Tales,* 35.

42. *Pasquil's Jestes, Mixed with Mother Bunches Merriments* (London, 1609), sig. A2r–v.

43. William Basse, *A Helpe to Discourse. Or, A Miscellany of Merriment* (London, 1619), 39–40.

44. Behn, "The Dumb Virgin," in *Works,* vol. 3, 335–60.

45. *A Compleat Collection of Remarkable Tryals of the most Notorious Malefactors, at the Sessions-House in the Old Baily, for near Fifty Years Past,* 4 vols. (London, 1718–21), 2:146–47. The men were acquitted.

46. Row-Heyveld, "'The Lying'st Knave in Christendom,'" n.p.; see also Gāmini Salgādo, *Cony-Catchers and Bawdy Baskets: An Anthology of Elizabethan Low Life* (Harmondsworth, UK: Penguin, 1972). For similar themes in artistic representation see Tom Nichols, "The Vagabond Image: Depictions of False Beggars in Northern Art of the Sixteenth Century," in *Others and Outcasts in Early Modern Europe: Picturing the Social Margins* (Aldershot, UK: Ashgate, 2007), 37–60.

47. [Robert Chamberlain], *The Booke of Bulls, Baited with two Centuries of bold Jests and Nimble Lies* (London, 1636), 6.

48. Hicks, *Oxford Jests,* 15.

49. Row-Heyveld, "'The Lying'st Knave in Christendom,'" n.p.; see also Paul Griffiths, *Lost Londons: Change, Crime and Control in the Capital City, 1550–1660* (Cambridge: Cambridge University Press, 2008), 121, 255.

50. M. M. Bakhtin, *Rabelais and His World* (Cambridge, MA: MIT Press, 1968); see also Paster, *Body Embarrassed,* 15.

51. Baker, "Praising Ugliness," 103; see also Julia Kristeva, *Powers of Horror: An Essay on Abjection* (New York: Columbia University Press, 1982).

52. Chamberlain, *Booke of Bulls,* 70.

53. Le Strange, *Merry Passages and Jeasts,* 93.

54. Nicholas Tyacke, *Anti-Calvinists: The Rise of English Arminianism c.1590–1640* (New York: Oxford University Press, 1987); Nicholas W. S. Cranfield, "Wren, Mat-

thew (1585–1667)," *Oxford Dictionary of National Biography,* Oxford University Press, 2004; online ed., Oct 2008. http://www.oxforddnb.com/view/article/30021. Accessed 27 September 2010.

55. Zall, *Hundred Merry Tales,* 251. See also *Poor Robin's Jests,* 59–60.

56. Copley, *Wits,* 194.

57. Lund, "Laughing at Cripples," 109; Turner, *Disability in Eighteenth-Century England,* 69-73.

58. Armstrong, *Banquet of Jeasts,* 58 (deaf hostess); 23–24, 45, 59, 160 (noses).

59. [Archie Armstrong], *A Choice Banquet of Witty Jests, Rare Fancies, and Pleasant Novels* (London, 1660), esp. 46, 55, 69, 82, 101.

60. Bryson, *Courtesy,* chap. 7.

61. Thomas Otway, *Friendship in Fashion* (London, 1678), 3.1. On Rochester, see William Pinkethman, *Pinkethman's Jests, Or, Wit Refin'd,* 4th ed. (London, 1735), 81.

62. Hicks, *Oxford Jests,* esp. 2, 3, 15, 49, 80, 90, 102, 126, 147–48, 171.

63. Dickie, "Hilarity and Pitilessness," 14.

64. Tom Shakespeare, "Joking a Part," *Body and Society* 5, no. 4 (1999): 48.

65. Gary L. Albrecht, "Disability Humor: What's in a Joke?" *Body and Society* 5, no. 4 (1999): 67–74.

CHAPTER 4

Antic Dispositions

Mental and Intellectual Disabilities in Early Modern Revenge Tragedy

LINDSEY ROW-HEYVELD

n their 1980 study of revenge tragedy conventions, Charles A. Hallett and Elaine S. Hallett argue that madness is "the central symbol that binds all of the motifs [of revenge tragedy] together."[1] At the same time, however, the Halletts identify madness as "perhaps the most misunderstood revenge tragedy convention."[2] They take issue with many scholars' literal approach to early modern madness, specifically the then-popular habit of drawing parallels between descriptions of distraction and contemporary phobias or psychoses. Attempting to diagnose fictional characters four hundred years after the fact, the Halletts insist, limits interpretative possibilities. While the Halletts' specific assertion here is accurate, in the years since their study, scholarship investigating the complexities of early modern madness has broadened the scope of "literal" interpretation. Research by Michael MacDonald, Carol Thomas Neely, and Ken Jackson, among others, has proven that understanding madness as a real condition experienced by real people, with specific medical and cultural valences, can illuminate a wide variety of early modern texts.[3]

For all the great strides that have taken place in the study of madness in the past thirty years, few scholars have situated early modern mental impairment within the context of disability,[4] and, especially strangely, in spite of the fact that it was emerging as a distinct legal and social category in the unfolding English Reformation.[5] Neither have scholars reconsidered the role of mental and intellectual disabilities within the tradition of revenge tragedy; three decades later, the Halletts' assertion that madness is the most important and least understood convention of revenge tragedy still holds true.[6]

Madness is often undcrexamined and undertheorized in studies of revenge tragedy because critics have frequently regarded it as a simplistic narrative necessity. As Fredson Bowers asserts, "For there to be any play at all, the revenger must delay," and madness, real or feigned, delivers that delay.[7] Madness provides an exceptionally convenient dramatic deferral since it facilitates the bloody conclusion it simultaneously puts off. Avengers such as Hieronimo, Hamlet, and Antonio adopt disability as a disguise so they might safely observe the villains they hope eventually to punish. Nevertheless, because their feigned distraction blurs into real derangement, these avengers potentially jeopardize their concluding revenge by means of the madness they take on to complete it, turning what looks like an instrument of action into an instrument of deferral. It is a slick dramatic maneuver, and the seemingly self-explanatory justification for the inclusion of madness and foolishness in revenge tragedies has often precluded further investigation.

But madness and foolishness are more than just vehicles for dramatic delay. An analysis of plays such as *The Spanish Tragedy, Titus Andronicus, Hamlet,* and *Antonio's Revenge* makes clear that mental and intellectual disabilities played a critical role in making the morally ambiguous revenge tradition palatable for early modern audiences. These disabilities weave together a number of the central thematic occupations of revenge tragedy, and, in so doing, present a paradoxical version of revenge that allowed audiences simultaneously to indulge in and condemn the bloody actions of the drama. Mental and intellectual disabilities also serve a similar narrative function. Through the inclusion and eventual elimination of disability, mad avengers are protected from the guilt of the violence they enact, while mad villains' guilt is affirmed and the violent ends they meet justified. Disability provides revenge tragedy with something of a literary loophole, facilitating the consumption of its ethically compromised but emotionally cathartic plot for audiences trained to condemn but hungry for vigilante justice.

Disability as a Thematic Instrument

Examining the cultural construction of madness in early modern England reveals a number of attributes that made it a valuable thematic instrument in revenge tragedy. To begin with, medicine regularly granted mental and intellectual disabilities performative qualities. Medical authorities, for instance, believed madness could be caused by simply pretending to be mad and could be cured by similarly theatrical means.[8] Widely circulated case studies reported doctors operating more like stage managers than physicians, using elaborately theatrical machinations to cure their "brain-sick" patients by gulling them into simply believing they were cured.[9] Revenge tragedies seize on the possibilities of this connection between madness and theatricality, featuring characters whose mental impairments entertain audiences and whose conditions blur the lines between real and feigned impairments. These plays also employ theatrical "cures" to end the avenger's madness: the play-within-a-play that is a frequent feature of revenge tragedy either affirms the guilt of the villain or, more often, facilitates the violence that frees the avenger from his maddening pain of injustice.

In addition to being theatrically resonant, early modern constructions of madness carried contradictory cultural associations shared by revenge tragedies; for example, madness reinforced the familial connections it also severed. Not only were family members usually the primary caregivers for persons with disabilities, especially those labeled "mad" or "foolish," but an individual's capacity to acknowledge and abide by familial ties was one of the primary factors in assessing his or her mental fitness. The failure to recognize a family member—or even the failure to recognize the authority of a family member—could lead to a label of "witlessness" or "insensibility."[10] This contradiction made the presence of mental impairment in revenge tragedy particularly apt, since the central conflict of the drama often hinges on an avenger's clash of familial obligations: in order to earn bloody justice for one family member, Hamlet, for instance, has to kill another. Mental and intellectual disabilities throw into relief both the avenger's shattering of familial bonds and his absolute commitment to those relationships.

The conflicts of duty highlighted by madness's familial connections are further teased out in its contradictory religious associations. In early modern England, the image of the fool could not be easily divorced from its negative sacred connections: the opening words of Psalm 52—"The fool hath said in his heart, 'There is no God'"—and the accompanying illustrations in psalters cemented the link between the person with mental impairments and the atheist.[11] Renaissance humanists, who associated reason with the divine, literalized this allegorical treatment of mental disability by characterizing the loss of reason as a break with God.[12] Paradoxically, mental impairments were also believed to facilitate an intimate connection with God; "holy fools," who lacked a fixation on earthly things, were thought of as uniquely Christlike. Erasmus plays up this contradiction of associations in *The Praise of Folly* when he has his Folly, previously depicted as the source of vice, declare herself the only true wisdom, since salvation is itself a type of divine madness.[13] These conflicting connections made persons with mental and intellectual impairments difficult to interpret in early modern England, and, therefore, especially rich parallels for avenging counterfeiters who walked that same difficult line between defying God and doing God's will. In John Marston's *Antonio's Revenge,* for example, Antonio's prolonged performance as a fool reinforces the play's fixation on divine censure versus divine consent since it mirrors the way Antonio repeatedly figures his act of personal retribution as an act of judgment ordained by God—in spite of his (and his audience's) awareness of the biblical injunctions against revenge.

The questions of guilt and innocence raised by the religious contradictions of madness find earthly counterparts in links between madness, revenge tragedy, and violence. One of the qualities frequently used to identify (or at least qualify) early modern mental disabilities, especially those categorized as "madness" or "lunacy," was the threat an individual posed to the peace. As Peter Rushton points out, mental disabilities often went unlabeled during the English Renaissance until the danger of physical harm was evident.[14] Claudius alludes to this potential for violence when discussing Hamlet's madness—"I like him not, nor stands it safe with us / To let his madness range" (3.3.1–2)—a potential that Hamlet fulfills in the murder of Polonius.[15]

Although madness and lunacy threatened physical danger, paradoxically, they also resisted the responsibility for that violence. One of the most popular euphemisms for mental and intellectual disabilities in early modern England was "innocent," a term that implied both a purity that would not entertain the possibility of violence and a lack of responsibility for any potential harm that might occur.[16] Revenge tragedies fixate on this duality, exploring the simultaneous guilt and innocence of the avenger, who must engage in unlawful violence in order to restore justice. In this way, having the avenger take on or be overtaken by madness increases the dramatic expectation of violence—and the ethical conundrum—inherent in revenge tragedies. Madness heightens the question of "Will he or won't he take revenge?" by transforming it into "Will he be too innocent to commit the required vengeance or will he be so guiltily enraged that he would be unable to stop himself from killing even if he wanted to?" Rather than serving simply as a somewhat unlikely diversion for the avenger, disability becomes a vital part of the anticipatory deferment of violence and its ethical complications.

The simultaneous visibility and invisibility of mental disabilities compounded the paradox of mad avengers' guilt and innocence. Unlike other impairments whose representations on the stage were almost entirely contingent on costuming, mental disabilities were invisible. At the same time, mental disabilities were also granted visual cues, which developed over the centuries into nearly emblematic forms: madmen wore very few clothes or none at all; had either wild, unkempt hair or were entirely bald; and traditionally carried a weapon, usually a club.[17] Fools wore striped or checked robes or cloaks, usually in green or yellow (the well-known "fool's motley"), with a belled or tasseled cap and also brandished a weaponlike item, although fools' accessories were distinctly nonthreatening.[18] This contrast of eye-catching costume and invisible impairment not only made for effective theater through its playful, layered substitutions, but also lent itself particularly well to revenge tragedies that were obsessed with uncovering the unseen.

The conundrum of madness's in/visibility is just one iteration of the revenge tradition's larger preoccupation with testing the scope of knowledge. Revenge has as much to do with revelation as it does with justice, and questions of epistemology, like those raised by the absence and presence of mental disabilities' visual signals, recur throughout the plays. When Hieronimo discovers the body of his murdered son in *The Spanish Tragedy,* he fears that Horatio's death shall pass both unrevenged and unrevealed. Yet the proof of guilt needed to reveal and revenge his son's murder proves strangely difficult for Hieronimo to acquire. A letter written in blood from an eyewitness is not enough; Hieronimo needs the duration of the play to confirm the identities of Horatio's murderers for himself. And he is not alone. The Ghost tells Hamlet of Claudius's crime, but Hamlet still needs to stage *The Murder of Gonzago* to confirm his supernatural sources. Titus Andronicus cannot act upon his desire for revenge until his mutilated daughter can find a way to communicate the names of her attackers without the use of tongue or hands. The disguise of disability, then, is often how avengers finally establish the proof of guilt that frees them to become vigilantes, even as it resonates with the epistemological uncertainty central to revenge tragedies. It allows avengers the time and the freedom to confirm the guilt of the villain while avoiding suspicion themselves. Simultaneously, putting on disability further complicates the issue of discernment raised by revenge tragedies since the very presence of madness undermines avengers' ability to serve as accurate and just judges. Because feigned madness so often perfectly resembles— and even bleeds into—the real thing, avengers compromise their claim to authority and blur the line between a righteous execution of justice and a maddened frenzy when they pretend disability. Mental impairment, then, undercuts the very certainty it is employed to secure.

Mental and intellectual disabilities assist these plays in negotiating the difficult ethical conundrum they stage. Critics have long debated how early modern audiences responded to the technically unlawful yet potentially satisfying actions of revenge tragedy. Did they see those raging avengers as agents of evil, as Lily B. Campbell and others have argued?[19] Or did audiences look past their Christian context to read avengers as heroic exacters of a necessary blood payment, as Fredson Bowers and his adherents have contended?[20] The answer may be that madness allowed playwrights and audiences the best of both worlds: they could indulge in revenge while condemning it, too, since mental impairments paradoxically heralded a break with family and religion, a tendency toward violence, a sense of perpetual indistinction and invisibility, and a failure of judgment—even as they also affirmed strong relationships with God and family, resisted violence, were easily identifiable, and facilitated reasonable judgment. Thanks to the construction of madness during this period, avengers could be always guilty and innocent, punishable and praiseworthy.

Disability as a Narrative Instrument

Just as mental and intellectual disabilities aided avengers in their efforts to interpret the guilt of their enemies, so these disabilities are themselves evidence to be interpreted. As disability scholarship has proven, the nonstandard body in literature is never allowed to be simply a fact but always serves as a sign of some deeper meaning that requires interpretation. This was particularly true in the early modern era, where disability could be read theologically, as a sign of God's wrath or as a wonder that indicated the powers of nature; physiognomically, as a physical indicator of spiritual corruption, or, in reverse, as a nearly sacramental outward sign of inward graces; or humorally, as the corporeal result of "excess" or "lack," both physical and moral. Disability was also often linked to the social problems that plagued England during the Tudor-Stuart period, specifically the rapid urbanization and vagrancy that spiked in the late sixteenth century. Disability invited interpretation, and the madness and foolishness found in revenge tragedies were no exception. Not only do characters (and audience members) have to decipher if a character is genuinely disabled, but they also have to determine what that disability means.

Scholars have engaged similar questions about what mental and intellectual disabilities are and what they signify within the context of revenge tragedy. Charles and Elaine Hallett, for instance, posit that madness was both the symptom and the symbol of emotional excess, implicitly condemning rage, grief, lust, despair, and other strong emotions while acknowledging the disruptive effects of psychological trauma and moral chaos. The Halletts also suggest that madmen and fools are used to provide a counterpoint to the "sanity" of normal conduct: "the extravagant behavior of the true lunatic was a natural symbol for that ordinary everyday madness to which all men are subject."[21] Other critics, such as Barbara J. Baines, suggest that madness serves as a foil, not to the behavior of sane characters and playgoers but to the image of Stoic acceptance so often presented as an ideal response to trauma in revenge tragedies.[22] Because the body was such an important political metaphor in early modern England, scholars such as Alan Thiher argue that madness is a symbol of governmental instability, particularly in revenge tragedies where the crux of the drama rests on the loss of a legitimate recourse to justice.[23] The "dislocation in consciousness" that Jonathan Dollimore asserts is frequently showcased in revenge tragedies can be the result of "a dislocation in the world,"[24] but, as Anne Duprat demonstrates, early modern mental disabilities were also granted the power to reorder the world, creating rich alternate versions of reality.[25]

While these are insightful observations on the presence and purpose of madness and foolishness in revenge tragedy, these disabilities also served a very specific narrative function: which characters succumb to madness and which do not guide responses to vigilante justice enacted in these plays. When the revenger is mad, his madness facilitates a nominal approval of his actions; when the tyrant is mad, his madness verifies the necessity of vengeance enacted against him. Disability in such cases is indeed a sign to be interpreted, and deciphering its meanings provided audiences with helpful navigation through the complicated ethics of the revenge tragedy.

David T. Mitchell and Sharon L. Snyder have theorized the role of disability in Western literature, identifying a pattern they call "narrative prosthesis" by which the nonstandard body acts "as a crutch upon which literary narratives lean for their representational power, disruptive potentiality, and analytical insight."[26] Mitchell and Snyder outline the fourfold structure of this narrative contrivance: (1) A marked physical difference is introduced to the reader. (2) The narrative accounts for the inclusion of this difference by recounting its origins. (3) This marked difference is brought from the periphery of the narrative to the central focus of its concerns. (4) There is an effort to rehabilitate or eliminate this difference, thus resolving the central narrative conflict in a purgation of the social body or a redefinition of essential states of being.[27] As Mitchell and Snyder have asserted, the nonstandard body functions in narrative art as the metaphorical embodiment of various types of social and individual aberrance, a phenomenon they call "the mate-riality of metaphor."[28] Just what metaphor the specific disability embodies often determines the fate of the character and the outcome of the story; that outcome, however, is usually limited to either eliminating the disability or eliminating the character with the disability (the so-called cure or kill princi-ple). The deterministic metaphorical power of disability is decidedly evident in revenge tragedies, where the multiplicity of meanings assigned to early modern madness directs the narrative and, especially, the audience's ethical interpretations of that narrative.

When the avenger experiences madness, the narrative prosthesis of dis-ability provides audience members with an interpretive strategy that allows them to elide the ethical problems raised by the actions of revenge. Many avengers—Hieronimo, Titus Andronicus, Hamlet, and Antonio, specifi-cally—initially engage in madness as a ruse. The fraud allows them to avoid the suspicions of the very men they are observing and plotting against. As Hieronimo explains in *The Spanish Tragedy:*

> Thus therefore will I rest me in unrest,
> Dissembling quiet in unquietness,
> Not seeming that I know their villainies,
> That my simplicity may make them think
> That ignorantly I will let all slip.[29] (3.13.29–34)

Enacting his machinations in the "rest" provided by the disguise of mental "unrest," Hieronimo and other avengers participate in the classical tradition of putting on madness to overthrow tyranny. Junius Brutus famously feigned madness in order to take down the evil Tarquin, and, as we are reminded in *Antonio's Revenge,* even Machiavelli suggested that, when seeking out one's enemies, "He is not wise that strives not to seem fool" (4.1.25).[30] Of course, their control over their costume quickly disintegrates, and it becomes diffi-cult for the avengers and others to determine their genuine mental condi-tion. Titus Andronicus, for instance, comes so close to genuine madness that he never officially sets out to feign it. His nemesis Tamora simply mistakes his behavior for derangement, and he takes deadly advantage of her error. In this way, these dramas swiftly move through the first three phases of narra-tive prosthesis, introducing the disability as an initially peripheral issue, giv-ing it a justifying origin, and then centralizing it as the fraudulent disability bleeds into reality.

In these plays, the avenger's madness motivates the plot and leads to its inevitable conclusion, but, paradoxically, madness is a pointedly inadequate justification for the actions of the plot and the machinations of the characters. Charles and Elaine Hallett assert that madness is crucial to revenge tragedy's bloody finale because it grants the avenger a potentially delusional but necessary sense of divine approval for his violent actions.[31] This assessment of madness in revenge tragedy comports with Mitchell and Snyder's assessment of the role of disability in narrative art, wherein "the inherent vulnerability and variability of bodies serves literary narratives as a metonym for that which refuses to conform to the mind's desire for order and rationality."[32] This statement is particularly true of mental disabilities, which, in revenge tragedies, become laden with symbolic meanings. Yet, at the same time, while madness is used to justify the actions of the avenger (to himself and to the audience of the play, as well) and to symbolize the social deviance the avenger has experienced and will cause, madness is also an insufficient explanation: revenge narratives destabilize early modern cultural assertions about the fixity of earthly and divine authority, but they do so by relying on the deterministic nature of disability. By depending on the fixity of disability to reveal the instability of order and lawfulness, revenge tragedies vividly illustrate Mitchell and Snyder's assertion that in prosthetic narratives "disability may provide an explanation for the origins of a character's identity, but its deployment usually proves either too programmatic or unerringly 'deep' and mysterious. . . . Their disabilities surface to explain everything or nothing."[33] Avengers who show up the artificiality of unchanging justice and authority through the predestined actions of their madness enact a similarly circular logic.

The conclusions of these dramas highlight their lack of explanation, since the resolutions of revenge tragedies rely on the motivation of madness; yet madness is often surprisingly absent from these scenes. By the time each avenger finally wreaks his revenge, he appears to have discarded the lunacy that he demonstrated earlier in the play. In the case of avengers such as Hieronimo and Hamlet, it is unclear whether they simply choose to abandon the pretense of madness—suggesting that they had control of it all along, however much their actions might belie that—or whether they were somehow cured of their condition, although no cure is ever identified. The obvious answer appears to be that they are cured by engaging in the final act of cathartic violence, which is contradictory, if, in fact, their madness facilitates their willingness to participate in that violence in the first place.

The ultimate fate of these avengers affirms the circular explanation of the prosthetic narrative, comporting with Mitchell and Snyder's assessment that disability explains "everything or nothing"—or, in the case of the revenge tragedy, everything *and* nothing. Instead of being cured or killed, protagonists of revenge dramas appear to be cured *and* killed: they enter into the final bloodbath free of their mental impairment and then they die in the attack that they instigate.[34] Both their curing and killing seem necessary to the narrative and ethical resolutions of these dramas. Avengers must be cured because, even if we agree that their madness motivates their violence, their lack of sanity would obliterate the scrim of justice that covers their brutality; similarly, they must be killed in order to punish them appropriately for their transgression of the law and return the narrative to a state of equilibrium. With these two conditions in place, the protagonists can be honored after their death in spite of their disability and unlawful actions—or, rather, because of their disability and unlawful actions. At the end of *The Spanish Tragedy,* the spectral Don Andrea promises to "lead Hieronimo where Orpheus play, / Adding sweet pleasures to eternal days" (4.5.23–24). Titus Andronicus is exonerated by his nation and honored by his remaining family members, who cover his mangled body with kisses. Hamlet, of course, is carried from the scene of his carnage by four captains, "like a soldier" (5.2.398); the "flights of angels" (5.2.362) Horatio invokes suggest that in his disability-free death he is not only "most royal" (400), as Fortinbras suggests, but also most Christian.[35] Valorizing the avengers after they have completed their revenge also guides the reactions of the audience members who have been presented with a complex moral task in deciphering these dramas. The application and elimination of madness allows spectators the transgressive pleasure of vigilante justice while exempting them from the moral quandary the violent and violating actions of the protagonist provoke.

Avengers, however, are not the only characters in revenge tragedy to experience mental disability. In a number of revenge tragedies, the object of revenge—the villain—succumbs to madness while the avenger remains sane. In Cyril Tourneur's *The Atheist's Tragedy,* the evil D'Amville loses his reason as he begins to lose his power and descends into madness by the end of the drama. The Tyrant in *The Second Maiden's Tragedy* is driven to distraction by his grief over the Lady's suicide. Lycanthropy plagues Ferdinand, the evil twin brother of the wronged Duchess in John Webster's *The Duchess of Malfi.* The mental disabilities experienced by villains, like those experienced by avengers, are metaphorically loaded. However, villains' madness signifies differently from avengers' madness. For villains, their disability is a direct result of their crime; madness is a physical manifestation of their guilt. D'Amville goes mad because of the loss of his sons, whose deaths derive from his murderous power plays; the Tyrant loses his reason because the Lady, whom he ruthlessly pursued, killed herself rather than be possessed by him; and Ferdinand's distraction sets in immediately upon seeing the bodies of his sister and her children, whose murders he himself had ordered. The point-edly motivated madness of these villains demonstrates Mitchell and Snyder's theory of the materiality of metaphor, wherein deviance from a physical norm embodies social and/or individual deviance. As in the other revenge tragedies, madness provides a circular explanation for the actions of these tyrants: because villains are driven mad by guilt, their disability proves that they are guilty.

Plays where the villain becomes mad also follow the model of narrative prosthesis by first introducing the disability, then attributing it to a specific origin (namely, the evil perpetrated by these villains), before bringing it to the center of the narrative concerns and, finally, eliminating it. Again, dis-ability helps elide the ethical difficulty of revenge. Villains' madness both facilitates and justifies the concluding violence, eliminating both the villain and his disability. This elimination neatly resolves the dramatic conflicts of the drama while protecting the hero (and, in turn, the spectators of the play) from responsibility for the otherwise ethically compromised ending. In his distraction, D'Amville kills himself, thus sparing the hero any possible taint of guilt associated with taking revenge himself in *The Atheist's Tragedy*. In *The Second Maiden's Tragedy*, the Tyrant's deranged obsession with the Lady's corpse leads the avenger to paint her dead body with poison; the Tyrant's necrophilia does the rest. Ferdinand in *The Duchess of Malfi* dies when he attacks his evil brother, the Cardinal, and the henchman-turned-avenger, Bosola, mortally wounding them both and allowing the play to reach its appropriate conclusion without tainting the purer heroes by forcing them into violence. The materializing of metaphor in these dramas means that villains' madness testifies to the rightness of revenge, since it proves their guilt by embodying their social and moral aberrations, while also providing for the elimination of those villains and their physical/social aberrance. Vil-lains' madness makes revenge both appropriate and convenient. Uniquely, the madness experienced by villains also eliminates the guilt of revenge, since the tyrants in these plays bring about their own violent ends, either directly or indirectly. In these cases, madness serves as a prophylactic to protect the would-be avengers from the ethical mire of the bloody conclusion and to protect the audience members as well, since their presence authorizes the actions on stage.

Some revenge tragedies, it is important to recognize, do not feature mad-ness at all. In plays such as Christopher Marlowe's *The Jew of Malta*, Thomas Middleton's *The Revenger's Tragedy*, and John Ford's *'Tis Pity She's a Whore* there is no apparent mental or intellectual disability, or at least none that is clearly articulated. Without the presence of madness in the drama, the ethics of revenge become even more ambivalent and difficult for audiences to negotiate. In *The Revenger's Tragedy*, after finally completing his seemingly justified and hard-won vengeance, Vindice publicly confesses to revenge and is therefore immediately shipped off to a "speedy execution" (5.3.123). His justification for his bizarre actions demonstrates that Vindice has not lost his reason but is, in fact, so reasonable he recognizes the way his quest for revenge has eliminated any moral superiority he might have once claimed: "'Tis time to die," he insists, "when we are ourselves our foes" (5.3.130). This unreasonable reason is also enacted by Giovanni in *'Tis Pity She's a Whore*, who rationalizes incest. His vengeance on his sister/lover and her husband is, like Vindice's, strangely self-defeating: he kills the one person whom he truly loved and then proceeds to take on a whole roomful of his enemies single-handedly, leaving little possibility for an outcome that does not include his death. Barabas, the titular *Jew of Malta*, meets a more straightforward end— he falls into a cauldron of boiling liquid after finally being apprehended by some of the many people he has harmed—but his position as a Machiavellian protagonist makes his death distinctly problematic. Like Giovanni, Barabas's revenge is motivated as much by his own evil actions as those done to him, and his attempt to restore his version of justice makes things more unjust than ever. In the revenge tragedies that feature madness, disability mediates and/or clarifies the actions of the protagonist; in dramas without madness, the protagonists tend to acknowledge the evil of their own actions, complicating the dramatic pleasure and ethical equilibrium of their resolutions and making it difficult even to group these plays within the revenge tradition.

Through a complex network of thematic and narrative connections, madness helped playwrights and audiences both indulge in and shield themselves from the dangerous pleasure of revenge tragedy. Capitalizing on the many contradictions of mental and intellectual disabilities in the early modern era, authors could stage avengers who were always both guilty and innocent. Taking this overdetermination of disability even further, madness could be employed to approve the violent actions of some characters and, simultaneously, to condemn the violent actions of others. Mental and intellectual disabilities could show the audience who to honor as a hero and who to castigate as a villain, however similar their behavior. Madness is, indeed, the central symbol that binds all the motifs of revenge tragedy together—but it is more than just a symbol. It is the empty center on which the project of the revenge tragedy turns: it can justify the avenger even as it signals his deviance; it can motivate, condemn, and eliminate tyrants; it can free audiences to revel in and revile the play's bloody actions. Revenge may be a dish best served cold, but it is madness that allows audiences of revenge tragedy to have that dish and eat it, too.

Notes

1. Charles A. Hallett and Elaine S. Hallett, *The Revenger's Madness: A Study of Revenge Tragedy Motifs* (Lincoln: University of Nebraska Press, 1980), 9.

2. Ibid., 41.

3. Michael MacDonald, *Mystical Bedlam: Madness, Anxiety, and Healing in Seventeenth Century England* (Cambridge: Cambridge University Press, 1981); Ken Jackson, *Separate Theaters: Bethlem ("Bedlam") Hospital and the Shakespearean Stage* (Newark: University of Delaware Press, 2005); and Carol Thomas Neely, *Distracted Subjects: Madness and Gender in Shakespeare and Early Modern Culture* (Ithaca, NY: Cornell University Press, 2004).

4. Because of their complicated definitions, madness and foolishness are often excluded from discussions of disability. I categorize them here as disabilities for a number of reasons: (1) to identify my allegiance with the project of disability studies, which does not segregate physical and mental disabilities; (2) to maintain historical accuracy, since early modern medicine, although it did treat madness differently than other impairments, did not impose a Cartesian separation of body and mind in its diagnosis and therapeutics; (3) to comport with emerging early modern legal definitions of disability, which grouped madness with impairments such as blindness, deafness, lameness, etc., in its categorization and distribution of financial compensation.

5. There is not a perfect correlation between "madness" and "foolishness" and what we today term mental or intellectual disability. As C. F. Goodey has demonstrated, words such as "fool" and "madman" were not limited to psychiatric impairments, but could also indicate social, economic, or religious status; see Goodey, "'Foolishness' in Early Modern Medicine and the Concept of Intellectual Disability," *Medical History* 48 (2004): 289–310. Yet because these terms primarily described mental disability, I use them as such. Importantly, the two terms were not identical in the Renaissance: "madness" tended to indicate a more volatile and often temporary loss of reason, while "foolishness" signaled a wide spectrum of longer-term mental incapacities; even so, given the imprecision of early modern medical terminology, they were often used interchangeably. I attempt to strategically differentiate between them where appropriate in order to retain their historical and cultural implications.

6. Throughout this article I use the conventional term "revenge tragedy" to refer to those early modern plays that engage issues of justice and retribution, follow a classically tragic model, and often repeat a set of Senecan tropes; early modern playwrights and audiences would not have used this term to designate these plays as a distinct category.

7. Fredson Bowers, *Elizabethan Revenge Tragedy, 1587–1642* (Princeton, NJ: Princeton University Press, 1940), 89.

8. Montaigne offers an entire essay on the dangers of pretending impairment, because "I have heard many examples of people falling ill after pretending to be so." See Michel de Montaigne, "On not pretending to be ill," in *The Complete Essays,* ed. M. A. Screech (New York: Penguin, 2003), 782.

9. For more on theatrical early modern medical case studies, see Winfried Schleiner, "Justifying the Unjustifiable: The Dover Cliff Scene in *King Lear*," *Shakespeare Quarterly* 36, no. 3 (1985): 337–43; for musical performance in early modern medicine, see Peregrine Horden, *Music as Medicine: The History of Music Therapy since Antiquity* (Aldershot, UK: Ashgate, 2000).

10. MacDonald, *Mystical Bedlam*, 126.

11. David A. Sprunger, "Depicting the Insane: A Thirteenth-Century Case Study," in *Marvels, Monsters, and Miracles: Studies in the Medieval and Early Modern Imaginations*, ed. Timothy S. Jones and David A. Sprunger (Kalamazoo: Western Michigan University Press, 2002), 231.

12. Allen Thiher, *Revels in Madness: Insanity in Medicine and Literature* (Ann Arbor: University of Michigan Press, 1999), 74.

13. Desiderius Erasmus, *The Praise of Folly*, ed. and trans. Clarence H. Miller, 2nd ed. (New Haven, CT: Yale University Press), 132–38.

14. Peter Rushton, "Lunatics and Idiots: Mental Disability, the Community, and the Poor Law in North-East England, 1600–1800," *Medical History* 32 (1988): 40.

15. William Shakespeare, *Hamlet*, *The Complete Works of Shakespeare*, Ed. David Bevington, 5th ed. (New York: Pearson/Longman, 2003), 1091–1149. All play citations hereafter are quoted within the text via act, scene, and line.

16. Rushton notes poignantly that "innocent" as a euphemism for mental/intellectual disabilities was particularly popular among the relatives of people with those impairments ("Lunatics and Idiots," 37).

17. Sprunger, "Depicting the Insane," 231–33.

18. John Southworth, *Fools and Jesters at the English Court* (London: Sutton, 1998), 163–74.

19. See Lily B. Campbell, *Shakespeare's Tragic Heroes, Slaves of Passion* (Cambridge [Eng.]: The University Press, 1930) and "Theories of Revenge in Renaissance England." *Modern Philology* 38 (1931): 281–96.

20. See Bowers, *Revenge Tragedy*.

21. Hallett and Hallett, *The Revenger's Madness*, 51.

22. Barbara J. Baines, "*Antonio's Revenge*: Marston's Play on Revenge Plays," *Studies in English Literature* 23, no. 2 (1983): 277–94.

23. See Thiher, *Revels*.

24. Jonathan Dollimore, *Radical Tragedy: Religion, Ideology and Power in the Drama of Shakespeare and His Contemporaries*, 3rd ed. (New York: Palgrave, 2004), 34.

25. Anne Duprat, "*Stultitia loquitur*: Fiction and Folly in Early Modern Literature," *Comparative Critical Studies* 5, nos. 2–3 (2008): 141–51.

26. Mitchell and Snyder, *Narrative Prosthesis*, 49.

27. Ibid., 53–54.

28. Ibid., 48.

29. Thomas Kyd, *The Spanish Tragedy*. *English Renaissance Drama*, ed. David Bevington (London: Norton, 2002), 3–73.

30. John Marston, *Antonio's Revenge*, ed. W. Reavley Gair (Manchester: University of Manchester Press, 1978).

31. Hallett and Hallett, *Revenger's Madness*, 78.

32. Mitchell and Snyder, *Narrative Prosthesis*, 48.

33. Ibid., 50.

34. In his reading of Shakespeare's *Othello*, David Houston Wood identifies a similar "cure and/or kill" phenomenon at work in that play's use of the prosthetic narrative. Yet because of the humoral practice of characterizing "health" or "normalcy" as an essentially unattainable state of being, Wood notes that disability was "an implicitly ubiquitous feature of early modern English life." In this case, Wood argues that the version of disability we encounter in early modern prosthetic narratives tends to be more "inward and covert" than those identified by Mitchell and Snyder. The dual protective measures implied by the "cure *and* kill" practice of revenge tragedy seem to affirm Wood's suggestion that early modern disability was indeed more inward and covert, since the narrative strategies that incorporated disability also necessitated a more stringent elimination of that disability in order to provide narrative resolution; see "'Flustered with Flowing Cups': Alcoholism, Humoralism, and the Prosthetic Narrative in *Othello*," *Disability Studies Quarterly* 29, no. 4 (2009): n.p. http://dsq-sds.org/article/view/998/1182.

35. The exception here is Antonio in *Antonio's Revenge*, who is freed of his disability but does not die after exacting his vengeance. For explanations of this atypical ending, see Dollimore, *Radical Tragedy*, and Phoebe Spinrad, "The Sacralization of Revenge in *Antonio's Revenge*," *Comparative Drama* 39, no. 2 (2005): 169–85.

CHAPTER 5

Disabling Allegories in Edmund Spenser's *Faerie Queene*

RACHEL E. HILE

n *The Rule of Metaphor,* Paul Ricoeur explores the philosophical and linguistic significance of metaphors that lose their status as metaphors by
means of "lexicalization," a process by means of which "dead metaphors
are no longer metaphors, but instead are associated with literal meaning."[1]
Without directly referencing Ricoeur, George Lakoff and Mark Johnson
address the issue of dead metaphors and arrive at the opposite conclusion:
"Expressions like *wasting time, attacking positions, going our separate ways,*
etc., are reflections of systematic metaphorical concepts that structure our
actions and thoughts. They are 'alive' in the most fundamental sense: they are
metaphors we live by."[2] Pervasive as they are, such lexicalized metaphors can
provide insight into the conceptual frameworks underlying a given culture's
language and thought, including ideas about bodies and bodily differences.
Lexicalized metaphors that associate sight with knowledge and blindness
with ignorance,[3] for example, or standing erect with moral and intellectual
merit and slouching or sitting with sloth[4] indicate a negative social valuation
of physically impaired persons so ingrained that such metaphors have hard-
ened for English speakers into "literal" expressions.

Judith Anderson, weighing in on the dead-metaphor question in regard
to early modern England, argues that the multilingual educational system
of the Renaissance would mean that many people, aware of etymological

roots of words, would be able to recognize a word or expression's genesis in metaphor.[5] Further, Katharine Eisaman Maus points out that early modern belief in Galenic (i.e., humors-based) theories of the human body means that it is difficult to know, in encountering expressions that we read as dead metaphors (e.g., references to "hot-headedness" for an angry, "choleric" person), "when we are dealing with metaphor and when with a bare statement of fact."[6] Michael Schoenfeldt echoes this conclusion, noting that "by urging a particularly organic account of inwardness and individuality, Galenic medical theory gave poets a language of inner emotion whose vehicles were also tenors, whose language of desire was composed of the very stuff of being."[7] Despite present-day difficulties in assessing the "liveliness" to early modern readers of metaphors that have since become formulaic, the elaboration of metaphor into allegory certainly serves to enhance a reader's awareness of metaphor as metaphor. One can breathe new life into a dead metaphor by extending it into an allegory, giving it characters and plot.

In this essay, I discuss the ways that Edmund Spenser revivifies dead metaphors of physical impairment, creating impaired allegorical figures that lead readers to his intended moral judgments by calling on his audience's shared biases and preconceptions related to bodily differences. Spenser sometimes uses impairment allegorically to elicit an intellectual response, using the image of physical or bodily privation to signal a moral incapacity essential to the plot of the allegory, as in the case of Corceca and Abessa. More often, however, Spenser's allegories of physical impairment aim to create emotional rather than intellectual reactions from the reader—specifically, emotions related to disgust and rejection—to lead readers to the desired moral interpretations.

In this manner, Spenser "imports" the full weight of social stigmatization of bodily differences in early modern England into the text in order to convey moral meanings that have nothing to do with physical impairment. Spenser takes for granted that his readers share stigmatizing ideas about and rejecting emotional attitudes toward physical impairment; transferring these ideas and attitudes allegorically from representations of impaired bodies to abstract ideas serves as an efficient means of conveying meaning, because preexisting cultural biases perform some of the work. The social model of disability posits a dichotomy between "impairment," defined as "a problem in body function or structure," and "disability," defined with reference to the social process that turns impairment, understood as neutral, into a socially stigmatized and undesirable state; "disability" thus reflects "an interaction between features of a person's body and features of the society in which he or she lives."[8] Thus, Spenser often creates impaired allegorical figures, taking for granted that his readers will perform the work of "disabling" those figures, and they must do so in order to glean the correct interpretation of the allegory.

Cognitive Metaphor Theory and Allegory

In conceptualizing metaphor as a figure of *thought,* the cognitive metaphor theory developed over the past three decades (and its extension to allegory) represents a break with earlier theories of metaphor that understood it as a figure of language only. George Lakoff and Mark Johnson define metaphor as involving the mapping of ideas and images from one conceptual domain (the "source domain") onto another (the "target domain"). Although this definition differs substantially from earlier twentieth-century theories of metaphor, Lakoff and Johnson's definition fits strikingly well with that put forth by George Puttenham in *The Art of English Poesy* (1589) when he asks, drawing upon the etymological background of the term, "for what else is your *Metaphor* but an inversion of sense by transport."[9] But what is transported? Although the number of possible source domains is as limitless as the number of possible target domains, metaphor has a tendency to describe the abstract in terms of the concrete. Research from the present moment finds much metaphorical meaning transported from the domain of the human body to other conceptual domains, and this was true as well during the early modern period.

Metaphors of the body enable one to "conceptualize the nonphysical *in terms of* the physical."[10] The importance of body metaphors is borne out by Zoltán Kövecses's study of the most common source domains of metaphors; he places "The Human Body" and "Health and Illness" first and second, respectively, in his list of the thirteen most common source domains.[11] To the extent that two people experience similar bodily actions, the body as source domain can help in sharing understandings of more abstract concepts, as noted by numerous scholars addressing the significance of embodied action to metaphorical mental structures. In a discussion of metaphors that draw on physical orientation, Lakoff and Johnson argue that a spatial orientation as source domain depends upon "the fact that we have bodies of the sort we have and that they function as they do in our physical environment."[12] Similarly, Mark Johnson follows an analysis of embodied understandings of CONTAINMENT, FORCE, and BALANCE with the summary statement that "certain abstract inference patterns are the result of metaphorical projections of image schemata . . . which arise in our bodily experience" (note that I follow the usage of cognitive metaphor theorists in using small caps to notate cognitive metaphors and concepts).[13]

But of course these experiences, assumed to be universal, depend on the experience of unimpaired bodies, as Amy Vidali points out in her critique of Lakoff and Johnson's analysis of the KNOWING IS SEEING metaphor.[14] George Lakoff and Mark Turner acknowledge the nonuniversality of the experiences underlying conceptual metaphors in general (though the example they provide refers to sexual experience, not embodied ways of being in the world), noting that "Metaphors may be grounded not only in recurrent direct experience but also in knowledge. . . . basic metaphors vary in the degree to which they have a grounding in experience or cohere with commonplace knowledge."[15] Implicitly, Lakoff and Turner here acknowledge that a culture's collection of conceptual metaphors is created by the majority. Recent experiments by Daniel Casasanto suggest, though, that even when a minority group (in his study, left-handed people) follows the linguistic norms of a culture by, for example, using linguistic formulae that associate right with good and left with bad, their embodied experience can actually override this linguistic cultural blueprint. His experiments showed that "Right-handers were more likely than left-handers to associate *right* with positive ideas and *left* with negative ideas. Left-handers were more likely than right-handers to associate *left* with positive ideas and *right* with negative ideas."[16] He proposes that

> Good Is Right and Good Is Left mental metaphors are created in right- and left-handers, respectively, via correlational learning . . . over a lifetime of lopsided perceptuomotor experience. People come to implicitly associate good things more strongly with the side of space they can interact with more fluently (their dominant side) and bad things with the side of space they interact with less fluently (their nondominant side).[17]

Casasanto's research certainly offers suggestive possibilities for considering the distinctive qualities of physically impaired people's body-based conceptual apparatuses and how their experiences of metaphors derived from embodied action might differ as well.

Such research reminds us of the need to be attentive to the role of subjectivity in the creation and use of metaphors. Just as embodied experience can affect a person's ways of conceptualizing abstract ideas through metaphor, the imagined subject position of the receiver of a metaphoric message also contributes to the meaning of the metaphor. In the case of metaphors and allegories presented within a literary text, the author signals the expected subject position of the person encountering a metaphor: for metaphors based on bodily experience, the reader will be expected either to identify with the metaphoric representation or else to see it as Other.

Between the two types of early modern English impairment-based metaphors that I will discuss in this essay, the most important distinction arises from the way the reader conceives the meaning, whether it be primarily through intellection or primarily through emotion. The frequency in *The Faerie Queene* of metaphors that invite an emotional reaction of disgust for and rejection of the impaired body illustrates David Mitchell and Sharon Snyder's observation that "disability as a narrative device—an artistic prosthesis . . . reveals the pervasive dependency of artistic, cultural, and philosophical discourses upon the powerful alterity assigned to people with disabilities."[18] Many of Spenser's metaphoric representations of physical impairment assume that the reader will imaginatively reject as Other the body described; by importing into the reader's experience of the text preexisting cultural biases regarding impairment, these disabling metaphors exemplify Mitchell and Snyder's "narrative prosthesis," in that they allow Spenser to convey meaning with less work. They also illustrate the importance of emotion in the creation of metaphors or allegories; Spenser seems acutely aware of the emotional reactions his early modern readers are likely to experience in response to descriptions of physically impaired bodies, responses not entirely different from those identified by present-day theorists of the abject. Bill Hughes, for example, calls attention to the emotional responses of fear and disgust that result from the abjection of disability: "The role of fear . . . is hugely underplayed in personal tragedy theory. So [too] is the role of disgust, a mediating emotion in the relations between disabled and nondisabled people that is in need of considerable development."[19] Spenser expects readers to transfer the fear and disgust activated by his disabling descriptions of impaired bodies to abstractions such as, for example, "wrathfulness" and "divisiveness."

We can see evidence of Spenser's goal of eliciting emotional responses from his readers to the personifications that inhabit Faeryland in his curious departures from traditional emblematic representations of such figures as Occasion and Ate. Spenser chooses to make them hideous and physically impaired, presumably in order to call on predictable responses of disgust in his readers. In doing so, he exemplifies some of the methods of meaning-making that distinguish allegory from metaphor. Peter Crisp argues that the essential difference between the two is that allegory does not refer directly to the target domain; instead, all the language refers to the source domain: "Allegory brings the metaphorical source domain to life in a way that no other form of metaphorical language can. Its peculiar imaginative excitement . . . resides in the fact that a metaphorical source domain is given its own, strange and fantastic, fictional life, instead of just being mapped straight onto a target domain."[20] One way to help readers draw the correct target-domain inferences from the strange, fantastic fictional world developed out of the source domain is to elicit powerful emotional responses to guide their own analyses. Certainly, as Mark Turner notes, "One of the most basic of the personification metaphors is AN ABSTRACT PROPERTY IS A PERSON WHOSE SALIENT CHARACTERISTIC IS THAT PROPERTY."[21] However, to make the personification compelling, an emotional reaction is desirable: "the way we feel about the appearance and character of the personification must correspond to the way we feel about the event."[22] Spenser illustrates these ideas, teaching his readers how to "fashion a gentleman or noble person in virtuous and gentle discipline" in part by holding up *un*-gentle, *ig*-noble personifications and inviting his readers to judge and reject them.[23]

Impairment-Based Allegories of Bodily Difference

Although recent theorists have analyzed the philosophical and political problems with the dichotomy between "impairment" and "disability" described earlier,[24] I find the dichotomy useful for identifying two qualitatively different kinds of allegory based on bodily difference. In what I call "impairment-based allegories," an allegorical figure's physical inability to perform some task leads to an intellectual interpretation of the allegorical situation, whereas in "disability-based allegories," the allegorical figure's bodily differences elicit a rejecting emotional reaction from the reader, and the reader's emotions guide the interpretation of the allegory. All of the allegorical figures I will discuss here depend upon an implied acceptance of the metaphor A MORAL STATE IS A PHYSICAL STATE, and all of them take for granted that an impaired body is less valuable than an unimpaired body, but there are nevertheless important qualitative differences between allegories based on the intellect versus the emotions as the source of meaning-making.

A well-known example of impairment-based allegory appears in *Everyman,* where Good Deeds's inability to walk plays a significant part in the plot. Good Deeds lies on the ground, "sore bound" by the sins of Everyman, so that she "cannot stir."[25] Her mobility impairment makes it impossible for her to attend Everyman on his journey to Death, despite her twice-expressed willingness: "I would full fain" (498) and "fain would I help you, and I were able" (515). Because other allegorical figures have falsely indicated willingness to accompany Everyman, the impairment is necessary to convince the audience that her repeated expressions of desire to help are not lies. She tells him, "I cannot stand, verily" and "on my feet I may not go" (498, 518). Throughout the play, Good Deeds is presented as a wholly positive character; her impairment prevents her from helping as much as she would like to, but she is always unambiguously good. The author here expects the audience to apprehend the meaning through intellection; the concept of privation is assumed to be connected with impairment in the audience member's mind, and transferring the idea of privation to the abstraction "good deeds" leads to the intended allegorical meaning: Everyman's spiritual heedlessness means that his good deeds are insufficient to help him achieve a good death.

Another example of impairment-based allegory, which will be relevant to the next section's discussion of Spenser's allegorical treatment of Ate, appears in Andrea Alciato's early sixteenth-century emblem representation of Ate, the goddess of discord. The emblem "Remedia in arduo, mala in prono esse" depicts Ate in flight, her wings making her even more capable of bodily movement than the average person, while the Litae, representatives of prayers and thus of goodness, chase after her despite their physical impairments:

> Once Jupiter had cast Ate down from the heavenly abode, what an evil bane thereafter assailed poor man! Ate flies out fleet of foot with fast-beating wing and leaves nothing untouched by mishap. So Jove's daughters, the Litae, accompany her as she goes, to mend whatever ill she has brought about. But they are slow-footed, poor of sight and weary with age, and so they restore nothing until later, after long passage of time.[26]

The illustration shows two of the three Litae using canes to support them in their pursuit of Ate. The process of allegorical meaning-making here again proceeds through an intellectual process of transfer of ideas, in the same manner as the example of Good Deeds in *Everyman:* the desire of the Litae to do good is inhibited by a physical impairment, again illustrating the metaphoric concept A MORAL STATE IS A PHYSICAL STATE.

These two examples, *Everyman* from the late fifteenth century and Alciato from the early to mid-sixteenth century, invite the audience to map meanings from the impaired body onto the moral and theological domain primarily through a transfer of ideas rather than through a transfer of emotional reactions. Similarly, in *The Faerie Queene* Spenser creates in the Corceca and Abessa episode an allegory based on bodily difference in which the reader's meaning-making depends upon intellect rather than emotion.

In this episode, physical impairments represent the lack of spiritual under-standing that Spenser sees as typical of the Roman Catholic believer. The brief episode of Una's encounter with the blind Corceca (literally, "blind heart"), her deaf and mute daughter Abessa (presumably derived from Latin *abesse,* "absence of being"; reminiscent of "abbess" or "abbey"), and Kirkrap-ine ("plunderer of churches") serves as a clear allegorical indictment of Catholicism. Abessa's and Corceca's impairments are allegorically significant. Corceca, thrice referred to as "blind" (1.3.12.3, 1.3.18.3, 1.3.22.2), sits "in eternall night" (1.3.12.4), and her daughter Abessa "could not heare, nor speake, nor vnderstand" (1.3.11.4);[27] allegorically, Corceca's physical blind-ness maps metaphorically to a spiritual state of unthinking superstition, as becomes clear from references to the 900 paternosters and 2,700 aves she says daily, to her use of sackcloth and ashes, and to her regular fasting prac-tice. Despite this impressive array of spiritual practices, however, upon the arrival of Una at the cottage, Corceca "for feare her beads . . . did forget" (1.3.14.5). Abessa meets Una and the lion by a well, and her inability to hear or speak renders her unteachable, in contrast to the Samaritan woman at the well described in the Gospel of John (John 4:3–42). Although the Samaritan woman at first reacts with confusion to the statements of Jesus, she eventually understands, believes, and evangelizes, whereas Abessa never overcomes her initial fear at meeting Una and the lion.[28] Abessa's impair-ments are understood by Spenser and his contemporary audience as making it impossible for her to learn and understand the truth. Darryl J. Gless con-nects Abessa with "various New Testament figures whose sensory deficiencies declare their need for the grace that roots out sin and enables perception of spiritual truth. Yet Christ heals these biblical figures,"[29] whereas Abessa's and Corceca's encounter with true faith in the form of Una leaves them unchanged.

The impairments of Corceca and Abessa are more germane to the alle-gorical plot than are the impairments of Occasion and Ate, but these are by no means positive characters. Spenser includes unattractive characterizing details for Corceca and Abessa, in line with the emphasis on eliciting from the reader an emotional reaction that matches the negativity of the allegori-cal idea. Notably, however, the impairments themselves are not treated with disgust. Instead, we are invited to judge Abessa harshly because of her sexual and financial dealings with Kirkrapine, who

whoredome vsd [with her], that few did know,
And fed her fatt with feast of offerings,
And plenty, which in all the land did grow;

Ne spared he to giue her gold and rings:
And now he to her brought part of his stolen things. (1.3.18.5–9)

As for Corceca, she transforms from a superstitious but mild-mannered old woman into a railing hag when she pursues Una away from her house, where the Lion has slain Kirkrapine. Mother and daughter accost Una and begin to "loudly bray, / with hollow houling, and lamenting cry, / Shamefully at her rayling all the way" (1.3.23.1–3).[30] Criticizing a young female allegorical figure for "whoredome" is as unsurprising as attaching a negative evaluation to an older female allegorical figure by connecting her with the many hag-figures who people Faeryland, but here at least physical impairment does not figure prominently in the negative emotional value Spenser attaches to these figures.

Disabling Allegories of Bodily Difference

Whereas the examples discussed in the previous section illustrate impairment-based allegories, some allegories are "disabling" in the sense that, as the social model of disability posits, they focus on eliciting emotional reactions to the disabled body based on social stigma and disgust. Spenser, with his reliance on emotional effects on the reader to convey allegorical meaning efficiently, creates a number of disabling allegories. I will consider here his personifications of Occasion and Ate; in both cases, Spenser's figures differ from contemporary emblems of the same abstractions in representing them as having physical impairments. These departures from emblem-book treatments of Occasion and Ate support my contention that Spenser consciously aims to elicit feelings of disgust and stigmatizing reactions in readers; I argue that Spenser's efforts to engage his readers' emotions to convey his allegorical meaning exemplify Philip Sidney's ideas about the ability of poetry to *move* readers to virtue.

I focus here primarily on Spenser's use of disgust to encourage readers to turn away not simply the intellect but also the will from the vices portrayed in the allegorical figures of Occasion and Ate. Much scholarly work on early modern emotions has focused on melancholy and sadness, presumably because the period's intense interest in and textual representations of melancholy make it a more knowable topic for transhistorical emotional analysis.[31] Analyses of Spenser's ideas about emotion have tended to follow this general emphasis on melancholy, but he certainly provides nuanced explorations of a multitude of emotions and affective states. Both Douglas Trevor and

Christopher Tilmouth see Spenser as endorsing the importance of reason in reining in strong emotions.[32] Trevor argues that although Spenser lauds "sadness" as a positive emotional state, he sees humoral psychology's ideas about melancholy as enabling people to shirk spiritual responsibility for emotional self-indulgence. Similarly, Tilmouth finds in Spenser a "psychomachic" view of the human soul, in which reason should be victorious over passion. Yet, perhaps in line with Trevor's discovery of positive "sadness" in Spenserian characters such as Redcrosse, Jennifer Vaught argues that Spenser presents men's weeping as a source of strength for Redcrosse and for the emotional male figures in book 6, the Legend of Courtesy.[33]

Yet these analyses, which focus on the sorrowful emotional experiences and expressions of allegorical figures *within* Spenser's epic, do not address the issue of Spenser's understanding of the role of emotion in conveying allegorical meaning or, more generally, in leading readers to virtue. Although, as Tilmouth argues, many Renaissance humanists did endorse a Stoic-inspired quelling of all affect, other ideas on emotion also influenced the discourse on emotion and thought. As Richard Strier points out, "insofar as self-consciously 'Renaissance' figures defined themselves as committed to rhetoric over against 'mere' philosophy or logic, they were committed to stressing the importance of the emotional and affective in life."[34] The rhetorician's emphasis on the importance of the emotional appeal in persuasion serves as secular support for the value of emotional experience, but religious ideas supported this as well, as Strier notes and as Gail Kern Paster develops in her discussion of Bishop Edward Reynolds's *Treatise of the Passions and Faculties of the Soule of Man* (1640), in which Reynolds compares Christ's emotions to human emotions in order to argue, in Paster's analysis, that "it is human sinfulness that makes immoderate passions an instrument of self-harm . . . not the passions themselves."[35] Spenser himself seems to argue for the importance of emotions in the episode at the Castle of Alma, when Arthur and Guyon meet the bevy of female personifications of passions in the heart, and each chooses the one who represents his own emotional makeup. Michael Schoenfeldt argues that "this strange . . . encounter involves a wary affirmation of emotion in the well-regulated moral life. Where temperance could sometimes be imagined to entail the rejection of passion entirely, Spenser here situates the passions at the heart of his temperate self, as spurs to the very virtue he depicts rather than as forces opposing it."[36]

In *The Defense of Poesy*, Philip Sidney's claims regarding poetry's ability to teach virtue rest on the importance of emotional responses to the situations depicted by the poet, with depictions of virtue leading to emotional attraction and those of vice leading to rejection, so that readers learn virtue "ere themselves be aware, as if they took a medicine of cherries."[37] In line with Sidney's prescriptions, when creating allegorical representations of virtue, Spenser aims to make them attractive to the reader; for the same reason, he emphasizes the unattractive qualities of allegorical representations of vice, and one way of creating an unattractive personification and thus eliciting a rejecting emotional response in his reader is to give a personification a physical impairment. In creating Occasion, Spenser both alludes to and departs from the emblematic tradition for this personification; in line with tradition, he gives her a long forelock and makes the back of her head bald, but unlike emblematic depictions of Occasion, Spenser's is ugly, old, and physically impaired:

> And him behind, a wicked Hag did stalke,
> In ragged robes, and filthy disaray,
> Her other leg was lame, that she no'te walke,
> But on a staffe her feeble steps did stay;
> Her lockes, that loathly were and hoarie gray,
> Grew all afore, and loosly hong vnrold,
> But all behinde was bald, and worne away,
> That none thereof could euer taken hold,
> And eke her face ill fauourd, full of wrinckles old. (2.4.4)

The iconographic detail of the forelock makes her identity clear to a knowledgeable reader, whereas the references to poverty, physical impairment, and her ugliness from age clarify Spenser's intention to make Occasion a symbol of vice rather than an opportunity for good. Sheila Cavanagh's feminist analysis of the hags in *The Faerie Queene* could fruitfully be extended to account for the impairment markers of many of the hags: "The poem's insistence upon marking the sex and gender of these creatures allows a thread of misogyny to weave through denunciations of their behavior. In fact, it is often difficult to distinguish slurs against individual hags or witches from those against women in general."[38] Just as the references to her clothing, hair, and face elicit a disgust reaction by activating stereotypes of old women that the audience already held, the references to her limp and the staff she uses to walk transfer to this personification the social stigma that Spenser can expect his contemporary readers already to associate with impaired bodies. Spenser creates an even more unpleasant association with Occasion's impairment by connecting it with her violence in instigating Furor to harm Phaon: "Somtimes she raught him stones, wherwith to smite, / Sometimes her staffe,

though it her one leg were, / Withouten which she could not goe vpright"
(2.4.5.5–7).

Scholars have noted the difference between Spenser's Occasion and the
emblem tradition on which he draws for the iconographic detail of the forelock and bald occiput. James McManaway summarizes the typical details
that identify Occasion in emblem books: "the figure of a young, vigorous
woman with winged feet (or standing on fortune's wheel or on a ball and
a dolphin). Her head is bald save for a long forelock, and in her hand she
usually holds a razor."[39] Both McManaway and Manning and Fowler have
attempted to explain Spenser's divergences from the traditional iconography
of Occasion by finding other emblematic sources that, combined with details
from emblem representations of Occasion, might add up to Spenser's Occasion. McManaway argues for Spenser's use of iconographic details from Discord and Envy, and Manning and Fowler add to this argument the assertion
that Spenser draws as well on emblem representations of Penitence.[40]

It seems to me that these analyses underestimate the complexity of Spenser's inventing imagination, tying him to emblems as though these were his
only source of inspiration for personifications. Surely, Spenser owes a huge
debt to the emblem tradition, but a principal concern in his creation of
these personifications is the importance of signaling not only intellectually,
not only visually (ekphrastically, that is), but *emotionally* as well, the allegorical meaning of the personifications. Paul Alpers, commenting on Spenser's
allegorical method in this episode, hints at this idea in his suggestion that
Spenser, in creating the episode, began with an image, not a verbal formula.
Alpers argues that emblem creation begins by translating words into images,
and he provides emblem examples of physically impaired women (including
Alciato's "Remedia in arduo," discussed earlier) to arrive at an interpretation
in line with my distinction between impairment and disability in metaphor:
"The lameness of these personifications is a metaphor for the slowness with
which . . . prayers and punishment take effect. But the lameness of Spenser's
hag . . . has no conceptual equivalent, and we therefore cannot assume that
the formula 'Occasion is lame' produced this part of Spenser's description."[41]
Alpers posits that Spenser, instead of beginning with some verbal formula
such as this, began instead with the image of "an allegorical hag who provoked wrath" and added details and iconographic signifiers from there.[42] I
am less concerned with the genesis of Spenser's creativity than with its out-
comes, especially the ways that readers come to understand the intended allegorical meanings. But to add to Alpers's emphasis on the allegorical function
of the *image,* as opposed to the *idea,* I would call attention to the reader's

emotional response as another important part of Spenser's goals for this figure. Words such as "filthy," "feeble," and "loathly" do more than create an
image—they also elicit negative emotions.

Like Occasion, Ate is one of Spenser's many "allegorical hags," and her
representation is designed in part to illustrate an idea, but the process of
meaning-making for this figure is not solely intellectual but emotional as
well. Ate symbolizes discord and division among people, and Spenser represents this allegorically by giving her a discordant and divided body—her
"monstrous shape" makes it clear that she "was borne of hellish brood"
(4.1.26.7, 9):

> And as her eares so eke her feet were odde,
> And much vnlike, th'one long, the other short,
> And both misplast; that when th'one forward yode,
> The other backe retired, and contrarie trode. (4.1.28.6–9)

This allegorical personification differs significantly from Alciato's "Remedia
in arduo." A woman who walks forward and backward at the same time
would seem unable to wreak as much mischief as Alciato's flying Ate, and
yet both Alciato and Spenser use physical impairment to make connections
between source and target domains. However, whereas Alciato's connection
is logical, Spenser's is emotional. The description includes numerous examples of words that convey not just an image but also a negative emotion:
Ate's "squinted eyes contrarie wayes intended" (4.1.27.2); she has a "loathly
mouth, vnmeete a mouth to bee" (4.1.27.3); and she hears with "matchlesse
eares deformed and distort" (4.1.28.2). Spenser repeatedly uses this kind
of emotional "argument" based on disgust reactions to personifications to
lead his readers to the correct moral judgment of the allegorical situation at
hand. I have discussed here the examples of Ate and Occasion because the
fact that Spenser diverges from established emblem conventions provides evidence that Spenser was conscious of the meaning-making effects he hoped to
achieve by creating physically impaired allegorical figures that his audience
would read through the lens of disabling social stigma.

Emotional impact plays an important role in creating an effective personification, and for personifications in *The Faerie Queene* meant to represent moral failings, Spenser relies to a great extent on the emotion of disgust.
William Ian Miller defends disgust as an emotion, noting that although it
does have a "more 'embodied' feel than other emotions," it fits the definition of an emotion: "Emotions are feelings linked to ways of talking about
those feelings, to social and cultural paradigms that make sense of those feel-

ings by giving us a basis for knowing when they are properly felt and properly displayed. Emotions, even the most visceral, are richly social, cultural, and linguistic phenomena."[43] The details that Spenser uses to elicit disgust reactions from readers to his personifications of Occasion and Ate of course are not limited to their physical impairments—Cavanagh ably demonstrates the misogynist ideas and imagery that contribute to these figures, and one could easily make an argument about the ageism underlying Spenser's depictions of hags as well. These overdetermined sources of disgust reactions provide signposts regarding both the emotional and ideological responses of early modern English people to categories of people understood as Other. Miller notes the wide-ranging, indiscriminate nature of such disgust, which "judges ugliness and deformity to be moral offenses" and "knows no distinction between the moral and the aesthetic, collapsing failures in both into an undifferentiated revulsion."[44] For Spenser, to describe a category of people by his culture understood to be ugly—the disabled, the old, the poor—is automatically to create a moral revulsion to the allegorical situation. Georgia Brown notes the significance of disgust in bringing together the physical and the ideological in this way: "Since disgust grounds the moral and political in sensory and emotional impulse, it embodies ideology, in the dual sense of expressing a particular ideology, and in the sense of giving ideology a material existence."[45] Spenser can count on the reader's revulsion in response to the disgusting, frail bodies he presents in so many of his allegorical personifications; he thus calls on the ideology of the Other's body in order to further his own, moral ideological agenda.

I HAVE AIMED to demonstrate two ideas in this essay. First, I argue in favor of finding and analyzing the distinctions among metaphors and allegories that use physical difference and impairment as source domain. Given the prevalence of the body as source domain for metaphors,[46] it is unrealistic to police the output of new metaphors and quite simply impossible to do so for the early modern period. It seems more fruitful to turn attention to the question of *how* these metaphors mean, and I have here metaphorically extended the distinction between impairment and disability to address the question of whether a metaphor or allegory derives its meaning solely from the mapping of a specific impairment onto another situation or whether the meaning derives as well from the stigmatizing emotional response associated with that impairment by the culture in which the metaphor or allegory originates.

My second point pertains specifically to Spenser's allegorical practice with personifications, which frequently rely a great deal on emotional impact to convey allegorical meaning. For this reason, these allegories based on physical difference are *disabling* metaphors, metaphors that serve to increase the audience's sense of the Other-ness of, and hence the necessity of rejecting, those with bodily differences. It is important to note, however, that Spenser does not single out physical impairment as the sole marker of Other-ness in his allegory; rather, stigmatizing disability is quite consistent with Spenser's use of disgusting details associated with other categories of people—women, the Irish, the lower classes, to name a few—to quickly elicit the necessary rejecting emotional response to clarify the negative valence to be attached to the allegorical figure. With this allegorical method, Spenser puts into practice the ideas of literary theorists such as Sidney, who argued for the supremacy of poetry—with its greater power than philosophy to move and its greater freedom than history to celebrate virtue—in spurring readers to virtue. His un-self-conscious reliance on preexisting cultural biases against unprivileged groups, such as disabled people, allows Spenser to import a whole system of emotional reactions to human difference into the moral world of Faeryland, leading, he hopes, to greater virtue in his ideal reader even as he reifies inequality and bias in his epic poem.

Notes

1. Paul Ricoeur, *The Rule of Metaphor: Multi-disciplinary Studies of the Creation of Meaning in Language,* trans. Robert Czerny with Kathleen McLaughlin and John Costello (Toronto: University of Toronto Press, 1977), 290.

2. George Lakoff and Mark Johnson, *Metaphors We Live By* (Chicago: University of Chicago Press, 1980), 55.

3. See Georgina Kleege, *Sight Unseen* (New Haven, CT: Yale University Press, 1999).

4. See Nancy Mairs, *Waist-High in the World: A Life among the Nondisabled* (Boston: Beacon Press, 1997).

5. Judith H. Anderson, *Translating Investments: Metaphor and the Dynamic of Cultural Change in Tudor-Stuart England* (New York: Fordham University Press, 2005), 14.

6. Katharine Eisaman Maus, *Inwardness and Theater in the English Renaissance* (Chicago: University of Chicago Press, 1995), 196.

7. Schoenfeldt, *Bodies and Selves,* 8.

8. See World Health Organization, *Disabilities* (Geneva: World Health Organization, 2010). Web. 28 July 2010. http://www.who.int/topics/disabilities/en/.

9. George Puttenham, *The Art of English Poesy,* ed. Frank Whigham and Wayne A. Rebhorn (Ithaca, NY: Cornell University Press, 2007), 238.

10. Lakoff and Johnson, *Metaphors We Live By,* 59.

11. Zoltán Kövecses, *Metaphor: A Practical Introduction,* 2nd ed. (New York: Oxford University Press, 2010), 18–19.

12. Lakoff and Johnson, *Metaphors We Live By,* 14.

13. Mark Johnson, *The Body in the Mind: The Bodily Basis of Meaning, Imagination, and Reason* (Chicago: University of Chicago Press, 1987), 96.

14. Amy Vidali, "Seeing What We Know: Disability and Theories of Metaphor," *Journal of Literary & Cultural Disability Studies* 4, no. 1 (2010): 33–54.

15. George Lakoff and Mark Turner, *More Than Cool Reason: A Field Guide to Poetic Metaphor* (Chicago: University of Chicago Press, 1989), 84.

16. Daniel Casasanto, "Embodiment of Abstract Concepts: Good and Bad in Right- and Left-Handers," *Journal of Experimental Psychology: General* 138, no. 3 (August 2009): 360.

17. Ibid.

18. Mitchell and Snyder, *Narrative Prosthesis,* 51.

19. Bill Hughes, "Wounded/Monstrous/Abject: A Critique of the Disabled Body in the Sociological Imaginary," *Disability & Society* 24, no. 2 (2009): 408. The concept of "the abject" as rejected Other bears many affinities with the ideas regarding disgust that I use here, and I commend Bill Hughes and Minae Inahara for their works extending Kristeva's comments on abjection to the field of disability theory; see also Minae Inahara, *Abject Love: Undoing the Boundaries of Physical Disability* (Saarbrücken, Germany: VDM Verlag Dr. Müller, 2009). I do believe that Spenser creates and recreates abjection in his allegorical personifications, including abject representations of disabled bodies, but I find Kristeva's ideas about abjection, as expressed in *Powers of Horror,* too broad to serve as a precise analytical tool for understanding this process, and so I choose here to focus on disgust as an emotion; see William Ian Miller, *The Anatomy of Disgust* (Cambridge, MA: Harvard University Press, 1997).

20. Peter Crisp, "Allegory: Conceptual Metaphor in History," *Language and Literature* 10 (2001): 10. Crisp asserts that although named personifications might seem to be examples of "direct linguistic reference to target domain entities," they are not, because such terms "function [not] as abstract nouns but as personal names. Idleness, Gluttony and Death . . . are named persons existing fictionally in their metaphorical source domains, from whom one maps onto the relevant abstract entities" (16, 17).

21. Mark Turner, *Death Is the Mother of Beauty: Mind, Metaphor, Criticism* (Chicago: University of Chicago Press, 1987), 21–22.

22. Lakoff and Turner, *More Than Cool Reason,* 79.

23. Spenser, *The Faerie Queene,* 714.

24. See Bill Hughes, "What Can a Foucauldian Analysis Contribute to Disability Theory?" in *Foucault and the Government of Disability,* ed. Shelley Tremain (Ann Arbor: University of Michigan Press, 2005), 78–92, and Shelley Tremain, "On the Subject of Impairment," in *Disability/Postmodernity: Embodying Disability Theory,* ed. Marian Corker and Tom Shakespeare (London: Continuum, 2002), 32–47.

25. *The Moral Play of Everyman,* in *Everyman and Medieval Miracle Plays,* ed. A. C. Cawley (London: J. M. Dent/Everyman, 1993), lines 487–88.

26. Andrea Alciato, *Emblemata: Lyons, 1550,* trans. Betty I. Knott (Brookfield, VT: Ashgate-Scholar, 1996), 142. The original Latin reads:

Aetheriis postquam deiecit sedibus Aten
Iuppiter: heu uexat quàm mala noxa uiros?
Euolat hæc pedibus celer, & pernicibus alis,

Intactúmque nihil casibus esse sinit.
Ergo Litæ, proles Iouis, hanc comitantur euntem,
Sarturæ quicquid fecerit illa mali.
Sed quia segnipedes, luscæ, lassæq[ue]; senecta,
Nil nisi post, longo tempore restituunt. (142)

27. Numeric references following quotations from *The Faerie Queene* refer to book, canto, stanza, and line numbers.

28. See Darryl J. Gless, "Abessa, Corceca, Kirkrapine," in Hamilton, *Spenser Encyclopedia*, 3–4.

29. Ibid., 3.

30. In stanza 23, Spenser seems to have forgotten that Abessa cannot speak, because "they gan loudly bray" (1.3.23.1); by the next stanza, the use of the pronoun "she" presumably refers to Corceca.

31. See Paster et al., in the introduction to *Early Modern Passions*, for a thoughtful discussion of the dangers of reading emotions across a divide of centuries (1–20).

32. Douglas Trevor, *The Poetics of Melancholy in Early Modern England* (Cambridge: Cambridge University Press, 2004); Christopher Tilmouth, *Passion's Triumph over Reason: A History of the Moral Imagination from Spenser to Rochester* (Oxford: Oxford University Press), 2007.

33. Jennifer C. Vaught, *Masculinity and Emotion in Early Modern English Literature* (Aldershot: Ashgate, 2008).

34. Richard Strier, "Against the Rule of Reason: Praise of Passion from Petrarch to Luther to Shakespeare to Herbert," in Paster et al., *Early Modern Passions*, 23.

35. Paster, *Humoring the Body*, 1.

36. Schoenfeldt, *Bodies and Selves*, 64–65.

37. Philip Sidney, *Sir Philip Sidney's Defense of Poesy*, ed. Lewis Soens (Lincoln: University of Nebraska Press, 1970), 25.

38. Sheila T. Cavanagh, *Wanton Eyes and Chaste Desires: Female Sexuality in* The Faerie Queene (Bloomington: Indiana University Press, 1994), 65.

39. James G. McManaway, "'Occasion,' *Faerie Queene* II.iv.4–5," *Modern Language Notes* 49, no. 6 (1934): 392.

40. John Manning and Alistair Fowler, "The Iconography of Spenser's Occasion," *Journal of the Warburg and Courtauld Institutes* 39 (1976): 263–66.

41. Paul J. Alpers, *The Poetry of* The Faerie Queene (Princeton, NJ: Princeton University Press, 1967), 214.

42. Ibid.

43. William Miller, *Anatomy of Disgust*, 7, 8.

44. Ibid., 21.

45. Georgia Brown, "Disgusting John Marston: Sensationalism and the Limits of a Post-Modern Marston," *Nordic Journal of English Studies* 4, no. 2 (2005): 137.

46. See Kövecses, *Metaphor*.

CHAPTER 6

Performing Blindness

Representing Disability in
Early Modern Popular Performance and Print

SIMONE CHESS

W hile scholarship has often attended to the metaphor of blindness in early modern literature, little attention has been devoted to instances in which literary texts present us with representations of individuals who are actually blind.[1] Disability theorists David T. Mitchell and Sharon L. Snyder argue that metaphors of disability, like blindness, within narrative are used to give a "tangible body" to abstract ideas.[2] But what are we to make of instances of "real" visual impairment, after having been so long conditioned to think of blindness less as a disability than a metaphor? What is the purpose of these blind characters on the stage and on the page? What can we learn from the textual specifics of their disabled bodies and of their use of adaptive language and technology? What does the spectacle of visual impairment mean for sighted (and for blind) readers or audiences?

As a metaphor, blindness—along with paralysis, limited mobility, cognitive difference, and other disabilities—is generally presented in negative

I am grateful to Wayne State University Humanities Center, the Wayne State Group for Early Modern Studies, and the Shakespeare Association of America's *Disabling Shakespeare* seminar and their participants for support of an early version of this essay. Jaime Goodrich, Lisa Maruca, and Michael Scrivener offered many helpful suggestions and ideas. Thanks especially to this volume's editors, for their smart and provocative feedback.

ways.[3] In their book *Narrative Prosthesis,* Mitchell and Snyder explain this pattern: "while literature often relies on disability's transgressive potential, disabled people have been sequestered, excluded, exploited, and obliterated on the very basis of which their literary representation exists."[4] And yet, in select textual instances where blindness is presented as a physical condition, the metaphorical trappings of visual impairment are reduced in a way that makes evident other, more material early modern concerns about disability. Rather than normalizing or erasing the presence of blind characters on the stage or page, these instances reveal early modern interest and investment in medical knowledge and in the lived experiences of the blind.

Using examples of blind and blinded characters in sources that include Shakespeare's *2 Henry VI* and the anonymous sixteenth-century play *Jacob and Esau,* sixteenth- and seventeenth-century scientific texts, and cheap-print ballads and broadsides, this essay explores how examining these representations of blindness on the stage and in print (and, alongside them, representations of the adaptive technologies used by early modern blind individuals) can unsettle the relationship between seeing and knowing, disability and agency, blindness as metaphor and as experiential. While it is unlikely that any of the blind characters were played by blind actors, I hope to show that physically blind characters, as opposed to metaphorically blind characterizations, had some of the same kinds of impacts as contemporary disabled performance artists who often use their own bodies on stage or in visual media as a way of "challenging both tired narrative conventions and aesthetic practices."[5] Further, by focusing on blindness as a real and embodied historical experience, these representations disrupt theoretical ideas of performativity, since, as Carrie Sandahl and Philip Auslander put it, "the notion that disability is a kind of performance is to people with disabilities not a theoretical abstraction, but lived experience."[6] If everyday life can be experienced as performance for people with visible disabilities, then early modern representations of disability on stage and in cheap print have the potential not only to displace metaphorical uses of disability with performances of actual disability but also to offer, through those performances, a glimpse at the everyday, lived "performance" of the early modern blind.

While perhaps the most attention to any moment of blindness in early modern drama has focused on Gloucester's blinding in *King Lear,* early modern attitudes toward blindness are more explicitly demonstrated in a strange (hundred-line) subplot of Shakespeare's less-discussed *The First Part of the Contention (2 Henry VI).*[7] In this subplot, the soon-to-be-overthrown King Henry is interrupted in his hunting by reports of a miracle at Saint Albans. This miracle, that one Simon Simpcox, born blind, has miraculously recovered his vision, is especially exciting to Henry, who immediately redirects his hunting party to see the supposed wonder.[8] When he hears that "a blind man at Saint Alban's shrine / Within this half-hour hath received his sight— / A man that ne'er saw in his life before now" (2.1.66–68), the king exclaims, "God be praised, that to believing souls / Gives light in darkness, comfort in despair!" (69–70). Though King Henry is willing to accept Simpcox's "miracle" based on his and his wife's testimonies, telling Simpcox that "God's goodness hath been great to thee" (86), his advisor and Protector, Gloucester is far more critical of Simpcox's recovery to sightedness. This attitude was realistic, informed by the medieval and early modern problem of beggars who feigned disabilities such as blindness.[9]

More than serving as a mere digression, then, Simpcox and his faked blindness provide Shakespeare with an opportunity to stage the scientific process through which this deception was famously uncovered. Though Simpcox's story of having been born blind has already been announced by the messenger ("ne'er saw in his life before"), confirmed by the king ("hast thou been long blind and now restored?"), and sworn by Simpcox and his wife ("Born blind, an't please your grace"; "Ay, indeed was he."), Gloucester repeats the question: "How long hast thou been blind?" (99). The play's intense focus on the fact that Simpcox claims to have been blind from birth makes him the perfect subject of scientific and philosophical inquiry. Georgina Kleege explains that "the hypothetical blind man" in philosophy "is always assumed to be both totally and congenitally blind," even though "real blindness, today as in the past, rarely fits this profile."[10] In emphasizing, through repetition, the fact that Simpcox is "born blind," Shakespeare allows for a performance of an important thought experiment in understanding blindness, conducted by Gloucester for the benefit of the audience at large.

This scientific spectacle takes place through an interrogation of Simpcox's story, his history, and his blindness. Curious over the fact that Simpcox is lame from a fall from a tree, Gloucester asks how he managed to climb it, if he was blind from birth. Unsatisfied with Simpcox's (lewd) answers, Gloucester launches into a rapid-fire volley of questions, designed to undermine the "subtle knave" (105). The speed and focus of Gloucester's investigation is striking, as is the dissonance between this dialogue and the rest of the scene, act, and play:

> GLOU: Let me see thine eyes: wink now, and open them.
>   In my opinion thou seest not well.
> SIMP: Yes, master, clear as day, I thank God and Saint Alban.

GLOUCESTER: Sayst thou me so? And what colour is this cloak of?
SIMP: Red, master, red as blood. . . .
GLOU: And what colour's my gown?
SIMP: Black, sir, coal-black as jet. . . .
GLOU: Tell me, sirrah, what's my name?
SIMP: Alas, master, I know not.
GLOU: What's his name?
SIMP: I know not. . . .
GLOU: What is thine own name?
SIMP: Simon Simpcox, an it please you, master.
GLOUCESTER: Then, Simon, sit thou there the lying'st knave
    In Christendom. If thou hadst been born blind
    Thou mightst as well have known our names as thus
    To name the several colours we do wear.
    Sight may distinguish colours, but suddenly
    To nominate them all—it is impossible.
    Saint Alban here hath done a miracle. (107–35)

Gloucester's examination of Simpcox, and his verdict against the man, is based on two major tests: the ability to recognize, differentiate between, and name colors; and the ability to recognize, sort, and identify people. As Gloucester sums up in his conclusions, this test is based upon the scientific or philosophical notion that "Sight may distinguish colours, but suddenly / To nominate them all—it is impossible." In this way, Gloucester outthinks Simpcox and proves that he is a fraud. But the scene renders visible some of the early modern stereotypes about vision loss, as well as some optical theories about the role that vision plays in determining color and identifying people.[11]

The scene of Simpcox's interrogation is enabled by the fact that Simpcox is posing as Kleege's "hypothetical blind man" so often used in philosophy: "He is the patient subject of endless thought experiments where the experience of the world through four senses can be compared to the experience of the world through five."[12] The Simpcox interlude, presented as it is as a pure thought experiment about the experience of blindness, requires Shakespeare to explore blindness on a physical and medical level.[13] The fact, for instance, that Gloucester is so interested in color reflects scientific interest in the ways that the eye could process, understand, and also misunderstand color. In his 1608 scientific text, *The Vanitie of the Eie*, George Hakewill discusses how the eye itself can offer false reports to the seer.[14] He likens the eye's trouble in discerning certain colors to our difficulty in seeing perspective:

Colours, in which reason by conclusions drawn out of her principles often checks & controules this sense for false reporting; for instance we need go no farther than those colours which appear in the rainbow, or on a doves neck by the reflection of the sunne's beames, those night-chasms & gapings in the firmament . . . These things all men knowe, and the greatest part acknowledge, to be errors of the eie, Though the learned only, search into and find out the causes of it.[15]

Hakewill understands the eye as an unreliable informant to the mind and understanding; even in cases of full sightedness, where the eye is functioning at its best, it can present confusing misinformation to the seer. At the same time, though, even as Hakewill enumerates the many untrustworthy qualities of ocular vision, he pushes for a single human understanding of sight when he asserts that "all men knowe" when they are being fooled by their eyes. This inconstancy between Hakewill's main point (that eyes are false informants prone to error) and his weak conclusion (that there is a universal agreement about which sight is authentic and which is fraudulent) reveals his hope that scientific inquiry can "search into and find the causes" of optical illusion, mis-sight, and, ultimately, visual impairments and idiosyncrasies. Indeed, by admitting the huge variety of visual misunderstandings that can happen in a sighted context, Hakewill reveals that full sightedness is unstable and that blindness and visual impairment, rather than being major variations from the norm, are actually the farthest points on a spectrum of inconsistent and unreliable sight.

Both Hakewill and Shakespeare approach their discussions of the nature of vision through the problem of misinterpreted visual data. In this manner, scientific analysis and dramatic representation are grounded in a shared interest in the working of the eye, and in interrogating the limits of vision and sight.[16] Though Simpcox was never actually blind, the evidence through which Gloucester reveals that he is faking simultaneously renders all vision and sightedness unfamiliar—Gloucester's questions reflect an early modern wonder at how it is that *anyone* can tell the difference between colors, or how any color can be a definitive thing, since even functioning eyes can deceive us (as Hakewill points out). Hakewill's casting of vision in this dubious light, according to Stuart Clark, is "the best example of the demolition of Renaissance optimism about vision."[17] In proving that Simpcox can see, Gloucester disrupts the audiences' intuitive sight, drawing attention to the act of looking and seeing, and potentially casting doubt on the efficacy of all sightedness. In this way, Simpcox's trial breaks down some of the seemingly clear distinction between able and disabled bodies; though the surface of the plot proves that Simpcox can see, and that his blindness was a false miracle, the mechanism for revealing this fraud causes more doubt than clarity.[18] Like Hakewill's *Vanitie of the Eie,* Shakespeare's *The First Part of the Contention* reveals that the idea of a pat universal visual ability is a false construction.[19]

In addition to exploring theoretical and philosophical aspects of vision and blindness, Gloucester's interrogation of Simpcox also offers a moment to consider early modern ideas about the experience of blindness. As a person claiming to be blind from birth, Simpcox says that he dreamed of regaining his sight but reports having led a rowdy, tree-climbing life. His blindness is not meant to reflect on his personality but rather to have been a disability that he lived with until the miracle. As a fraudulent blind person, Simp-cox's choice to be cured of his "blindness" hinges upon a fascination the sighted have with imagining what blindness, or living with a disability more broadly, is like. The overrepetition of the word "blind" and focus on Simp-cox's ostensibly congenital blindness reveals this fascination with difference; Gloucester's questions, then, reflect early modern questions about the way that blind people might experience the world. In this way, though Simpcox is not blind, the staged representation of his blindness, and the exploration of the nature of blindness through the device of uncovering the false miracle, reveals an interest in examining what blindness is all about. Unexpectedly, in trying to understand Simpcox's blindness, Gloucester reveals how sightedness is subjective and unstable; if all eyes are false informants, then all sight is as subject to doubt as Simpcox's. Finally, through staging a public performance of scientific inquiry into Simpcox's blindness, the play encourages audiences or readers to stare at the blind and, in so doing, to use the spectacle of visual impairment as a means through which to evaluate the limits of disability together with the possibility of adaptive strategies and possibilities.[20] Even though Simpcox is revealed to be sighted, and even though we learn that he was never technically blind, we also get to watch him embody the position of disabled individual and, from that space, challenge and undermine a king, an advisor, and an entire system of scientific evaluation for visual function. In the end, our pleasure in staring at Simpcox is predicated on the idea that the truest workings of his sight are ultimately unknowable.

IF THE Simpcox interlude allows the audience to observe an actor perform-ing blindness, and to think through what the experience of blindness might be, those issues are explored in a more material and sustained manner in the anonymous sixteenth-century Old Testament play *The Historie of Jacob and Esau.*[21] Though the play generally follows the parameters of the biblical story of Jacob and Esau, the anonymous author devotes great detail to the strategies that blind Isaac uses to maneuver in the world; the author even invents a boy character, Mido, who serves as a guide and narrator of events for Isaac. Perhaps because the story hinges on Isaac's blindness, and his subsequent inability to differentiate between his sons, the author takes pains to show how Isaac uses and refuses assistance. In this way, the play ultimately becomes as much about the limits or possibilities of perception for a blind person—or about the failure of Isaac's adaptive systems—as it is about Rebecca and Jacob's deceit.

In adapting the story of Jacob and Esau, the play's author creates an original character called "Mido, the ladde that leadeth blind Isaac." When we first see Isaac on stage, he is calling for Mido to lead him. The dialogue shows us how Isaac uses Mido as a guide who helps him navigate in the world; in their first appearance, Mido instructs Isaac to "lay your hande on my shoulder, and come on this way" (284). In staging a blind character, the author finds it necessary to represent his adaptive or assistive navigation system as well.[22] In fact, the idea of leading or guiding the blind, an idea not rooted in the biblical source, becomes a central concern of the play. This addition is refreshingly direct and based in material realities. While Isaac's blindness certainly represents anxieties about life with a disability—after all, his blindness causes him to make a tremendous and weighty error—the play also focuses on what his disability means in a more pragmatic way. The primary focus on the mechanics of adaptation, rather than or in addition to the emotional and metaphoric trappings of Isaac's blindness, offers a frank analysis of disability that resists becoming purely didactic or representational.

When Mido considers the possibility that he may become blind when he is old, he asks, "How shall I grope the way, or who shall leade me then?" (329); he is worried not about making life-changing decisions like Isaac's but about getting around. The play certainly exploits the metaphorical potential of Isaac's need for leadership: when Rebecca takes over the job of leading Isaac, she says, "it is my office as long as I am by. / And I would all wives, as the worlde this day is, / Woulde unto their husbands likewise do their office" (467–69). Here the distinction between metaphor and representation is especially clear since Rebecca will metaphorically lead Isaac toward giving Esau the birthright, even as she literally fulfills her job as a physical guide. And when Isaac is about to be fooled by Jacob, Mido observes that "Jacob leadeth Isaac" (1307).

But even as *Jacob and Esau* plays with the metaphor of leading blind Isaac, it also presents, again and again, the blind man navigating the stage with the help of his boy guide. The play thus differentiates between Isaac's ability to be misled and the fact of his blindness. We observe that Isaac can adapt to being blind with the right kind of assistance; he has a much harder time dealing with metaphoric blindness. In fact, including adaptive technology in the world of the play is one way that the author plays up the disjuncture between blindness as a disability and a metaphor.[23]

When Mido is Isaac's guide, he provides more than just navigational aid. He frequently narrates or describes situations for his blind master. So, for instance, he helps Isaac spy on Rebecca by reporting to Isaac, "Yonder she is speaking; whatever she doth say: / By holding up his hands, it seemeth she doth pray" (394–95). Though this observation obviously promotes the plot development, it also provides a glimpse at the assistive purpose of a real guide to the blind; Mido provides not only basic facts (where Rebecca is) but also visual detail that carries implications for Isaac's understanding of the situation.[24] At one point, Isaac tells Mido that he can do nothing without Mido's help. But rather than making Isaac seem helpless, the author's inclusion of a devoted and trained guide for Isaac actually demonstrates the efficacy of assistance for a person who is blind. In fact, Isaac starts being blind only in the metaphoric way—not understanding what he's doing or who he's blessing—after he sends Mido out of the room. In the end, it is Mido who reveals Rebecca and Jacob's plot to Isaac, and who helps him navigate as he attempts to repair the situation. By adding Mido's character to the play, the author hints at a pragmatic alternative to the biblical story of paternal deception: an option in which Isaac, though blind, has the resources and assistance to avoid deception. Indeed, though Mido is presented as silly and boyish when he is "off duty" in the play, he also performs his work for Isaac with apparent honesty and transparency. Even as the audience understands that Mido might at any point accidentally or intentionally mislead Isaac, the play presents the possibility that access to good, responsible, adaptive assistance can work. In fact, when the technology of Mido-as-guide is working, the focus is redirected away from the boy and toward Isaac and his actions and decisions.

In *Jacob and Esau,* Isaac deals with the kind of total blindness that Simpcox was feigning in *2 Henry VI.* His blindness is depicted as very real and, in many ways, limiting. Isaac explains, for example, that "Saving that what so ever God doth is all right, / No small griefe it were for a man to lacke his sight" (301–2). Part of the spectacle of this play would have been the uncomfortable pleasures of watching the blind man negotiate the stage and story of the play. Mido himself draws attention to the impulse to stare at difference, and to the distinct specificity of blindness as an embodied disability. As Rosemarie Garland-Thomson explains it, "When we do see the usually concealed sight of disability writ boldly on others, we stare in disbelief and uneasy identification."[25] In *Jacob and Esau,* the audience is already uneasily identified with Isaac, watching helplessly and with dramatic (and biblical) irony as he heads unknowingly toward giving the mistaken birthright to Esau from the start of the play. And yet, the author also uses the character of Mido to showcase the kind of uneasy identification with disability that Garland-Thomson suggests. At several points in the play, Mido imitates Isaac's movement and reports, "I have done so ere now both by day and by night / As I see you grope the way, and have hitte it right" (332–33). Interestingly, Rebecca chides Mido for these impressions, accusing him of "couterfaiting" (337) his blind master, an accusation that predicts the kind of false miracle scene depicted by Shakespeare in *2 Henry VI.*[26]

At the same time as the play encourages its audience to stare at Isaac's non-normative negotiations (reemphasizing the non-normative ways that Isaac moves and gropes), and even as it showcases his major blindness-based error (blessing the wrong son), it also stages blindness as a disability that can be managed and, with adaptation, successfully negotiated. Further, it maintains the audience's uneasy identification with Isaac and his blindness; at one point, Isaac tells Mido: "For who so to old age whill here live and endure, / Must of force abide all such defautes of nature" (326–27). In his scientific treatise, Hakewill marvels at the vulnerability of the eye, which he claims is "subject to far more diseases from within, and casualties from without, than any other member," in part because of the complexity of its "diverse pieces," each of which can be diseased; plus "to these internal diseases we joine those externall accidents, offensive to it, winde, dust, bruses sometime to the dimunation, and sometime to the deprivation, and not seldome to the total losse and perishing of the sight."[27] Hakewill's description supports Isaac's claim that anyone who could live long enough would likely outlive his sensitive eyes. Like Gloucester's examination of Simpcox's visual experiences, Isaac's candid assessment of visual vulnerability exposes the blurry boundaries of visual disability; not only are eyes false informants that show us sights our minds recognize as misleading, but eyes are also always already in the process of failing, either gradually or entirely. Rather than functioning as the norm, sightedness is exposed in *Jacob and Esau* to be inconsistent and transitory, while blindness and visual impairment become the general expectation.

Writing about blindness in the medieval period, Edward Wheatley confirms that "varying degrees of visual impairments must have been so widespread as to be unremarkable, especially before the Italian invention of eyeglasses for the nearsighted in the 1280s and for farsightedness in about 1450."[28] At the same time, this idea resonates with the disability studies model in which the term "able-bodied" is replaced by "temporarily able-bodied," acknowledging that even with medical advances, we are still all likely to experience disability as we age.[29] In both early modern and contemporary contexts, then, the experience of watching Isaac negotiate his disability is perhaps instructive as well as voyeuristic. For the audience who stares at Isaac's negotiations of the stage (as represented, perhaps, through Mido's mimicry of Isaac's way of walking), the experience of uneasy identification with a blind man is rendered even more powerful by the gradual realization that his disability is neither unique nor avoidable. Instead, the audience acclimates to Isaac's blindness and learns that sightedness is unstable and incomplete.

SOME OF THE most explicit sources for an investigation into the material realities of early modern blindness and the public reception of assistive technologies are evident in cheap-print texts such as ballads, which, because of their short form, huge proliferation, and broad popular circulation, often capture thematic elements, such as ideas about disability, that are less transparently addressed by more formal print and performance cultures.[30] I now turn, therefore, to two seventeenth-century ballads from the Pepys collection, each with an unexpected take on blindness.[31] In these ballads, even more than in *Jacob and Esau,* blindness is taken as a medical or physical reality that informs, but does not necessarily define, the characters that are blind. Further, the woodcut images that accompany the texts fill in missing information about adaptive tools for the blind while simultaneously providing the reader with an uninterrupted look—an opportunity to stare—at a blind person in action. These ballads, then, while certainly not accurate reports on actual, lived experiences of blind individuals, can perhaps take us one step further from metaphorical blindness toward a consideration of how real people might have negotiated loss of sight. The ballads would have been read and heard by able-bodied and disabled audiences alike: for blind audience members, these blind characters provide models of adaptive living and potential messages of solidarity and unity; for sighted audience members, blindness ballads enable an empathetic and experiential connection with blindness.

The woodcut for "The rarest Ballad that ever was seen, / Of the blind beggar's Daughter of Bednal-Green" offers an image of a blind man navigating with perhaps the most complete suite of adaptive technologies that I've found thus far.[32] More autonomous that Isaac could be when he relied on Mido, here the blind beggar's tools include a bell, a dog, and a long cane.[33] The woodcut suggests, even before we read the ballad, that this blind beggar has many resources at his disposal. For this reason, though the ballad initially highlights the man's deficits, the visual evidence of his autonomy and adaptation undercuts this message and instead demands that the beggar be recognized and admired for his obvious capacity and agency. The woodcut emphasizes the beggar's blindness but also emphasizes his mobility and centrality in his own story, thus resisting the idea that his agency is dependent upon sight.

Over the course of the ballad, the beggar's young and beautiful daughter, Bessee, decides to leave Bednal-Green because none of her suitors will marry "a Beggar his heir." In a new town, she gathers a collection of suitors, all begging to marry her. She then reveals her family origins:

> My father quoth she, is plain to be seen,
> The silly blind begger of Bednal-green,
> That daily goes begging for charity, . . .
> He always is led with a dog and a bell. . . .

One by one, each of Bessee's suitors turns her down when they hear who her father is; readers are encouraged to empathize with unmarriageable Bessee, and, by extension, with her father the blind beggar, whose disability and status make her undesirable. Later, when Bessee meets a knight who is willing to marry her, a merchant suitor challenges the marriage at the beggar's doorstep. In defense of his daughter, the blind beggar speaks up and offers a financial challenge to Bessee's enemy: "Rail not against my child at mine own door, / Though she be not deckt with Welbet and Pearl, / Yet I will drop Angels with thee for my Girl." It is an incredible scene, in which the beggar miraculously and inexplicable produces three times as much gold as the rich man who has insulted his daughter. Though blind, he defends his own, reveals remarkable resources, and even seems able to count coins without impediment: "Then there's (quoth the begger) for pretty Bessee, / With that an Angel he cast on the ground, / And dropped in Angels full three thousand pound."

Here, the beggar provides his daughter's dowry in a showy display of wealth, literally showering her and her suitor in gold coins such that "So as the place whereas he did sit, / With gold was covered every whit." If his patriarchal and masculine powers have been undermined elsewhere in the ballad, here he aggressively competes with the suitor, ultimately humiliating him by outpacing him in the tossing of coins. The scene is a triumphant one for the beggar, and for audience members identifying with him. But it is also the turning point in the ballad where the already hyperbolic tale moves toward pure fantasy. In terms of the beggar's disability, though the beggar is literally blind, he suffers from none of the metaphorical weaknesses generally attached to blindness. As his woodcut suggests, he is savvy, forward thinking, and totally in control despite (or because of?) his physical disability, adaptive tools, and apparent class status; so much so, in fact, that he causes jealousy and admiration:

> The Gentleman all that this treasure had seene,
> Admired the begger of Bednal-green.
> And those that were her suitors before,
> Their flesh for very anger they tore.

Here, the beggar is not even described as blind anymore, and his other characteristics seem more important. For a mixed reading and listening audience that included working-class and disabled individuals, this ballad offers a moment of identification and validation as the beggar impresses and outdoes the very gentlemen who dishonored his family.

Though the ballad reduces references to the beggar's blindness as his power and control increases, the author does not include disability in the list of ways that the beggar is not who he seems: though the beggar seems poor, he is revealed to be rich; though he seems without social capital, he is revealed to be gentry; though he seems to be emasculated, he is revealed to be a powerful patriarch; conversely, the beggar not only seems but is blind, all the way to the end of the ballad. The woodcut image of the beggar navigating with his dog and his bell, then, can equally represent the seemingly disenfranchised beggar of the start of the ballad or the victorious hero of the ballad's conclusion. The signifiers of blindness are as much a mark of accomplishment as weakness, since both beggar and beggar-hero are equally blind. By resisting the potential of curing the beggar's blindness as part of the ballad's pat, fairy-tale ending, the author prevents a neat conclusion that the beggar has somehow "overcome" disability. Instead, his blindness proves to be among his only core identity qualities and, as such, is presented as part of his victory.[34]

The ballad closes with Bessee's wedding to her knight at which her father is first notably absent (she excuses him by saying that he is too "base" to attend), then present as a singer, and, finally, he reveals himself through his song to be a noble who, blinded in battle, has lived for forty years as a beggar. The ballad's conclusion resolves the mystery of the beggar's heaps of gold (and the tension of the beggar's daughter so quickly becoming a lady) by revealing his class background. While this ending may seem like a cheat, the text resists an entirely conventional conclusion by leaving the noble man as blind as the beggar: the beggar never stops being blind, nor does he seem to regret his blindness. His song ends on a triumphant note: "Full forty long winters thus have I been. / A silly blind Begger of Bednal-green." To the end, the beggar names his own blindness as part of his identity, and that blindness is meant only as a description of his inability to see. Though blind, the beggar is noble; though blind, he is honorable; though blind, he can see his daughter's beauty and worth.[35]

Blindness represented with adaptive technologies, as in the case of Isaac with Mido or the beggar-turned-noble with his dog, stick, and bell, is taken to perhaps its furthest extreme in a ballad called "The Scoulding Wife, or, The Poor Man's Lamentation of his Bad Market in His Chusing Him a Wife,"[36] in which the long cane is used as a weapon. This ballad, which Pepys included in his category on "Marriage," describes an unhappy domestic scene in which a jealous wife attacks her husband's former sweetheart after the husband gives the sweetheart an "innocent" kiss. After this brutal fight between women, the ballad takes a dark turn when the husband, tired of his wife's constant scolding, replaces her medicinal eyedrops with "a liquor . . . 'twas Henben and steep't in Whay." When the husband treats his wife with the switched eye drops, "she Curst and Swore, well she might, / For never since that day she got her sight." Thus, the ballad gives us a backstory for the wife's blindness, which was caused by her husband's malicious intent. The ballad likewise claims that, through becoming blind, the wife is transformed from a scold to an obedient spouse. The husband explains:

And I provided a dog and a Bell,
To carry her about, from place to place:
Then she cries Husband, I hope all is well:
But before it was Togue, add Cuckold to thy Face.
The blessed be Heaven, and Mercury strong,
They made a change in my Wifs Tongue;
For it is a medicine, both certain and sure,
To bee cured of a Scold, but I'le say no more.

On the surface, the conclusion of this ballad is deeply disturbing, simultaneously misogynistic and ableist in its implications that the wife deserved to be blinded because she was a scold and that her condition of blindness would lead to a submissive personality. In the text of the ballad, as narrated by the seemingly triumphant husband, the wife is given a guide dog and bell and then expected to serve as an example for other scolding wives.[37] The

"I'le say no more" at the end of the ballad seems a nod to an audience of henpecked husbands who, the narrator hopes, may try the "certain and sure" medicine of blinding their own wives. And yet, the woodcut that accompanies the ballad undermines all of these messages, providing sighted readers of the ballad with a visual anecdote to the text.

In this remarkable image, the cuckolded husband, horned, kneels and cowers before a wife, who is poised to strike him. But, while the image ostensibly shows the wife *before* blindness has cured her of her bad behavior, the weapon she raises against her husband looks suspiciously like one we have come across before: the guidance cane used by early modern blind individuals. If we take the weapon to be this cane, a marker of blindness and an adaptive tool that helps blind people move autonomously through the world, then the woodcut serves as a *post*script to the ballad: the blind wife's revenge against her husband. Since the cane's threat is exclusively visual, it is inaccessible to fully blind ballad audiences; nevertheless, it is a powerful reminder to sighted readers that blindness is neither a successful disciplinary tool nor a sign of weakness. The cane's double use as adaptive and defensive provides a model (albeit a violent one) for empowerment for a blind woman and also functions as a threat to those who might attack or abuse her.

The early modern period marked a moment where visuality and the ability to see were becoming increasingly important and central to cultural production, in part because of the proliferation and dissemination of images and texts meant to be seen. In his 1616 *Mikrokosmographia,* Helkiah Crooke declared that, amongst all of the senses, "sight is the principall. . . . For those who either by Nature or by Accident are blinde do account themselves therin miserable."[38] And yet, the texts and images discussed here, through their serious consideration of the ways that a character might use human, animal, and material tools to adapt to being blind in a visual world, begin to reframe early modern disability as less about limitation and more about strategy. Indeed, the more that a text dismantles the correlation between the use of blindness as metaphor and the loss of power for a blind person, the less blindness has to *mean* something else. The more deeply we can find evidence of the experience of blindness itself, moving away from the idea of blindness as a tragic punishment and toward blindness as a biological fact, the more clearly blindness becomes one of many characteristics that contribute to selfhood and identity. The fraudulent blind man who could climb trees, the biblical father who used a guide, the blind beggar-hero of a single ballad, and the revolutionary image of a raised cane are hardly enough to suggest that blindness was ever considered an *asset* in early modern representation. But these representations do serve to complicate the discourse and meanings of early modern blindness and to suggest that, by reducing the "trappings of metaphor" and attending to disability and the adaptive tools that come with it, we might perceive a fuller picture than mere metaphor can provide.[39] This fuller picture suggests that the experience of staring at disability, on the stage or in a woodcut, may be less about didactic messages and more about the invitation for identification and instruction. In their discussion of the often-fraught relationship between literary analysis (or, more broadly, the humanities) and disability studies, Mitchell and Snyder claim that "while the representational portraits we investigate [through literary analysis and historicism] often prove unsatisfactory, they allow us to viscerally encounter disability in a way that we could not otherwise."[40] Indeed, these representations of physically blind persons in plays and cheap print allow an encounter, however flawed, with early modern attitudes toward, and lived experiences of, blindness.

Notes

1. For a broad history of Western attitudes toward disability, see Stiker, *History of Disability*. Stuart Clark gives a thorough cultural history of vision in *Vanities of the Eye: Vision in Early Modern European Culture* (Oxford: Oxford University Press, 2009), and Moshe Barasch, in *Blindness: The History of a Mental Image in Western Thought* (New York: Routledge, 2001), analyzes representations of blindness from antiquity through the eighteenth century. In *Narrative Prosthesis* Mitchell and Snyder use the term "narrative prosthesis" to describe the twofold function of disability in literary narratives: "first, as a stock feature of characterization and, second, as an opportunistic metaphorical device" (47).

2. Mitchell and Snyder, *Narrative Prosthesis*, 56.

3. Mitchell and Snyder call this sort of representation, and the critical approaches which reveal and theorize it, "Negative Imagery"; ibid., 17–21.

4. Ibid., 8.

5. This description of the work of some disabled performers and theater artists comes from Carrie Sandahl and Philip Auslander, *Bodies in Commotion: Disability and Performance* (Ann Arbor: University of Michigan Press, 2005), 4. For more on contemporary disability performance studies, see Telory Davies, *Performing Disability: Staging the Actual* (Germany: VDM Publishing, 2009); Bruce Henderson and Noam Ostrander, eds., *Understanding Disability Studies and Performance Studies* (New York: Routledge, 2010); and Petra Kuppers, *Disability and Contemporary Performance: Bodies on Edge* (New York: Routledge, 2003), *The Scar of Visibility: Medical Performances and Contemporary Art* (Minnesota: University of Minnesota Press, 2007), and *Disability Culture and Community Performance: Find a Strange and Twisted Shape* (New York: Palgrave Macmillan, 2011). Previous to these modern disability performances, staged public performances in madhouses and asylums showcased the mentally ill and disabled; see Jackson, *Separate Theaters*.

6. Sandahl and Auslander, *Bodies in Commotion*, 2.

7. Quotations from *2 Henry VI* are from Greenblatt et al., *Norton Shakespeare*, 203–91. Subsequent references will appear within the text.

8. For a detailed history of the Simpcox story, see Row-Heyveld, "'The Lying'st Knave in Christendom.'" As Row-Heyveld observes, this story had been in circulation since at least 1529 when Thomas More recorded the incident in his *A Dialogue Concerning Heresies*, claiming to have heard the story from his own father, Sir John More. Simpcox's story was included in Richard Grafton's *A Chronicle at Large* (1562), John Foxe's *Actes and Monuments* (in the 1570, 1576, and 1583 editions), and finally in Shakespeare's play, probably written in 1591.

9. Wheatley discusses medieval anxieties about feigned blindness in *Stumbling Blocks*, 22. Rosemarie Garland-Thomson situates the start of law focused on disabled fakery to the "inception of the English Poor Laws in 1388" in *Extraordinary Bodies: Figuring Physical Disability in American Culture and Literature* (New York: Columbia University Press, 1997), 48. See also Susan M. Schweik, "Dissimulations," *The Ugly Laws: Disability in Public* (New York: New York University Press, 2009), 108–40.

10. Kleege, *Sight Unseen*, 396.

11. Stuart Clark (*Vanities of the Eye,* 2) explains the disruption of an Aristotelian link between seeing and knowing, and the particular crisis in certainty about vision that marked the European Renaissance.

12. Kleege, *Sight Unseen*, 391.

13. Kleege offers the example of Descartes's 1637 *La Dioptrique,* in which a hypothetical blind man calculates the distance between two objects by using two walking sticks; ibid., 391–92.

14. George Hakewill, *The Vanitie of the Eie* (Oxford: Joseph Barnes, 1608), 49–53.

15. Ibid., 50.

16. See Stuart Clark, *Vanities of the Eye,* esp. 9–38, for a discussion of Hakewill and developments in Renaissance theories of vision.

17. Ibid., 25.

18. For further discussions of the history of "miracle cures" for the blind, see Wheatley, *Stumbling Blocks,* esp. 155–85; and Barasch, *Blindness,* esp. 45–66.

19. Thanks to Allison Hobgood for her suggestion that Simpcox's interrogation and its resulting doubt of visual efficacy breaks down the seeming difference between able and disabled bodies such that, in a radical shift, "disability becomes the norm."

20. The term "stare," an "interpersonal action through which we act out who we imagine ourselves and others to be," is Garland-Thomson's in *Staring,* 14.

21. The 1586 title page gives the full title of the play as *A newe mery and wittie Comedie or Enterlude, newely imprinted, treating upon the Historie of Iacob and Esau, taken out of the xxvi Chap. Of the first booke of Moses entituled Genesis.* For a discussion of the play's fraught publication history, see Paul Whitfield White, ed., *Reformation Biblical Drama in England: An Old Spelling Edition* (New York: Garland, 1992), xxxiv–xlv. References to the play within the text are cited by line and refer to White's edition, 67–133.

22. For a historical examination of visual representations of guides for the blind, see Barasch, *Blindness,* 103–14. David Houston Wood rightly points out the connection between Isaac led by Mido in *Jacob and Esau* and Samson led by a "guiding hand"

(line 1) in Milton's *Samson Agonistes* (1671); see *Time, Narrative, and Emotion in Early Modern England* (Burlington, VT: Ashgate, 2009), 139–70.

23. Discussing Jaehn Clare's modern performances of disability, which incorporate her wheelchair, for example, Johnson Cheu argues that "such actions help viewers to see the permanence of the disabled body, while asking viewers to redefine able-bodied notions of what it means to be disabled. The viewer begins to understand disability as both a corporeal entity (impairment) and as a social construction." "Performing Disability, Problematizing Cure," in Sandahl and Auslander, *Bodies in Commotion,* 135–46.

24. For a brief discussion of the problems of adequate and respectful service providers for the blind, see Harlan Lane, "Construction of Deafness," *The Disability Studies Reader.* 2nd ed. (New York: Routledge, 2006), 82–83.

25. Garland-Thomson, *Staring,* 20.

26. Barasch (*Blindness,* 105–6) argues that while the guide has been a familiar element in depictions of the blind since antiquity, the motif of the guide shifts in the early middle ages.

27. Hakewill, *Vanitie of the Eie,* 92–94.

28. Wheatley, *Stumbling Blocks,* 8.

29. For a discussion of the notion that we are all Temporarily Able Bodied (TAB), see Carol A. Breckenridge and Candace Volger, "The Critical Limits of Embodiment: Disability's Criticism," *Public Culture* 13, no. 3 (2001): 349–58.

30. Tessa Watt, *Cheap Print and Popular Piety, 1550–1640* (Cambridge: Cambridge University Press, 1991), estimates that ballads at this time were similar to the modern newspaper, printed in the millions, 11. See also Natascha Würzbach, *The Rise of the English Street Ballad, 1550–1650* (Cambridge: Cambridge University Press, 1981); Dianne Dugaw, *Warrior Women and Popular Balladry, 1650–1850* (Chicago: University of Chicago Press, 1996); Joy Wiltenburg, *Disorderly Women and Female Power in the Street Literature of Early Modern England and Germany* (Charlottesville: University of Virginia Press, 1992); and Steve Newman, *Ballad Collection, Lyric, and the Canon: The Call of the Popular from the Restoration to the New Criticism* (Philadelphia: University of Pennsylvania Press, 2007).

31. The entire Pepys collection is available through the English Broadside Ballad Archive at the University of California, Santa Barbara, at http://emc.english.ucsb.edu/ballad_project/.

32. Pepys 1.490–91, http://emc.english.ucsb.edu/ballad_project/ballad_image.asp?id=20231. Hereafter, all in-text quotations come from this source or, subsequently, "The Scoulding Wife, or, The Poor Man's Lamentation of his Bad Market in His Chusing Him a Wife," Pepys 4.136.

33. Little is known about the historical trajectory of each of these adaptive technologies. The bell was the most common sign of blindness in the early modern period, used to alert sighted individuals to clear the way for the blind and as an accessory to begging. Generally, seeing-eye guide dogs became popular following World War I, while the white cane came into popular use in the 1970s. Still, images of guide dogs and adaptive canes go back as far as the classical period and can be found in many medieval and early modern visual and literary texts. For other markers of blindness in visual representation, see Barasch, *Blindness,* especially the sections on veils and blindfolds (82–92), guides (99–101; 103–14), and stumbling or groping (101–3).

34. The beggar's victory here is impressive and joyful, but it also participates in what Eli Clare terms "supercrip stories," which focus on disabled people "overcoming" disabilities; see *Exile and Pride: Disability, Queerness, and Liberation* (Cambridge: South-End, 1999).

35. The blind beggar ballad ultimately resists the rehabilitative resolution outlined in Mitchell and Snyder's *Narrative Prosthesis,* esp. 53–54, by retaining the beggar's disability despite his restored reputation.

36. Pepys 4.136, http://emc.english.ucsb.edu/ballad_project/ballad_image.asp?id =21800.

37. For more on domestic dispute and spousal violence in early modern literature, including ballads, see Frances Dolan, *Marriage and Violence: The Early Modern Legacy* (Philadelphia: University of Pennsylvania Press, 2008), esp. 67–96.

38. Helkiah Crooke, *Mikrokosmographia,* 2nd ed. (London: W. Iaggard, 1618), 535.

39. I borrow the phrase "the trappings of metaphor" from Susan Sontag, *Illness as Metaphor and AIDS and Its Metaphors* (New York: Picador, 1989). Sontag suggests we can remove these trappings by reconnecting metaphors of blindness to the actual bodily disabilities from which they stem.

40. Mitchell and Snyder, *Narrative Prosthesis,* 45.

CHAPTER 7

"There is no suff'ring due"

Metatheatricality and Disability Drag in *Volpone*

LAUREN COKER

n the opening of Jonson's *Volpone,* the title character describes how he applies "ointment for [his] eyes" and impersonates symptoms and ailments as a form of manipulation: "Now, my feigned cough, my phthisic, and my gout, / My apoplexy, palsy, and catarrhs . . . this is my posture" (1.2.124–26).[1] While this description works as a comical instance of metatheatricality on the Renaissance stage, it simultaneously works as a performance of disability drag—a term introduced by Tobin Siebers to indicate instances in which an able-bodied person performs as a person with a disability.[2] The use of disability drag in *Volpone* is particularly notable, however, for this layered, metatheatrical deployment of imposture: unlike an able-bodied actor who performs as a character with a legitimate disability,[3] the suffering body's credibility in this early modern play works reciprocally with the character's staging of able-bodiedness.[4] Volpone's lack of legitimate disability at the play's outset—alongside the overt performance of an ailing body—undercuts the perception of disability as a material and lived bodily condition.

Volpone's metatheatrical staging of disability drag brings issues of corporeality or bodily deceit to the forefront. His bodily imposture makes problematic Jonson's representation of the disabled body: a disconnect surfaces between his character's decision to appear ailing on stage while simultaneously choosing to acknowledge his able-bodiedness to the audience, and this disconnect poses a problem regarding the legitimacy of disabled bodies in early modern culture. More specifically, a fracture develops between the actor's bodily performance, which is an intentional fiction, and the real or lived body, as the stage fiction can lead to the perception that the lived body and its apparent disabilities, too, are unreal. Interpreting Volpone's metatheatrical representations of disability drag on the early modern stage thus calls for return to a question raised by Ato Quayson: "What happens to our interpretation when we examine the status of disability within a representational system in which *the discomfort of disability is* not *accounted for?*"⁵ Quayson's question resonates in *Volpone* because the play positions "discomfort" as a satirical performance of stereotypes related to disability—stereotypes that do not address the physical or mental suffering that may accompany a bodily condition. Moreover, the staged mimicry of discomfort in *Volpone* offers a metadramatic representation of comedy as "another site for disabled body viewing" that "hinge[s] upon narrow ideas about unacceptable bodies that encourage freak-show like titillation."⁶ In *Volpone,* the suitors who experience the "freak-show like titillation" brought about by Volpone's "unacceptable" body are in fact victims of a con artist. Volpone's false and exaggerated coughs, paired with his token "sick dress," thus allow the play to become a metaspectacle, a mimetic image of the outwardly unnatural construction of discomfort or pain and its observation by other characters on stage as well as the audience.

Much of my reading of *Volpone,* particularly in social or cultural contexts, is indebted to Mark Breitenberg's *Anxious Masculinity in Early Modern England*⁷ and Gail Kern Paster's work in *Humoring the Body* and *The Body Embarrassed,*⁸ as these texts focus on the material fluidity of early modern selves. But while both critics engage the staging or fashioning of bodies (through humoral and gendered perspectives), the metatheatrical performance of the disabled body—along with its social and physical resonances—deserves further investigation. Representations of false disability in the dramatic sphere, after all, can expound on contemporary attitudes toward offstage interpretations of disability as imposture. Jonson's depiction of the body in *Volpone* satirizes the credibility of disability; Volpone's body sends one message to the characters on stage and another to the audiences who recognize the metatheatricality of that same body's performance.

In addition to questions of material corporeality and bodily construction that come about with *Volpone's* metatheatrical use of disability drag, I focus on this play for its insight into how wealth and social status affect the credibility of the drag performance. The imposture of disability in *Volpone,* alongside its references to the containment of syphilitics near the drama's conclusion, accentuates the manipulation—through bodily deceit and disguise—of social practices or institutions intended for the ailing poor during the early modern period while also highlighting attempts to contain or control those disabled bodies. Volpone, exposed for feigning illness among people who desire to see his "sick dress," portrays physical impairments as performances negatively spurred by greed and manipulation, and his treatment of disability as performance influences early modern social structures that contain poor pox sufferers within hospitals for the *Incurabili*. And, again, although the metatheatricality of this play reinforces social models of disability, its deployment of disability drag calls into question the embodied nature and, at times, painful bodily *experience* of disability that can, in reality, affect people of all social strata.

Social Stigma and Dismantling Disability Drag

Volpone is a fictional representation of disability drag; he is also a figure of wealth. Performances of disability imposture were not limited to the early modern stage, and responses toward those of lower social standing who engaged in disability drag often involved physical and visual objectification.[9] Exposure of the drag performance rendered the impostor's body a spectacle and became another tool for denying the physically embodied nature of disability (and disease) while perpetuating the notion that it was largely performative. French surgeon Ambroise Paré's *On Monsters and Marvels*, for example, recalls a beggar feigning illness.[10] In "The Imposture of a Woman Beggar Who Pretended to Have a Canker on Her Breast," Paré's brother spies a begging woman with "a great amount of foul matter" flowing out onto a cloth in front of her breast. The brother then describes the beggar as "plump," and he claims her face has a "good lively color," which seems to indicate sound health. Thinking the beggar is an impostor, Paré's brother physically uncovers the woman's breast and finds a "sponge soaked and imbued with animal blood and with milk" that is "conducted through fake holes" in an "ulcerated canker." He then knows for "sure that the canker is artificial."[11] The brother's visually charged assessment of the beggar's body resembles an invasive and penetrating medical gaze,[12] but it strays in the undoing of an impostor's symptoms, thereby reversing a diagnosis of cancer into health—and a bodily condition into an artificiality.

The beggar presents herself as "hideous" and laden with "foul matter," but she does not present herself (and, by extension, her breasts) as prepared to be "uncovered" as a medical patient seeking a diagnosis or treatment might.[13] Paré's beggar, as an object of social derision and skepticism, puts an image of illness on display by means of her disguised body—and though not in a theater, she engages in acting, and in spectacle, through her dress and performance. However, insofar as she does not intentionally situate her naked breasts as observable objects, this account deviates from the theatrical in its physical undoing of costume and construct. The brother separates the beggar's plumpness and color from her other observable bodily symptoms, taking it upon himself to expose her feigned illness and disguise. Because the brother has "[taken] some warm water and [has] fomented the breast, having moistened it," and later has "found the teat healthy and whole and in as good condition as the other,"[14] he crosses the border between passive observer (akin to an early modern audience member) and physically invasive violator. The safe distance of "theatricality" collapses in his exposure of, and attendance to, her healthy breast. The beggar's disability drag is violently dismantled.

Although bodily exposure can lead to anxiety for spectators, the unveiling of the beggar's healthy breast arguably makes onlookers and the surgeon *less* anxious, as exposing a drag performance confirms the idea that pain, illness, and disability (particularly among someone of a lower class) are constructed tools for self-promotion and, further, evidence of a lack of moral character. Moreover, exposing disability as performance helps secure the viewer's own sense of health; in this case, the beggar's ailment no longer reminds one of his or her own physical vulnerability. As such, the beggar's undoing confirms Rosemarie Garland-Thomson's sense that starers perceive disability with "fascinated disbelief";[15] rather than validating an illness or an onlooker's perceived susceptibility to a bodily condition that may result in pain or discomfort, the female beggar's exposure fosters the incredibility of her illness while simultaneously validating her low social status and subsequent punishment. Her disability drag, in turn, is "providing an exaggerated exhibition of people with disabilities but questioning both the existence and permanence of disability."[16] At the same time, the perception that her disease lacks materiality is bound up with the perception that her performance puts a strain on the larger social body.

More specifically, the construction and exposure of disability as performance in "The Imposture of a Woman Beggar" places observers in a position of power and promotes the containment and isolation of marginalized figures after situating them on visual display. Paré concludes the narrative about the beggar by indicating that his brother "condemned the slut to get the whip," prior to banishing her from the country.[17] Here, the abject beggar

who feigns disability becomes even more abject: she is cast out of the country's boundaries due to the surgeon's exposure of her able body. This social
domination over those of abject classes—particularly among persons with a
disability, real or impersonated—reflects vexed attitudes toward beggars during the early modern era. As William Carroll explains, "Of the genuinely
poor, diseased, and destitute there was little dispute: it was a Christian duty
to give them relief"; nevertheless, many "were united at least in their perception that the wandering poor were a real social and spiritual problem and
that the existing system had not contained them."[18] The cultural preoccupation with beggarly infiltration and the focus on helping only the *genuinely*
poor and ailing adds yet another dimension to Paré's depictions of the beggar (and, arguably, of other marginalized persons): the performance and construction—and subsequent deconstruction—of the beggar and her cancerous
disguise demands that those in positions of power decide and determine
the fate of disabled individuals (even those feigning disability) primarily by
visual dissection.[19] The dismantling of the beggar's drag evidences how the
disabled poor are made objects of derision, skepticism, and intrusive spectacle, while other more wealthy impostors—such as the fictional Volpone—are
allowed, at least initially, to maintain agency and control over their disguises
and dis/abilities.

Undressing Volpone's "Sick Dress"

Instances of disability drag in *Volpone* are manifested not by beggars and
other socially abject characters but rather by the upper echelons of early
seventeenth-century society, and this reversal demonstrates social hypocrisy
toward the affluent impostor as opposed to the abject impostor. Volpone,
a wealthy character in disability drag, is perceived unconditionally by his
fellow onstage onlookers as embodying both legitimate and wholly material disability. Yet this perception, as we will see, does not extend to offstage
audiences who cannot—for their insider status—witness his disabled body as
a corporeal truth; in Volpone's metatheatrical construction of his sick guise,
early modern viewers continue to perceive his disability as lacking materiality. More precisely, bodily materiality—or, to recall Quayson, the discomfort of disability—is not merely disregarded or undermined in Jonson's
play; rather, the onstage viewers who believe Volpone is in pain are scath-
ingly labeled, as the character Mosca puts it, "harpies" (1.2.123). Their initial
belief in Volpone's material discomfort counters Elaine Scarry's notion that
pain fosters disbelief; though sufferers are certain of it, she explains, others

remain in doubt of that person's experience.[20] While Scarry's assertion might illuminate the surgeon's undoing of the female beggar's costume in "The Imposture of a Woman Beggar," Volpone's suitors trouble her claim, for they *desire* to see the character in "sick dress" and wholeheartedly believe that he is "turning carcass" (1.2.90). Volpone's performance of ailments makes him a spectacle of bodily suffering that suitor-spectators such as Corbaccio and Voltore pay to stare at in *fascinated belief.* And because Volpone is described in the Argument's opening line as wealthy and as one who "feigns sick" (1) as a means of gaining wealth and gifts from various potential heirs, an intentional hypocrisy emerges in which Jonson employs a disability drag most often considered characteristic of the early modern poor and desperate to the wealthy and privileged.

In this employment, Jonson creates an important distinction between Paré's beggar and Volpone. In Paré, the beggar's dismantled drag permits viewers to distance themselves from an often anxiety-inducing disabled body that supposedly has the potential to become a drain on social wealth. Here, instead, Volpone explicitly recounts his scheme to "delude" (1.2.123), by pretending to approach death:

> This draws new clients daily to my house,
> Women and men of every sex and age,
> That bring me presents. . . .
> With the hope that when I die . . .
> it shall then return
> Tenfold upon them. (1.1.76–81)

Volpone, from the outset, frames his ostensibly disabled body as a commodity, a symbol not of the depletion of wealth or status but of its possibility. As such, Volpone's drag performance fosters indulgence, belief, and even celebration of his (illegitimate) pain. Volpone's elaborate description of his costume, or "sick dress," and performance of "Uh! [*coughing*] uh! uh! uh! O" (1.2.124–29) offer a comparable theatricality and demonstration of disability as the female beggar's. Yet his social position does not undermine but rather legitimates his "disability" when he encounters those who would attempt to believe, observe, or diagnose his condition: Volpone's potential heirs express assurance and excitement over his seemingly impending death and distribution of wealth, and as Mosca lists Volpone's symptoms to Corbaccio while observing Volpone in costume, Corbaccio exclaims "good" five times (1.4.42–48).

While Corbaccio identifies with the representation of bodily discomfort in Volpone's "Uh! [*coughing*] uh! uh! uh! O," the same cough-laden exclamation prevents the audience from identifying with or understanding this pain. Instead, the performance becomes for them a mere imitation of what Paster calls an unintentional "bodily event."[21] The theatricality of Volpone's discomfort satirizes an individual's attempts to master the ailing body since Volpone *is* actually in control while his body appears to be suffering and uncontrollable.[22] Moreover, Volpone's falsely ailing body remains on display, but, unlike Paré's beggar, no one attempts to undo his costume or guise; Volpone eventually strips his disguise autonomously (5.12.83). During these scenes of observation and excitement surrounding Volpone's outwardly dying body, audiences likely recognize the metatheatricality: an able-bodied actor plays an able-bodied Volpone who feigns turning "carcass." Disability is, yet again, rendered wholly performative.

Further, the implications of disability drag as an imitation of a body approaching death in *Volpone* would have a particular discursive resonance with early modern audiences given alternative definitions of "carcass" circulating at the time. The *Oxford English Dictionary* glosses "carcass" in its spiritual contexts as "anything from which the 'life,' 'soul,' or essence is gone."[23] Based on this characterization, Volpone-as-carcass becomes both a physical shell and a spiritual vacuum: Volpone's "essence is gone." And even though I read much of Volpone's disability drag performance in terms of the character's dialogue and actions within the play itself, this fundamental notion of a lack in essence matters especially in the context of Volpone's overarching performance and its place in a cyclical, repetitive Renaissance theater characterized by actors' consecutive performances.[24] The comedy, first performed by the King's Majesty's Servants, starred Renaissance actor Richard Burbage as Volpone.[25] Burbage's performances in other play cycles (such as Shakespeare's *Othello*) as an able-bodied person, but also his repeat performances as the able-bodied Volpone who feigns illness, complicate the nuances of his staged imposture. The recurrence of disability drag performances by either the same actor in an uninterrupted period or a different actor reinforces the perception of deception, construction, and performativity of the material body—and echoes Volpone's self-description as "carcass." Volpone, already void of "life" or "essence," cannot suffer; the character, embodied by the well-known able-bodied actor playing him, is a construct, too, and this construction renders any potential suffering on his part strictly performative as well.

Whereas Volpone's credibility amidst other characters arguably does little to undermine the negative treatments of socially abject characters in the play, his lack of credibility amidst early modern audiences—both in his character's performance of sick dress and in his player as a known, able-bodied person—does much to undermine positive and credible treatments of socially powerful yet morally corrupt characters. In other words, Volpone, in spite of his wealth and status, is through his greed and performance of illness nothing more than an impostor and an upper-class rendering of the beggar figure. The Avocatore claims that Volpone, "by blood and rank a gentleman," cannot receive the punishment that those of lower social statuses may endure (5.12.118); yet the play's later description of Volpone's character undercuts this elevated rank, as the Avocatore uses the term "imposture" to characterize Volpone's performance—a term explicitly likening him to Paré's beggar-impostors.[26]

Volpone, "by feigning lame, gout, palsy, and such diseases," must "lie in prison, cramp'd with irons, / Till [he] be'st sick and lame indeed" in the *Incurabili* hospital (5.12.120–24). Through this punishment,[27] the Avocatore condemns Volpone to a space where his *criminal* body will be contained, and yet his insistence that the Fox becomes "lame" emphasizes contemporary denotations for the term, including crippled, impaired, and maimed,[28] and hence indeed marks Volpone as a person with a disability. Furthermore, Volpone's relocation to the hospital of the *Incurabili* situates him in a place typically reserved for impoverished syphilitics. According to Kevin Siena, hospitals of the *Incurabili* initially served to isolate and care for victims of the pox during this time: "Italians . . . define[d] the disease as 'incurable' and develop[ed] special hospitals to cater to the poor so afflicted." Siena explains that with the growth of mercury treatments for venereal disease came the perception that the pox could be treated, but he adds, "The *Incurabili* hospitals continued to provide the most important service of housing and treating the infected poor."[29]

As a result, Volpone's containment among the Italian poor near the drama's conclusion plays with the conventional social ordering of early modern bodies. The punishment evidences how the judges have a *desire* for Volpone to become truly "lame indeed." Unlike the beggar whose guise of disabling illness is stripped away, Volpone's drag intentionally is reassembled by a social institution (the judicial system); the wealthy Volpone in his disability drag is forced into a place for people with "real" disabilities. The judges in the play hence reconstruct the *construct* of disability for Volpone in order to justify his corporeal performance. This reconstruction is, again, an exact inversion from what happens to Paré's female beggar; her body is violated and her drag costume torn apart in ways that disrupt the distance between observer and observed. *Volpone's* judges, who must also look, dissect, and decide his character's fate, take the opposite approach: though the drag has been exposed to everyone on stage by this point, the judges endeavor to reinstate the suspension of disbelief underscored in his consistent theatricality. The stage and its characters are (once more by way of metatheater) reassembled and redressed. Isolated and contained like the beggars—and, in the case of Volpone, the impoverished syphilitics—of their time, abject subjects are not redeemed through Jonson's treatment of Volpone, particularly the socially abject who may be ailing. A wealthy person, exposed for imposture among people who want to believe his "sick dress," destabilizes the important materiality of bodily suffering among all social strata—in the hospital of the *Incurabili* or elsewhere. The play's final aim to make someone "lame indeed" increasingly betrays unequal social structures and a perverse pleasure in theatricality rather than honest attention to individuals' actual material conditions and suffering.

Paré's "The Imposture of a Certain Beggar Who Was Counterfeiting a Leper" further substantiates the tenuous and socially hypocritical sense of justice made visible in *Volpone* through performances of false disability. Like the female beggar, the "big knave of a beggar" in Paré has a face that "shows no sign of leprosy."[30] The same brother from the previous narrative again strips this beggar and "condemns him to get the whip." This false leper then undergoes public torture and death: he is "banished forever from the country by the halter," and "the people [have] shouted at the top of their voices to the executioner: 'Strike, strike, officer! *He can't feel anything: he's a leper!'* wherefore at the voice of the people the executioner was cruelly bent on whipping him so hard that shortly afterward he died" (emphasis added).[31] The spectacle of this beggar's death is distinct, of course, from Volpone's public condemnation but private punishment. Regardless, however, the viewers' *denial* of the beggar's ability to feel discomfort or pain—coupled with their paradoxical reinforcement of his feigned status as a leper—parallels how he and the Fox both are linguistically made "lame" while, in many ways, perceived simultaneously by audiences as incapable of actual physical suffering.

Volpone's ending, too, affirms the perceived instability of disability and pain while underscoring its performativity. Volpone usurps the Epilogue of the drama, reminding audiences again of the metatheatricality of his punishment to ail among the poor:

> The seasoning of a play is the applause.
> Now, though the Fox be punish'd by the laws,
> He yet doth hope, *there is no suff'ring due,*
> For any fact which he hath done 'gainst you;
> If there be, censure him; here he doubtful stands:
> If not fare jovially, and clap your hands. (1–6, emphasis added)

Volpone once more asserts to the audience that the entire drama is a performance; he seeks to detach his character's legal punishment from physical embodiment, claiming, "there is no suff'ring due." "Due," implicating both monetary payment and justice, works in this instance as another pun that allows Volpone's character to escape the condemnation of the masses by calling for applause over "censure." Finally, the character also escapes material embodiment of any kind by invoking the third person. No longer does the actor playing Volpone refer to his body and actions using "I" or "me"; he instead affirms detachment by invoking "he" and "the Fox." This detachment becomes further compounded by the invocation that "here he . . . stands." Audiences see an actor playing Volpone, and the actor acknowledges that a representation of the character stands before them. The speaker fails to link materially to the body he enacts. By concluding the drama in this way, Jonson utterly eliminates the potential for legitimate representations of discomfort or suffering and reinforces the initial problem of material embodiment revealed in disability drag and its metatheatricality.

VOLPONE FAILS to redeem the material credibility of the ailing body in both social and corporeal spheres by satirizing disability and its discomfort and rendering the disabled body a tool for exaggerated performance, spectacle, and manipulation. Moreover, images of ailments, particularly when revealed as costumes and performances on the Renaissance stage, remind audiences of the metatheatricality of disability—even when the drama ends. The notion of disability as performance gets internalized: as Volpone's character asks his audience to "censure" or "clap," viewers are encouraged to look, unveil, and pass judgment. While some spectators may "jovially" applaud the drag performance of illness *on*stage, offstage and in "real life" these sorts of judgments likely lead to punishment and containment of those who were either truly disabled or socially abject.

The metatheatrical manifestation of disability drag in *Volpone* destroys the boundary between actor and audience. This destruction ironically empowers viewers outside dramatic spheres while disempowering the object of their view—as is the case with Paré's beggars. The spectator's gaze becomes rooted in skepticism and disbelief, and people with physical or mental ailments become spectacles for analysis and eventual containment. As a result, the metatheatricality of drag performances such as Volpone's extends beyond the stage, both shaping Renaissance ideologies around disability and discomfort and reflecting early modern social structures that encouraged the elimination of impostors and containing of syphilitics. Lastly, it is worth noting that disability drag is not unique to *Volpone:* Antonio feigns mental illness in Middleton and Rowley's *The Changeling,* and Beaumont's *Knight of the Burning Pestle* employs boy actors to play adult men who then transform into characters such as George, a dwarf, and Sir Pockhole, a syphilitic. These Renaissance dramas, among others such as Shakespeare's *King Lear* (in which Edgar famously fashions himself into a beggar with mental illness), can serve as a broader cultural window into how disability drag, particularly when acknowledged as a metadramatic performance, often problematically engenders doubt about the lived materiality of disability in the early modern period.

Notes

1. All references to this work come from Ben Jonson, *Volpone,* ed. Brian Parker and David Bevington (Manchester: Manchester University Press, 1999). Subsequent citations appear within the text.

2. Siebers explores the idea of disability drag as well as passing: the choice to hide disability or to make it visible. In terms of disability drag, Siebers has also suggested that viewers of the performance perceive disability as temporary or merely a construct. See *Disability Theory,* 114–16.

3. An example of this type of drag performance (one lacking metatheatricality) in early modern contexts might include, for instance, the amputation of Lavinia's hands in *Titus Andronicus.*

4. It could be asserted that most performances of bodily discomfort in comedic genres are metatheatrical in their imitation of suffering for laughter. However, *Volpone* takes the metatheatricality even further by exposing and explaining his performance of discomfort directly to the audience.

5. Quayson defines discomfort as a "euphemism for the broad range of perturbations that afflict the character with disability, from embarrassment to physical discomfiture to pain, both mental and physical"; see *Aesthetic Nervousness,* 54. Because Volpone's metatheatrical performance of disability hinges on his mimicry of "discomfort," this type of disability drag conflates with other fakers of bodily ailments, including the illness faker and the deathbed faker.

6. Mitchell and Snyder, *Cultural Locations of Disability,* 166. As Mitchell and Snyder have argued, "*disabled bodies have been constructed cinematically and socially to function as delivery vehicles in the transfer of extreme sensation to audiences*" (162, italics original). In the case of *Volpone,* the "*transfer of extreme sensation*" to the spectators happens within the plot, rather than to the viewers offstage.

7. Breitenberg posits that the early modern male body's construction is rooted in regularity and fluidity, arguing that it is a "signifier of cultural tensions and contradictions"; see *Anxious Masculinity,* 3.

8. Paster, *Body Embarrassed* and *Humoring the Body.* She argues that how one's body comes across in early modern culture owes as much to the passions and Galenic humors—and one's struggle for control over them—as it does to "the realities of social . . . hierarchy everywhere in the period" (*Humoring the Body* 21).

9. While there are various early modern examples of anxiety about false disability and illness, similar instances can be seen as early as the medieval period. For scholarship on such accounts and cautionary tales toward disability counterfeits, see, for example, Metzler's *Disability in Medieval Europe*, 151–52.

10. Paré, *Monsters and Marvels*.

11. Ibid., 74–75; chap. 22.

12. This term is from Michel Foucault, who characterizes the medical gaze as a process of extrapolating various symptoms or signs of illness that then pieces them back together to form a holistic diagnosis; *The Birth of the Clinic*, trans. A. M. Sheridan Smith (New York: Vintage Books, 1973), 14.

13. A facet of this surgeon's gaze can be explained via Rosemarie Garland-Thomson's *Staring*: "Staring is a conduit to knowledge. Stares are urgent efforts to make the unknown known"; she adds, "Knowledge gathering is the most productive aspect of staring in that it can offer an opportunity to recognize one another in new ways" (15). Though I conflate this instance of staring with the gaze due to the surgeon's diagnostic approach, Garland-Thomson distinguishes between the two actions: "The stare is distinct from the gaze, which has been extensively defined as an oppressive act of disciplinary looking that subordinates its victim" (9). For Garland-Thomson, the process of staring, especially when the object of the stare returns the look, has more reciprocity between subject and object.

14. Paré, *Monsters and Marvels*, 75.

15. Garland-Thomson, *Staring*, 20.

16. Siebers, *Disability Theory*, 116.

17. Paré, *Monsters and Marvels*, 75.

18. William Carroll, *Fat King, Lean Beggar* (Ithaca, NY: Cornell University Press, 1996), 27.

19. Lindsey Row-Heyveld has drawn attention to early modern disability as "particularly effeminizing" within the social hierarchy and framed this feminization around passivity, claiming that "persons with disabilities became objects to be acted upon" ("The Lying'st Knave in Christendom," n.p.) Row-Heyveld also emphasizes the paranoia about counterfeiters who used false disability to garner charity.

20. Elaine Scarry, *The Body in Pain* (Oxford: Oxford University Press, 1985), 4. Quayson also uses Scarry's point in order to explain how discomfort can produce doubt: "The one not in pain may entertain some doubt about the veracity or intensity of what the bearer of pain claims to be feeling" (*Aesthetic Nervousness*, 79–80).

21. Paster, *Body Embarrassed*, 12. She further asserts that "bodily events that . . . we ordinarily regard as trivial . . . might in the humoral body be fraught with significance as *unwilled* alterations of the body's internal state" (12, emphasis added).

22. Volpone's controlled imposture of suffering becomes even more complex at the outset of act 5. Privately, Volpone confesses that his "left leg 'gan to have the cramp," claiming "some power had struck" him "with a dead palsy" while performing as ailing for an audience (5.1.5–7). While this could be taken as a legitimate performance of discomfort, the character's emphasis on a public performance versus a private expression of pain remains a product of metatheatricality; the audience still observes the able-bodied actor making this claim. After expressing this discomfort, moreover, Volpone turns to wine as a means of controlling the pain, saying he "shall conquer" and "prevent" any "villainous disease" (5.1.9–13).

23. *Oxford English Dictionary*, 2nd ed. (Oxford: Oxford University Press, 1989), def. 4.

24. In *Disability Theory* Siebers argues, "When actors play disabled in one film and able-bodied in the next . . . the audience also knows that an actor will return to an able-bodied state as soon as the film ends" (116).

25. See Brian F. Tyson, "Ben Jonson's Black Comedy: A Connection between *Othello* and *Volpone*," *Shakespeare Quarterly* 29 (1978): 61.

26. This is not the first instance in which Volpone has been equated with the immoral beggar-impostor. Bonario discovers Volpone's disguise earlier in the play, and Volpone responds, "I am unmasked, unspirited, undone, / Betrayed to beggary, to infamy" (3.7.77–78).

27. Stephen Greenblatt projects a similar reading onto Volpone's punishment, contending that the sentence prohibits the Fox's constant metamorphoses and disguises until "his being finally and irrevocably assumes the shape of his mask"; "The False Ending in *Volpone*," *Journal of English and Germanic Philology* 75 (1976): 102. Still, while Volpone's mask is indeed one of sickness, it retains its wealthy status, making it a slight departure from his character's earlier performances.

28. See *OED*.

29. Kevin Siena, *Venereal Disease, Hospitals, and the Urban Poor* (Rochester, NY: University of Rochester Press, 2004), 64. Jonson sets *Volpone* in Venice, rendering Siena's reading of Italian hospitals geographically applicable to the drama. At the same time, the application to English society also comes across for, as Siena posits, "The Italian hospital records pre-date London ones, but it is likely that the chronology of the English response parallels the case . . . in Italy" (64).

30. Paré, *Monsters and Marvels*, 76–77, chap. 23.

31. Ibid., 77.

CHAPTER 8

Richard Recast

Renaissance Disability in a Postcommunist Culture

MARCELA KOSTIHOVÁ

When I think of the intersection of the English Renaissance and the issue of disability, no one seems to come to mind as prominently as Shakespeare's Richard III. Indelibly categorized as "deformed" by Thomas More (a label faithfully maintained by Hall and Holinshed), the persona of Richard rearticulated by Shakespeare permeated Western popular consciousness far beyond the relatively narrow fields of history and drama. As Sharon Snyder remarks, thanks to Shakespeare, Richard has been infamously elevated to the position of the "arch-defective in all literature," the pinnacle example of "malevolent disability."[1] It is of course up for discussion whether Richard's reported physical disfigurement is historically accurate or inserted by pro-Tudor historians eager to heap damnation on the king.[2] In this essay, however, I choose to focus elsewhere, namely, on the culturally contextual reception of *Richard III*. I posit that Shakespeare's text, while forceful in its demonization of Richard's body and soul, is surprisingly ambiguous in describing the physical nature of Richard's deformity. This ambiguity is particularly perplexing considering that the text is destined for staging: after all, a theater audience needs to be both told *and* shown Richard's deformed body to subscribe to the larger early modern ideological linking between bodily and psychological evil. Even more importantly, this ambivalence challenges each production to invent its own bodily projection of Richard's evil interiority to attend to contextually specific modern perceptions of the correlative between disabled exteriority and psychological interiority. Inevitably, the play thus invites a series of stagings, each of which disables the Renaissance text on the par of current discourses of disability in a given cultural context. I will here examine one specific example—a wildly popular production of *Richard III* in the postcommunist Czech Republic—to pursue the ways in which a particular case of disabling the Renaissance may feed off of—and feed into—contemporary political tensions surrounding the normative discourses of humanity, masculinity, and citizenship.

Despite an immense cultural devotion to Shakespeare and a relative cultural notoriety for the formidable "hunchback" Richard, *Richard III* was rarely performed in communist Czechoslovakia.[3] The 1989 Velvet Revolution did not bring an immediate change in this trend, although Shakespeare performances in general multiplied on postcommunist Czech stages in the absence of ready material independent of the communist taint. This Richardian dearth came to an abrupt end at the very end of the second millennium, even as the first decade of political transition was expected to give way to the free democratic future promised by the impending acceptance into the European Union in 2004. In the midst of a general disenchantment with new political circumstances, which for much of the Czech population brought a worse standard of living than communism, *Richard III* seemed to offer a relevant opportunity for reflection on the trappings of political power and the futility of political engagement of the average citizen. The Czech late 1990s increasingly were plagued by undisguised battles for political control among the supposedly liberated postcommunist politicians. These battles frequently were punctuated by embarrassing performances of anxious masculinity and resulted in corruption charges that tended to equal or even supersede the "tunneling" scandals of the communist era. The three Czech productions of *Richard III* that opened in 1999 and 2000 (two of them competing with each other in the capital, Prague),[4] offered three more or less explicitly reflective mirrors of the current political power structure.[5]

Among these three *Richard*s, the longest-lived became *Richard III* produced by Divadelní Spolek Kašpar (Theater Guild Clown), which opened in September 2000 at Divadlo v Celetné (Theater in Celetná Street). This production made overtures toward Renaissance theatrical practices in a minimalist set as well as sophisticated and expensive "historic" costumes bristling with armor and showcasing voluptuous fabrics. Moreover, the production gestured toward Renaissance practices in that all but two of the actors doubled in multiple roles, often cross-gendered. The major draw of the production, however, rested on the interpretation of Richard's famed deformity in casting a well-known and well-liked actor, Jan Potměšil, in the leading role. Formerly a rising star of the Czech theater and film scene whose protagonists included romantic leads in films marketed to young viewers, Potměšil's career came to an abrupt (if eventually temporary) standstill once he began using a wheelchair after an accidental injury sustained while engaging in dissident activities against the communist regime. Hailed as possibly the sole "casualty" of the Velvet Revolution[6] and celebrated for "beating the odds" of whole-body paralysis, Potměšil in this role became an immense draw for both traditional and nontraditional theater audiences. Far from "disappearing" into his role, Potměšil's performance—buttressed by the theater collective and the media—blurred the boundaries between the actor and character by foregrounding the actor's past in all promotional and evaluative materials, frequently as the defining feature of the production and of the entire collective.

In what follows, I will both explore the ways in which this particular staging disables the Renaissance text and investigate the cultural implications of blurring Richard's ambiguous "natural deformity" with Potměšil's accidental disability acquired in the process of political activism. I am fascinated by the ways in which this production uses Shakespeare's text and cultural capital simultaneously to disrupt and to confirm contemporary stereotypes of disability, particularly as it relates to questions of normative masculine power, while commenting on embarrassing and greedy (if not as bloody, in the Richardian fashion) machismo of corrupt government officials whose scandals in fact shared newspaper pages with reviews of *Richard III*. Ultimately, I suggest that this production's version of Renaissance disability, in its multivalent ambiguity, uneasily captures a postcommunist transitionality wherein (corpo)realities are in flux, the future multiple and uncertain, and the narratives of the past uncomfortably unsettled.

Richard's (Un)fair Proportions

Postcommunist transitionality is not limited to the public political sphere. As the example of *Richard III* demonstrates, the transition from communism has permeated all spheres of public and private life, and profoundly affected intimate conceptions of individual humanity, particularly as it related to citizenship and attendant human rights. In the realm of categorizing and addressing the question of disability, obvious tensions arose from competing pressures: on the one hand, the state was entrenched in its communist and pre-communist past with its legacy of institutionalization—and disenfranchisement—of bodies deemed mentally, physically, sexually, or politically deviant; on the other, the Czechs needed to respond to the specific pressures of the European Union to impose Western discourses of equality, including disability. This conflict fueled the perception that the ability of Czechs to define the parameters of their own citizenship had been jeopardized, if not made impossible. This perception alone created profound cultural resentment and retrenchment to hostile conservative attitudes. Parallel pressures of the EU that sought to redefine postcommunist parameters of gender and sexuality[7] further intensified this backlash.

Stepping into these ubiquitous cultural tensions, Kašpar's *Richard III* brought to the table a host of conflicting interpretive possibilities. In presenting a "past" heartthrob in the title role, the production might challenge existing biomedical practices of pathologizing and disenfranchising nonnormative bodies. In contrast, the not-so-subtle engrained association of Richard's bodily materiality with evil might solidify existing stereotypes of disability. Potměšil, as the only visibly disabled person in the influential entertainment industry, could be read equally as an early champion of disability rights or as an exotic exception that, as a Czech maxim would argue, proves the rule of a dominant repressive norm. More widely, Richard's exacting hypermasculinity in Potměšil's articulation of Shakespeare's usurping ruler, in the context of neocolonial EU expansion, can serve as a warning against a national future in which an economically exploitive European Union damagingly exacts its power structure on its new (if vainly protesting) potential members. Or the spectacle of an empowered murderous deviant might fuel a growing paranoia that more inclusiveness in terms of citizenship—particularly as it rests on normative, able-bodied masculinity—would politically and socially empower those who previously were systematically disenfranchised.

In Shakespeare's textual template, the link between power, masculinity, and deformity is laid out in Richard's first soliloquy, which serves as a de facto prologue and thus establishes the organizing principles of the play. His disabled masculinity—or the inability to perform normative masculinity adequately—fuels his anxiety of disempowerment and subsequent disqualification from normative courtly activities. Posing the dual prongs of normative masculine power—military and heterosexual conquest—Richard seeks to supplement the shortcomings in the latter: instead of exerting sexual power, he sets out to manipulate his political surroundings through cunning, and sometimes brutal, intrigue. His bodily deformity, though never explicitly articulated, acts as the necessary linchpin that engenders his self-professed villainy. Yet the play's occasional commentary on other characters' comparable brutality (Margaret), duplicity (Buckingham), and selfish political agility (nearly everyone else) leaves the uncomfortable impression that Richard offends not because he is ruthless, per se, but rather because he dares to grasp for power for which his deformity makes him ineligible. In other words, claiming that which all of the other agents of power in the play seek, Richard temporarily transgresses the confines of the implicit imperative conflation of deformity with disempowerment from conventional venues of social and political power. Seen from this perspective, Shakespeare's ending seems to restore power to the Lancastrians not because they are more ethical than Richard but because they are normatively bodied.

The link between Richard's "misshapen" body and his ethics, particularly in the context of Renaissance ideology of interiority/exteriority, as Michael Torrey reminds us, is an ambiguous one. On the one hand, Torrey argues, Anne and Margaret believe that "his deformity is a clear sign that he is odious and wicked," suggesting their concurrence with the ideology of clear overlap between the normative aesthetics of exteriority and the interior moral code.[8] On the other, the play also poses the real problem of Richard's position as a "successful deceiver."[9] Despite his "deformity," Richard repeatedly leads others to suppose him virtuous, bringing forth a contrasting Renaissance view that hesitated to conflate one's visage and moral predispositions. Fluctuating between these two views in the course of the play, Richard's "body alternately does and does not seem to give him away."[10] Ultimately, Torrey suggests that "[a]lthough Richard's deceptions might at first seem a rejection of physiognomy[,] . . . they actually mirror an uncertainty about appearances that physiognomy itself betrays."[11]

Despite the importance ascribed to Richard's body, his deformity is a point of great textual ambiguity beyond the extent that Torrey allows. Richard describes his own body very little, usually as a rhetorical device that serves to underscore his unsuitability to public action. In the opening soliloquy, he tells the audience of his "rudely stamp'd" appearance that mars "fair proportion" (1.1. 16, 18), caused by a premature birth that left him "deformed, unfinished . . . scarce half made up" (20–21).[12] He mentions a more specific nature of this deformity twice: at the outset of the play, Richard refers to a limp (1.2.250), and, when in need of an excuse to behead Hastings, Richard produces a previously unmentioned "arm . . . like a blasted sapling, all withered up" (3.4.68–69). It is important to note that the positive correlation between Richard's deformity and his ability to achieve publicly—whether as a ruler or a lover—is more fictional than factual: as an aspiring ruler, Richard out-politics all his opponents; as a lover, he succeeds in wooing not just once, in one of the most spectacularly incredible seductions of the English stage, but nearly twice.

If Richard is unreliable in describing his disabled body or in outlining its cultural efficacy, other characters are equally unhelpful. His deformity is *never* mentioned by characters who harbor any real or feigned loyalty to Richard of York, later Richard the King. Those who lack such loyalty—mostly because they have been affected by his ruthless politicking—do not stint with negative epithets. It is crucial to note, however, that as a rule they resort to name-calling once they grasp the (negative) impact of Richard's machinations as well as their inability to take corrective action. This resort to opportunistic Othering therefore serves symbolically to disempower an unexpectedly—and presumably undeservedly—powerful agent. Even then, negative references to Richard's body consist of rather vague, general epithets ranging from the well-used "dog," to "devil," to "villain" and "toad," which seem commensurate with the anger of each speaker but do not provide a bodily description of the addressee. Even Margaret's more imaginative and more descriptive "bottled spider" and "poisonous bunch-backed toad" (1.3 241, 245), repeated later by Elizabeth (4.4 81), and relation-slandering "elvish-mark'd, abortive, rooting hog! . . . seal'd in [his] nativity! . . . the slave of nature and the son of hell! . . . slander of [his] heavy mother's womb! . . . loathed issue of his father's loins!" (1.3 225–31), seems to zero in on the non-normative aspects of Richard's bodily materiality only as *an afterthought* of his actions.[13] This deferred labeling suggests a culture of deep fear of the other, coated by a thin layer of political correctness (or, in Renaissance approximations, good breeding and manners) that breaks in an instant of power rupture. As much as other characters do not seem to ascribe any significance to Richard's non-normative body while he conforms to social expectations, his corporality becomes the central focus of the process through which his inappropriate assertions of power are explained.

The conflicting accounts of Richard's motives, combined with an absence of a definitive word on his bodily state in the text of *Richard III,* forces the discourse of embodiment, power, deformity, and disability into the exceedingly culturally determined stage-world of the play. When Richard refers to his body as "misshapen thus" (1.2 250), he foregrounds his own performativity, calling the audience's attention to the deformity it sees. Such visual deformity calls for a performance of physical deviance that is highly context- (and culture-) specific. Not explicitly articulated, such expression of a culture's commitment to normativity is perpetually lingering in the play's margins. Thus, each production of *Richard III* plays into the temporal expectations of its theatrical audience, contemporary discourses of (dis)ability and deviance, masculinity, citizenship, power, and sexuality. All are further blended with the cultural capital of transcendental Shakespeare, his own unreliable and ideologically tainted historical accounts, as well as the stage and film legacies of preceding productions. More than any other Shakespeare play, I propose, the definition of "monstrosity" and "disability" thus becomes a self-reflexive cultural text to be read, revealing the underpinnings of the cultural context in which the play is produced.

Postcommunist Disability

It is somewhat of an understatement to claim that a performance of an unexpectedly disabled Richard challenges the Czech normative discourse of disability, which—around the time of incorporation into the EU—was not favorably predisposed toward including persons with disabilities in the category of equal citizenry. The unwavering tendency to conceptualize disability biomedically as a pathology in the Czech context (and in Central Eastern Europe in general), as Daniel Holland has found, has resulted in an understanding of disability as an "impairment in psychological, physiological, or anatomical function."[14] Disability, thus categorized, becomes "a deficit that is 'possessed' by an individual and necessitat[es] individual treatment."[15] Consequently, it is possible to deny a group of such separate individuals—deprived of the benefit of structural collectivity of persons who depart from standards of bodily and mental "wholeness"—collective political platform that would help lessen some of the "particularly severe challenges to health status and quality of life" and, more broadly, elicit a shift in discourse delineating individuality and citizenship.[16]

The overwhelming majority of Czechs living with disabilities has been in the care of a state that has continued the communist practice of sequestering them from the able-bodied population in separate institutions where they are not likely to interfere with the accepted societal norm. As a result, departures from the norms of "ability" have remained invisible, sensationalized, deviant, abnormal, and taboo.[17] The removal of persons who do not meet standards of mental and physical normalcy from the normative collective eye into separate facilities has been strengthened further by the reluctance with which authorities have provided required public accommodations. The U.S. Department of State, for the first time in 2002, included disabilities as one of its foci in human rights reports on individual countries. According to this report, the Czech Republic performed poorly in providing necessary support for the disabled.[18]

The great reluctance to accommodate persons with disabilities, even in the face of potential sanctions by the European Union, speaks to a degree of cultural disruption that spans beyond mere logistical change. A shift in the level of provisions to persons with specific needs would inevitably open the question of equality of all, starting with the public education system. There, the engrained cultural practice since the nineteenth century has been an early separation (in the fifth or ninth grades, depending on school) into vocational tracks—academic, technical, vocational, special—that affirms a sociopolitical practice of constructing an intellectual hierarchy that divides the young citizenry into implicit tracks of (in)ability. In the great majority of cases, these tracks delineate the lifelong career options of each individual. After the fall of communism, as Mel Ainscow and Memmenasha Haile-Giorgis have charted in their research, changes to the Czech curriculum have made it "more demanding in the belief that this will raise standards in education" relative to international educational achievements.[19] This persistent practice of early categorization systematically discriminates against children from less affluent backgrounds, rural areas, and ethnic minorities. Ainscow and Haile-Giorgis point out that, for instance, "between 25 and 100 per cent of pupils in schools for children with moderate learning difficulties are from Romany backgrounds. In explanation of this, it has been argued that mainstream schools have too many socio-cultural/racial tensions and conflicts for Romany children."[20] As the elementary example of education attests, any discussion of disability is a discussion of enfranchisement that threatens to undermine the very classificatory system that fuels Czech culture and its society, economy, and political system. Alex McClimens, a Western disability scholar, proposed that accepting established Western discourse of disability would equal a "loss of national identity and culture" for many postcommunist societies.[21] In other words, the question of establishing individual norm of ability and humanity lies in the core of the national conception of citizenship, so much so that reorienting toward Western (dis)ability discourse would threaten to undermine the entire ideological system of a society.

It is not surprising, then, that the Czech tradition in which the Kašpar *Richard III* inevitably positions itself sees Richard mainly as an evil malcontent whose external physique merely reflects his inner malevolence. An eminent Shakespearean, Zdeněk Stříbrný, provided a more nuanced assessment of Czech Richards performed since 1945, calling the title character "both a Machiavellian titan and a cripple suffering from a deep-seated sense of inferiority, a raging tyrant and wisecracking comedian, God's chief enemy and the scourge of God avenging the old crimes of the Red and the White Rose upon the two houses and opening the way for historical progress."[22] Though broader in its interpretive possibilities than the unequivocal popular view, such interpretation continues to collapse implicitly Richard's behavior with his deviant body, reluctant to acknowledge the structural implications of damaging discourses of disability and deviance that permeate both worlds of the play and the Czech culture.

In a context where disability is a widely pathologized umbrella term that inadvertently catches all groups that are to be culturally disenfranchised, putting an explicitly disabled—yet profoundly able—body on ritualistic public display in a Shakespeare play is likely to create a rupture in existing discourse. This publicized non-normative body cannot escape, as Carrie Sandahl and Philip Auslander remind us, being understood as solely "about disability."[23] The superimposition of contemporary views of disability discourages—even actively prevents—the actor from "disappearing" into his role as is usually expected.[24] Instead, the overlay of disability inevitably demands additional narratives that inescapably interact with a plot of whichever play or character is onstage. Rosemarie Garland-Thomson argues that "the disabled body is novelty writ large for the captivated starer, prompting persistent curiosity and launching a troubling tangle of identification and differentiation," so that the able-bodied audience is perpetually "seeking a narrative that puts their disrupted world back in order."[25] Moreover, these narratives are always already circumscribed by the able-bodied mentality that requires narratives that, as Sandahl and Auslander maintain, articulate the balance of disability and power in that they "must inevitably show how we conquer our disabilities or how they eventually conquer us."[26]

Intriguingly, in the case of Kašpar's *Richard III,* the superimposed narrative of the disabled actor is in conflict with the traditional interpretation of the character he portrays. While Potměšil's commanding presence on stage provides unarguable evidence of his victory over the assumed limitations of his impairment, his stage persona Richard is gradually stripped of every last vestige of whatever power he temporarily grasped. Potměšil's Richard further disrupts the ingrained binary between the two apparently opposite discourses of disability, drawing together Richard's congenital difference, which left him "misshapen, scarce half made up" with the actor's "tragic" accidental disfigurement. This overlap is further strengthened by the perpetual rearticulation (by the theater and the press) of Potměšil's progression from Romeo to Richard, recalling that the fateful car accident caught the promising, handsome actor in the midst of rehearsals for the title role in Shakespeare's *Romeo and Juliet.* Since the only marker of Richard's deformity is a wheelchair, this performance offers a potential cognitive impasse that invites alternative interpretations of the character, normative difference, as well as of the wider social context. Have we just witnessed a Coriolanian tragedy wherein a national hero has been stripped of his just deserts, only to descend into villainous rage and lash out at his discriminatory environment? Or, have we witnessed another Iago-like treachery that reinforces the red flags that non-normativity presumably raises in any good citizen?

Richard's Romeo

The sheer success of the production, which kept it on stage for the last decade[27] and carried it through more than three hundred performances in the repertory theater, tells us little about the specific reaction of Czech audiences beyond their voracious appetite to see an exotic celebrity performance. More informative are the ways in which the production is promoted by the Kašpar collective and reviewed by the press. While wrapped in commendable rhetoric of equality, Kašpar unabashedly cashed in on its unique member, promoting his contributions to the collective efforts while charging disproportionally inflated prices for performances in which he appears. The reviews, in turn, divide between badly hidden condescension and admiring sensationalism. Thus far, the focus on all fronts is a surprise encounter with the previously unknown and, more so, a surprise at the ability in the presumed disabled that ironically parallels the discomfort felt at Richard's usurpation of state power.

Kašpar promotional materials seem to confirm the already cited assumption that "the disabled body is naturally about disability."[28] Since his first theatrical appearance in Kašpar productions after his accident, Potměšil was cast in a series of roles marked by various degrees of physical and mental deviance. For instance, in the case of the theatrical adaptation of Daniel Keyes's *Flowers for Algernon,* Potměšil's physical difference was to symbolize—or to accentuate—Charlie Gordon's considerable mental impairment. *Richard III,* then, is merely another in a series, one that Potměšil ironically deems the most "normal" compared to the others he performed previously. His presumed, and by now inevitably acquired, "expertise in disabled characters" provides an identity for the entire ensemble. Indeed, in all substantial interviews with the director, Jakub Špalek, whether about the production or the Kašpar company in general, Potměšil is its only member who is mentioned at any length.[29] In sum, regardless of whatever arrangement exists inside the Kašpar collective, the materials suggest a profitable exploitation of Potměšil's non-normative body to satisfy the public's craving for a safe spectacle of deviance that, despite its inroads into a deliberately uncharted territory, validates the boundaries of normative discourse of ability and citizenship.

With few exceptions, the overwhelming majority of reviews seem to share and fuel further this notion of an exciting non-normative spectacle neatly articulated for consumption by eager audiences. As if working from a template, most reviews of *Richard III* follow the introductory paragraph with an overview of Potměšil's accident and his subsequent recovery. While some depart into the specifics of overwhelming (and ultimately erroneous) medical prognoses, others stress Kašpar's generosity in providing a space for Potměšil to "resurrect" his craft, or offer accounts of the actor's personal life marked by consistent humility in face of public scrutiny and crowned with the birth of a son. All of these responses then tend to transition seamlessly into polite praise for the actor's performance as Richard, frequently mentioning—but failing to reflect on the effects or implications of—the discrepancy between the actor's positive attitude and Richard's villainy. Indeed, Karel Kříž calls Potměšil "an institution of goodness,"[30] and Zdeněk Tichý sees him as "predestined for protagonist roles."[31] Most also speak admiringly of Potměšil's ability to act *despite* his impairment. Some comment on his commendable ability to "make up" for his physical shortcomings: Martina Hrdličková, for instance, notes that Potměšil "balances out his physical handicap with the dynamism of his dialogues."[32] The reviews, as a rule, end with cursory courtesy nods to the rest of the cast, who appear as the more-or-less (depending on the reviewer) successful and/but necessary also-rans. All in all, the reviews equally underscore the narrative of an unfortunate-but-grateful gifted subject who is happy to be subjected to public personal scrutiny thinly veiled in the guise of theatrical performance.

Rather than *Richard III*, Richard III, or even Potměšil as a celebrity, it is Potměšil's non-normative body that is the heart of this sought-after spectacle that provides an audience with the unprecedented ability to indulge the otherwise forbidden (yet difficult to resist) urge to stare at the disabled body. Indeed, since staring here is a prerequisite of the exercise of theatrical performativity, such exercise is hardly to be questioned. Yet such a stare is not likely to produce the necessary familiarity that might lead to de-tabooization of the non-normative bodies in the larger social and cultural context. The unclear and unexplored link between bodily non-normativity and moral depravity in *Richard III,* together with the pervasive discourse of *inability* attendant upon the concept of "disability," undermines the potential this particular production could have had to begin renegotiating the categories of (in)ability in the Czech context. Potměšil's progress from Romeo to Richard, particularly in the framework of the transcendental Shakespearean cultural capital that is tapped to sanctify most Czech productions' ideological message, provides a clear narrative of cultural categorization that seems ready to counter the overtures of the European Union for cultural assimilation.

Notes

1. Sharon Snyder, "Unfixing Disability,'" in *Bodies in Commotion,* ed. Sandahl and Auslander, 272.

2. At the time of publication, this very question is being pursued subsequent to a recent archeological recovery of remains that are thought likely to be Richard's. Perhaps not surprisingly, the question of physical "deformation," pending a successful DNA identification of the remains, is paramount to the research agenda (Martin Wainwright, "Richard III: Could the skeleton under the car park be the king's? Remains at church near Bosworth Field battle site show signs of violent death and severe curvature of the spine," *The Guardian* online, 12 September 2012. http://www.guardian.co.uk/science/2012/sep/12/richard-skeleton-king-remains-bosworth).

3. Only nine Czech productions of *Richard III* have been noted between 1945 and 1999, a very small number in comparison to some of Shakespeare's more popular plays such as *Twelfth Night* (produced 97 times in the same interval), *A Midsummer Night's Dream* (91), or *Taming of the Shrew* (78).

4. The first to open was *Richard III* at Velké Divadlo (the Large Theater) by a regional theater in Plzen during the 1999–2000 season. The Kašpar production of *Richard III* ceremoniously opened the scaled-down Czech replica of the Globe Theatre during the 2000–2001 season.

5. For explicit references, see reviews by Eva Jeníková, "Richard Třetí odráží stav české politiky," *Zemské Noviny: Kultura,* 22 April 2000, "Potměšilovi slouží vozík jako exkluzivní rekvizita," *Zemské Noviny: Kultura,* 25 September 2000, and "Richard Třetí odráží stav české politiky," *Zemské Noviny: Kultura,* 22 April 2000; Martin Putna, "Shakespeare a klid na práci," *Mladá Fronta Dnes,* 25 September 2000; Zdeněk Tichý, "U Kašparů může být i zlo fascinující," *Mladá Fronta Dnes,* 13 October 2000, "Kašpar by měl s námi i vymřít, míní Špalek," *Mladá Fronta Dnes: Kultura,* 20 September 2000, and "Potměšil tasí meč jako Richard III," *Mladá Fronta Dnes: Kultura,* 20 September 2000; Jiří Kříž, "Prahou zní: Království za koně," *Právo,* 29 September 2000.

6. See, for instance, Ivo Toufar, "Říjen: Divadelní Blázinec," *Hospodářské Noviny,* 13–15 October 2000.

7. See Marcela Kostihová, *Shakespeare in Transition* (New York: Palgrave Macmillan, 2010), particularly chaps. 3 and 4.

8. Michael Torrey, "'The Plain Devil and Dissembling Looks': Ambivalent Physiognomy and Shakespeare's *Richard III*," *English Literary Renaissance* 30, no. 2 (2000): 123.

9. Ibid., 126.

10. Ibid.

11. Ibid.

12. This and all citations hereafter come from *Richard III* in *The Riverside Shakespeare,* 2nd ed., ed. Herschel Baker et al. (Boston: Houghton Mifflin, 1997), 748–804.

13. Further points of ambiguity complicate our understanding of Richard's bodily materiality. The young Duke of York relays an origin-less rumor that Richard "grew so fast / That he could gnaw a crust at two hours old" (2.4.27–28). This rumor is implicitly belied by Richard's mother, the Duchess of York, when she reports that he was "long a-growing" (2.4.19). And, despite her measureless disappointment at the discovery of Richard's involvement in the disempowerment of his other brothers, her report of Richard's growth does not allude to anything but a generally labor-intensive child:

> Thou cam'st on earth to make the earth my hell.
> A grievous burthen was thy birth to me,
> Tetchy and wayward was thy infancy;
> Thy school-days frightful, desperate, wild, and furious,
> Thy prime of manhood daring, bold, and venturous;
> Thy age confirm'd, proud, subtle, sly, and bloody,
> More mild, but yet more harmful—kind in hatred. (4.4.167–73)

14. Daniel Holland, "Grass Roots Promotion of Community Health and Human Rights for People with Disabilities in Post-communist Central Europe: A Profile of the Slovak Republic," *Disability and Society* 18, no. 2 (2003): 137.

15. Ibid.

16. Ibid., 133.

17. Holland's findings are echoed across Western research on the Czech Republic and Central Eastern Europe. Hannah Roberts, for instance, argues in parallel that "'Social care homes' in central and eastern Europe and the former Soviet Union were originally designed to hide away people with mental health problems, because such people were not supposed to exist in the utopia of the communist system. Today the lack of community-based care in the region means that beds in such institutions are still in demand, despite their frequently harsh living conditions and the severe restrictions they typically impose on residents' liberty"; see "Mental Health Care Still Poor in Eastern Europe," *The Lancet* 360 (17 August 2002): 552. The lack of basic rights was reflected in the overwhelming license given to legal guardians who "typically have unchecked powers to decide not only a person's place of residence, but also his or her financial affairs, legal actions, and medical treatments" (ibid.).

18. The report states that "persons with disabilities suffered disproportionately from unemployment[, even though] businesses in which 60 percent or more of the employees were disabled qualified for special tax breaks and the Government provided transportation subsidies to disabled citizens. . . . In Prague 24 of the 50 metro stations were wheelchair-accessible; however, most of those stations were in the suburbs, and the majority of stations in the city center remained inaccessible. . . . Access to education was a problem for children with physical disabilities due to the lack of barrier-free access to most public schools." See "Czech Republic: Country Reports on Human Rights Practices—2002," released by the Bureau of Democracy, Human Rights, and Labor (the US Department of State), 31 March 2003. http://www.state.gov/g/drl/rls/hrrpt/2002/18361.htm.

19. Mel Ainscow and Memmenasha Haile-Giorgis, "Educational Arrangements for Children Categorized as Having Special Needs in Central and Eastern Europe," *European Journal of Special Needs Education* 14, no. 2 (1999): 109.

20. Ibid., 115.

21. Alex McClimens, "lost in translation," *Learning and Disability Practice* 8, no. 6 (July 2005): 34.

22. Zdeněk Stříbrný, *The Whirligig of Time: Essays on Shakespeare and Czechoslovakia,* ed. Lois Potter (Newark: University of Delaware Press, 2007), 89.

23. Sandahl and Auslander, "Introduction," *Bodies in Commotion,* 4.

24. For more discussion of the implications of mainstream theater's requirement to "disappear" into a character for actors with disabilities, see Carrie Sandahl's "The Tyranny of Neutral: Disability and Actor Training," *Bodies in Commotion,* esp. 257.

25. Rosemarie Garland-Thomson, "Dares to Stares: Disabled Women Performance Artists and the Dynamics of Staring," *Bodies in Commotion,* 31.

26. Carrie Sandahl and Philip Auslander, "Rehabilitating the Medical Model," in *Bodies in Commotion,* 130.

27. At the time of final revisions of this article (fall 2010), the play was still on the active repertoire at Kašpar, though appearing only infrequently.

28. Sandahl and Auslander, *Bodies in Commotion,* 4.

29. Jakub Špalek, *Richard III,* Divadelní spolek Kašpar, Divadlo v Celetné, 20 September 2000.

30. "Prahou zní," 10.

31. "Kašpar by měl s námi i vymřít, míní Špalek," 23.

32. Martina Hrdličková, "*Richard III:* Jan Potměšil nehraje neřest v moralitě," *Reflex* 47 (2000): 87.

CHAPTER 9

The Book of Common Prayer, Theory of Mind, and Autism in Early Modern England

MARDY PHILIPPIAN, JR.

R ecent conversation about disability in the early modern period has largely concerned overt representations of disability, those for which Western culture has had a long taxonomic history—cultural historians using familiar terms for familiar conditions. This work has without question been useful to our understanding of nonstandard bodies and minds, but its tendency to identify and define according to familiar terminology has perhaps also limited the development of a disability heuristic that would otherwise allow for a more inclusive model for theorizing disability. In this emerging investigative field within early modern studies, a disability stud- ies[1] of the English Renaissance, Carol Thomas Neely's work has become the most notable example.[2] Neely shows that madness, figured in the various discourses of the Renaissance as "distraction," exemplified a fluidity and, sometimes, subtlety that study of Shakespeare's plays in particular and early modern subjectivities more generally ought to include. Neely argues that "early moderns drew on the traditional humoral discourses of Galen and Aristotle to rethink the parameters of the human by reimagining madness" and that "discourses of madness flourished because they were useful in recon- ceptualizing the boundaries between natural and supernatural, masculinity

I would like to thank my colleague Wayne Norman in the Department of Psychology at Simp- son University for directing me to several valuable resources on the subject of the autistic brain.

and femininity, body and mind, feigned and actual distraction."[3] In stark contrast to modern conceptions of madness that inform how we look at such cognitive disability, her investigation of the discourses that articulated the theorized sources and observable symptoms of madness and her close reading of its textual history in fifteenth- and sixteenth-century England evidences, as she claims, that early modern "discourses did not yet dehumanize distracted persons, as the concept of 'insanity' later would do."[4] Neely's work is inclusive of a range of discourses (medical, theological, literary) that converge and overlap to construct representations of early modern subjectivity and madness on the stage and is an example of how attention to nuanced discursivity can enable modern readers to attend more sensitively to historical constructions of difference and disability.

Yet for all of its sensitivity to the differences that characterize the historical distance between early modern and modern subjectivities, Neely's approach does at times overly rely for its identifications of "distraction" upon textual signifiers of difference: words that would act as labels or diagnoses for madness within a specific discursive history. And though Neely shows how "Shakespeare's tragedies . . . invent a new language for the mad, a stylistically italicized and culturally inflected speech peculiar to distracted characters,"[5] the inflection and italicization are nonetheless evidenced through language used by figures in the plays. Examples include a look at the anonymous Gentleman's description of Ophelia in *Hamlet* 4.5.6–8, in which her speech is described, for example, as "but half sense" and "nothing," and finally as "unshaped." And Neely's careful reading of period medical treatises also focus upon a writer's use of some native form of terminology to describe maladies that afflict body or mind (or both in some cases). She cites Timothy Bright's *Treatise of Melancholie* (1586) in which Bright discusses "the terrour of the afflicted minde."[6] Neely's work is illuminating, but it is also limited by its core methodological focus upon the linguistic sign.

Methodological logocentrism is not uncommon in the study of literary history, so concerned are scholars with material evidence in the form of a textual, if not often strictly linguistic, record. But as I hope to show, omissions in the textual history of a culture can also signify the presence of the scholar's topic of interest. The wider cultural and social uses of a specific text might overlap with possible therapeutic uses of that same text, so that a devotional text, for example, could be read as a behavioral script that ushered those of atypical cognitive development into corporate religious and social life. Scholars would thus practice a very different kind of logocentrism, one that focuses upon a text's uses as a sign of its participation in an early modern discourse of disability. And while attention to actual language enables scholars to trace out the various discursive locations that collectively speak of madness, for instance, as difference, it may also prevent them from noting silences or omissions in a discursive history that nonetheless would speak of forms of difference and disability that are present in a culture's historical record.

Stephen Dobranski has argued, for example, that a particular kind of Renaissance textual omission, one that "differ[s] from other unfinished or censored Renaissance works because their authors and/or publishers seem to want readers to notice the imperfections," acted for early modern readers as "ostensive stimuli," inviting them into "a cooperative relationship between writers and readers."[7] Dobranski's study contributes to the body of literature known as reception studies, but his insights into the cultural function of the textual omission in early modern England are suggestive for how we might also read omissions in the historical record, or for how we might again see, in Louis Montrose's famous formulation, the textuality of history.[8] The Elizabethan Book of Common Prayer functioned as a communicative mode that uniquely made accessible to those in the pews the emerging theological system of belief and the physical movements and utterances that comprised the church's liturgical service, despite the absence of commentary in the historical record concerning parishioners with receptive or expressive language differences.

Departing from the work done by some early modern disability studies scholars, the present essay considers the Book of Common Prayer in light of modern cognitive theory in an effort to explain more specifically how the prayer book functioned as a mechanism for wider social access for those with cognitive disabilities of a specific kind. In its capacity to standardize reformed rites within the church, the Book of Common Prayer simultaneously enabled willful, cognitively and socially atypical, prayer book conformists[9] to enter into broader normative participation in the larger social sphere. For these individuals, specific cognitive differences influenced their development of what modern cognitive science calls Theory of Mind, a term that refers to an acute inability "to take the perspective of another person" or the inability "to understand the different perspective of others."[10] Without this capacity, an individual is essentially locked within a perpetual state of egocentrism. To exhibit atypical Theory of Mind development meant that these individuals would also have been different in terms of their wider social acceptance. This would have been especially so in early modern England, since, as Christopher Haigh, Judith Maltby, and Ramie Targoff have shown, conformity to nominal religious practice also meant acceptance into the wider social fabric of a community,[11] especially after the passing of the

Act of Uniformity of 1559. For those individuals with limited, impaired, or simply atypical Theory of Mind, and for those with nonstandard language receptivity, the Book of Common Prayer functioned, quite literally, as a religious script and story that could be read and memorized, a script that detailed expectations for the church year, including all the relevant rites and ceremonies that constituted church life. This script/story enabled these individuals to be more than merely outwardly identified by members of their congregation as devotees of the faith, but ultimately, and more significantly, as self-identified and self-understood adherents to the faith and participating members in the wider social world of early modern England.

Cartesian Theory of Mind, Modern Cognitive Science, and Autism

While the term Theory of Mind has a long history, dating back to the writings of Augustine and, even earlier, Plato, the origins of the modern conception of Theory of Mind are found in the writings of René Descartes. In his now famous letter to Gibieuf, dated 19 January 1642, Descartes makes a rather auspicious claim that is the result of several years thinking and writing on the subject of human cognition, specifically its location, function, and capabilities. He writes:

> I am certain that I can have no knowledge of what is outside me except by means of the ideas I have within me; and so I take great care not to relate my judgements immediately to things, and not to attribute to things anything positive which I do not first perceive in the ideas of them. But I think also that whatever is to be found in these ideas is necessarily also in the things themselves.[12]

Locating the core of the human sense of self outside of the confines of the material body, Descartes argues that the mind is inherently immaterial, disembodied, and ineluctably separate from the corporeal. The theory of mind at the heart of modern cognitive science owes much to this formulation of the relationship of the mind to the body that also forms the core of Descartes' philosophical (or neurophilosophical) project. Yet he also nonetheless acknowledges that there is something like an interanimation of these, or that the mind and body echo one another's existence, so that neither one can be said to exist without the copresence of the other. He goes on to state,

We cannot have any knowledge of things except by the ideas we conceive of them; and consequently, that we must even think that whatever conflicts with these ideas is absolutely impossible and involves a contradiction.[13]

Arguing further, and by analogy, Descartes claims:

Thus we have no reason to affirm that there is no mountain without a valley, except that we see that the ideas of these things cannot be complete when we consider them apart; though of course by abstraction we can obtain the idea of a mountain, or of an upward slope, without considering that the same slope can be travelled downhill.[14]

For Descartes, and for the emerging early modern medical discourse, the psychological inheres in the physiological, though each remains distinct. In contrast to Augustinian theory of mind, Charles Taylor has argued that for Descartes reality is a product of perception. "A representation of reality now has to be constructed," Taylor writes, so that "As the notion of 'idea' migrates from its ontic sense to apply henceforth to intra-psychic contents, to things 'in the mind,' so the order of ideas ceases to be something we *find* and becomes something we *build*."[15] No longer should the individual struggle to orient himself or herself toward some identifiable cosmic order; the individual should instead recognize the impossibility in the first place of such an order ever existing outside of the mind whose sole purpose is to impose order upon the otherwise chaotic, to call order into existence. In his widely referenced analysis of what he calls Descartes's "Disengaged Reason," Taylor argues that "The order of representations must thus meet standards which derive from the thinking activity of the knower."[16] In his analysis of the sources and function of Descartes' *cogito,* Taylor finds that rationality results from following an internally defined set of procedures used to order what exists outside the individual's mind; thus, rationality results from employing a method for imposing the ordered self upon a disordered cosmos.

Reconsidering and responding to Taylor's analysis of Descartes' "source of the self," John Sutton has argued that the separation of the mind from the body-as-material accredited to Descartes in Western philosophy since the mid-seventeenth century is probably overstated. Sutton traces a thread of Galenism in more modern medical theory's understanding of mind through as late as the nineteenth century. He notes that the older "psychophysiological . . . frameworks were dynamic in the sense that they assumed the importance of what modern . . . cognitive science call[s], 'continuous reciprocal causation.'"[17] Citing the work of Andy Clark, Sutton points out that a resurgence of interest in "embodied cognition is particularly suggestive in the light of . . . the old fluid physiologies."[18] The mind may not be entirely disconnected from the body according to modern medical observation and theory. "As in jazz improvisation," Sutton writes, citing Clark, "the behavior of every part of the system changes continuously as the patterns of input within a dense web of causal complexity alter."[19] These scientists and researchers might even agree with literary and cultural historians of the early modern period such as Michael Schoenfeldt that "the lexicon of Galenic medicine has survived the demise of its intellectual framework in part because of its cogent experiential basis and its profoundly sentient terminology,"[20] recognizing the abiding explanatory potential of a pre-Cartesian theory of the mind as embodied. Gail Kern Paster, in writing about "embodied passions" in early modern England, has similarly shown that "For the early moderns, emotions flood the body not metaphorically but literally, as the humors course through the bloodstream carrying choler, melancholy, blood, and phlegm to the parts and as animal spirits move like lightning from brain to muscle, from muscle to brain."[21] Modern cognitive science, as Sutton and Clark show, may be returning to an earlier, ancient notion of mind/body interinfluence and moving away from the sharp division postulated by Descartes.

In modern cognitive science, neurobiology, and psychology, Theory of Mind (conveniently differentiated now from earlier conceptions of the term by the acronym ToM) is once again, as it was for Descartes in the early modern period, an *au courant* area of investigation, and while the modern ToM remains a hypothesis, it is a highly well-regarded one often cited by developmental psychologists and neuroscientists alike as an explanation for why the vast majority of individuals with significant language deficits, especially receptive language, demonstrate a profound unawareness of what others might think and feel.[22] Researchers such as Simon Baron-Cohen have found that ToM deficits are primarily typical of individuals with autism spectrum disorder (ASD). Baron-Cohen, an evolutionary psychologist at Cambridge University, describes ToM as the ability to infer "the full range of [another individual's] mental states from [observing his or her] behavior," and a key developmental feature that allows a person to distinguish between true and false belief.[23] The beginning of ToM, as Michael Tomasello's research would show, occurs in infancy, a point in an individual's development of intersubjectivity when intentionality is ascribed to others and to self.[24]

ASD is defined in the most recent edition of the *Diagnostic and Statistical Manual of Mental Disorders* (DSM-IV) as "The presence of markedly abnormal or impaired development in social interaction and communication and a markedly restricted repertoire of activity and interest"; the definition adds, "Younger individuals may have little or no interest in establishing friendships," and, further, "Older individuals may have an interest in friendship but lack understanding of the conventions of social interaction."[25] Regarding the ability to communicate effectively, the DSM-IV entry states, "The impairment in communication is also marked and sustained and affects both verbal and nonverbal skills."[26] The term "autism" was coined by Leo Kanner in 1943, yet he and many psychologists before him had noted peculiar inabilities in some individuals to access the social world that existed around them. Histories of the disorder note that in earlier times the disorder would have been categorized as profound emotional distress or "retardation."[27]

The causes for ASD and the attendant failure to develop ToM are currently hotly debated by a wide spectrum of specialists, including neurologists, neurobiologists, social psychologists, environmental biologists, and, most notably in recent years, immunologists. And although researchers presently do not agree on the causes of autism, there is wide agreement that so-called impaired social cognition and receptive and expressive language differences, characteristics of ASD that are comorbid with lack of ToM, result from problems with the interactivity between the superior temporal gyrus (STG), the amygdala, and medial prefrontal cortex.[28] As Bigler et al. explain, "In autism . . . the interplay between impaired social cognition and deficits in communication, including verbal and nonverbal aspects of social communication, comes via a link between the STG and the amygdala, and other frontotemporolimbic connections. Dysfunctions in this neural circuitry could easily contribute to . . . impaired language."[29] It is also widely held that the use of social scripts enables an individual with ASD and notably atypical ToM to begin "rewiring" his or her brain so that medically and socially defined normative social interaction is increasingly possible. Yet it should be noted that like ToM itself, the neurological substrates of this rewiring have not yet been identified.[30] Changes in an individual's behavior that are said to result from the intervening use of specific cognitive therapies, especially in children below the age of five, are cited as evidence that key neuropathways in the brain have undergone some fundamental alteration.

In the late decades of the twentieth century, researchers in autistic brain function designed therapies and strategies for increasing these individuals' awareness of pretense, but the longitudinal study of patients with ASD or those who exhibit atypical ToM development has revealed that this cognitive difference tends to remain pronounced throughout their lives.[31] Those who exhibit variable ToM often require visual modes of communication in order to compensate for nonstandard language reception if they are to understand what others may expect of them or how they are to complete a series of steps in a process.[32] And research into this inability to understand the motivations, perspectives, beliefs, and emotions of others has revealed that "initial impairments in theory of mind may be further exacerbated as time goes on by poor expressive and receptive language abilities," which then progressively limit their ability to engage in a wider social world.[33] For these individuals, mechanisms must be identified that will allow them to compensate for atypical neurology, a neurology that results in their identification, and categorization within the prevailing medical discourse, as cognitively disabled.

The primary cognitive therapy that interventionists use to catalyze the development of ToM is known as social skills training, and the main techniques used are the social script and the social story.[34] A social script is a written text that involves the individual with ASD in a scenario of verbal exchange, a back-and-forth conversation, matched to appropriate nonverbal communication such as appropriate hand gestures and predictable eye contact. Such scripts typically engage individuals in a customary conversation that allows him or her essentially to practice interacting with another person along fairly predictable patterns of verbal exchange. The effectiveness of the social script technique stems from the very predictability of future social interactions that directly imitate or are strongly reminiscent of the scripted version. Individuals are taught how to socialize through this experience and are encouraged to generalize the pattern of exchange to include future such encounters. Socializing becomes conventional. Like the social script, the social story is a written text but a narrative that depicts common social situations, such as the most acceptable way to greet someone, the proper way to respond when someone is upset, and what behaviors are involved in attending church. Because those with ASD and/or atypical ToM "struggle to read, interpret, and respond . . . to their social world," social stories are used by therapists to map out the kinds of interactions that are nearly autonomic for individuals who are neurotypical.[35] Social stories break the social world down into micronarratives that can be learned the way one learns, for example, about genre (or, in this case, genres of social interaction). The genre of lyric includes a variety of more specific poetic forms, or microgenres, such as the sonnet and the ode, with the sonnet exemplifying a more rigid form than the ode, which is defined more by tone and purpose than it is by line length, stanzaic pattern, and meter. Yet for all the differences between the various microgenres within the larger genre of lyric, it is nonetheless possible to learn to identify each as distinct, and, perhaps most importantly, one can learn the basic features of each in order to reproduce them.

The Early Modern Book of Common Prayer as Cognitive and Social Therapy

With its tripartite narrative design composed of an interweaving of the calendrical, doctrinal, and theological religious scripts that contain the story of the church, the Book of Common Prayer functioned for early modern individuals with atypical ToM (as well as for those who were neurotypical) as a macrosocial story, a collection of micronarratives that included the church's calendar, the litany (doctrinal instruction and statements), collects (a combination of basic theological tenets and prayer instruction),[36] and scriptural passages from both Old and New Testaments. To learn to participate in the common prayer service necessarily involved one in the larger social life of the church community, since the basic patterns of church life were outlined and scripted in the Book of Common Prayer, the communal touchstone that bound individuals together. John N. Wall notes on this subject "Aggressively linear, prayer book worship links past and present in terms of the promise that [parishioners] share a common future; it enables ancient texts to become what makes possible the saying of something vital to the present and to glimpse an as yet unsayable future while it also enables modern texts to become facilitators of such interchanges."[37] The prayer book, in other words, serves the people as a historical narrative of their theological identity, linking, as Wall points out, the past to the present. For those exhibiting atypical ToM, a historical narrative aids them in constructing a reasonable and longitudinal understanding of where they came from in a historical sense and what the larger community of which they are a part expects to do in the future, thus eliminating some confusion regarding who they might be within a larger body of believers.[38]

Thomas Cranmer, the primary architect of the Book of Common Prayer, was convinced that a prayer book and accompanying liturgy could unite English devotees of the Christian faith even as it spiritually transformed them. Cranmer believed that an ordered and theologically coherent narrative could standardize religious practice, a belief that reflects at least a nascent understanding of the formative power narrative held for shaping cognition and identity.[39] This point about early modern English reformers is too often neglected. Critical neglect of this kind may be a result of scholars' common assumption that individuals in the Elizabethan Church of England used the prayer book in merely a perfunctory manner. If scholars demonstrated instead that many individuals found the prayer book to be devotionally efficacious, then they might also come to acknowledge its larger social function for the cognitively disabled within the church and wider community.

Ramie Targoff notes, for example, "Despite the prominence of the liturgical reforms that the prayer book introduced, their impact on early modern
religious culture has often been underestimated," and that "when historians
have acknowledged the extent to which the prayer book sought to standardize the devotional voice of both the laity and clergy, they have frequently
represented this commitment to uniformity in terms of the religious estab-
lishment's political, and not devotional, motivations. . . . Those sympathetic
to 'traditional religion' have regarded common prayer as a superficial practice
that had no real meaning for most English worshippers."[40]

Citing Patrick Collinson's *The Religion of Protestants* as one well-known
study of early modern reformed prayer book religion, Targoff notes that Collinson acknowledges how use of the prayer book resulted in greater religious
conformity, though he "never imagines" that prayer book conformity no
doubt fundamentally remade congregants' devotional lives.[41] Collinson does
not conceive of prayer book conformity as desirable for many people, that
is, or as a positive influence upon their personal—and not merely politically and socially expedient—faith commitments. In contrast, however, to
this earlier work on Elizabethan prayer book religion, Judith Maltby treats
the prayer book as "the most pervasive agent of change . . . in the religious
consciousness and even affections of the English laity. Its success may be
explained in part by the element of continuity it gave its users along with
innovation."[42] Maltby's central claim is that the prayer book "succeeded as an
agent of change as well as of continuity from the middle of Elizabeth's reign
onwards," evidencing a widespread commitment to its use as an efficacious
devotional aid and not merely as a means of state-imposed conformity.[43]
While historians of early modern England continue to debate the relative
devotional significance of the Book of Common Prayer for those who were
expected to make use of it, their critical discussion of its reformative effects
upon parishioners, with few exceptions, continues to overlook the cognitive
influence of its overarching narrative.

In the 1559 edition of the prayer book is a section titled "Proper Lessons
to be Read," which details in the form of a chart, a kind of early modern
spreadsheet or desk calendar, exactly which Old and New Testament passages, including the Proverbs and Psalms, were to be read on each day of
the year. This was a programmatic approach to scripture instruction and one
that, in its starkness (no textual commentary weaved either into the readings
or in the form of notes at the bottom of the printed page), put readers into
direct contact with the holy scriptures. And so, in addition to this section
serving as the calendar for the church year, it exemplified a basic Reformation theological conviction that laity should be given direct access to scrip-

ture. The calendar readings also usually coincide with the remembrance of a particularly significant figure in the history of the life of the church; they marked the beginnings and endings of elongated purification rites (such as fasts) and compelled laity to celebrate Christ's birth, death, and resurrection. This calendrical narrative situated the passing of the days of the year within the larger symbolic history of the church and within the additional frameworks of biblical knowledge and Reformed theological conviction.

The church calendar is followed by scripted morning and evening prayers and then by the Litany, or the basic script for the church service that laity were to recite (or read) as a corporate body, thus subsuming individuals' voices within the larger communal one. The Litany begins with the solemn recognition, "O God the Father of heaven: have mercy upon us miserable sinners. O God the Father of heaven: have mercy upon us miserable sinners."[44] This structure of repeated lines is sustained throughout the Litany and would have been no doubt particularly effective at not merely reminding laity of their need for God's mercy and grace but also uniting them in an act of scripted contrition, especially memorable for the cognitively disabled who required reminding and verbal, if not experiential, reinforcement, the kind that actively shaped one's religious and social subjectivities.

The Collects, Epistles, and Gospels immediately follow the Litany and were to be read in accordance with the church calendar. These collects were intended by Cranmer to involve the laity in a kind of second layering of prayer that logically should follow the laity's corporate admission of sinfulness found in the Litany. But they were also micronarratives that piecemeal contributed to the prayer book's construction of the larger Christian narrative, and some even were intensely compressed narratives that would contain the entire story of Christ's sacrificial redemption of humankind. In the first collect, for example, it reads: "Almighty God, give us grace that we may cast away the works of darkness, and put upon us the armor of light, now in the time of this mortal life (in the which thy Son Jesus Christ came to visit us in great humility); that in the last day, when he shall come again in glorious majesty to judge both the quick and the dead, we may rise to the life immortal, through him who liveth and reigneth with thee and the Holy Ghost, now and ever. Amen."[45] For individuals with less acute ToM, this collect, repeated many times throughout the lifetime of the faithful, dutiful user of the prayer book, is an essential religious story that once learned marked the cognitively disabled person as a member of the larger social world accessed only through a corporately, publicly understood and privately embraced religious identity.

A careful reading of Cranmer's writings in the 1540s and 1550s on the topic of the prayer book's cognitive influence upon the people reveals that in his own thinking he made an important distinction between "heard" and read prayers, a distinction that further helps us understand the role of liturgy in the lives of individuals with cognitive disability. Cranmer's belief in the efficacy of narrative was limited to the hearing of it and not the reading of it.[46] His preface, for example, to the English litany of 1544, a precursor to the vernacular liturgy, makes clear that the laity's understanding should result from what "enters in at their ears,"[47] noting later in his Preface first added to the prayer book of 1552, "Whereas St. Paul would have such language spoken to the people in the church as they might understand and have profit by hearing the same, the service in this church of England (these many years) hath been read in Latin to the people, which they understood not, so that they have heard with their ears only: and their hearts, spirit and mind have not been edified thereby."[48] Cranmer does not appear to have been convinced that the practice of reading the church service was more effective at "edifying" congregants. He privileges the heard prayer over the written and read. Returning to the preface of his Litany of 1544, Cranmer had written then, "These holy prayers and suffrages following are set forth of most godly zeal for edifying, and stirring of devotion of all true faithful christian hearts: so it thought convenient in this common prayer of procession to have it set forth and used in the vulgar tongue, for stirring the people to more devotion: and it shall be every christian man's part reverently to use the same."[49] Cranmer's primary concern for prayer book use was that the congregation prayed as if with one voice: this was the source of the book's spiritual efficacy. Its power to "stir" primarily derived from hearing and not reading, from corporate voice that subsumed the individual. Conformity was key, and his comments regarding common prayer in the preface to his Litany and in the preface to the Book of Common Prayer demonstrate his belief that the aural was of greater value than the written and read.

For those congregants who could not access the aural as successfully because of their varied (or different) mechanisms for language reception, this would have often presented a problem, one that might even constitute a threat to the conformity Cranmer sought to establish among the laity. Yet since Cranmer did not inveigh against the practice of prayer book reading during a service, the possibility still existed for those who could read to access the larger subjectivity-shaping narrative that the prayer book represented. Moreover, one could also argue that because the reading of common prayer occurred within the context of the recitative church body, reading was a means of attending to the aural in a manner that would not otherwise be possible, thus fulfilling Cranmer's most basic goal for the use of common prayer.

I HAVE COMMENTED on important findings in neurobiology that offer scholars of the early modern era important insights into the role the Book of Common Prayer played for laity who were cognitively disabled. Yet the sciences are not the only disciplines to offer such insights. Scholarship in the field of narratology offers mutually confirming conclusions about the influence narrative has upon cognition and subject formation, whether an individual is neurotypical or struggling with language acquisition or related cognitive difficulties. This disciplinary interplay has rich potential for future investigations of cognitive disability and difference in the English Renaissance, and some theory of mind approaches to the study of literary texts and the reading experience are already under way.[50] Jerome Bruner argues that for the study of narrative and its effects upon the mind, "The central concern is not how narrative as text is constructed, but rather how it operates as an instrument of mind in the construction of reality."[51]

How might the early modern religious subjectivity of the cognitively different have been shaped by the narratives woven together in the Book of Common Prayer? This is at core a structural question. Bruner would respond that "the best hope of hermeneutic analysis is to provide an intuitively convincing account of the meaning of the text as a whole in the light of the constituent parts that make it up."[52] Combining calendrical, doctrinal, and theological narratives in a single text, and one to be used daily by nearly all those one knew, the early modern prayer book linked Protestant religious narrative to an individual's identity. But this religious narrative also served as a social story that invited the cognitively disabled into fuller public existence. On the role of narrative in this sense, neuroscience and narratology seem to agree, mutually confirming a similar, if not the same, conclusion via seemingly unrelated methodological and analytical approaches.

The argument I have offered here—that the early modern Book of Common Prayer functioned simultaneously as a religious and social script and story and, by extension, an enculturating textual mechanism for parishioners with atypical neurology—has much to suggest to modern historians of early modern England. It may be, for example, that theological statements and systems communicated in a homily or sermon were not enough to create points of access to religious life for those who exemplified noticeable cognitive differences in their undirected or spontaneous social interactions.

Some individuals may have also required a concrete religious script, one that would have facilitated in the form of printed words in a handheld book content that also communicated larger social expectations, a point that Thomas Cranmer's writings indeed suggest. A "social script" (to use the language of modern cognitive therapy), because it catalyzes comprehension in a way that the strictly aural cannot, may have been for early modern parishioners with variable ToM development the only effective means by which the abstract dimensions of public religious practice and private belief could be accessed, functioning then also as a primary facilitator of participation in the larger social sphere that was characteristically recognized, in the medically defined language of early modern England, as normative.

Written and circulated in parishes nearly one hundred years before Descartes formulated his famous phrase and theory of mind, the Book of Common Prayer nonetheless functions as a projection and materialization of the power of reason to impose itself upon scattered theological writings, church creeds, calendars, and rites. In the same way that institutions of all kinds commit to print their basic policies and procedures for self-governance, creating what might be usefully termed a paper infrastructure, the prayer book functioned as a paper infrastructure of the religious mind. It was, in other words, a textual apparatus that recorded the ordering capacities of human reason and reflexively and habitually, through repeated use, influenced the continued ordering of the mind and self, making no distinction between the mind of persons who were cognitively atypical and those defined by early modern medical discourse as "normal."

Notes

1. I take my definition of this phrase from James C. Wilson and Cynthia Lewiecki-Wilson's essay, "Disability, Rhetoric, and the Body," in *Embodied Rhetorics: Disability in Language and Culture,* ed. James C. Wilson and Cynthia Lewiecki-Wilson (Carbondale: Southern Illinois University Press, 2001): "Disability studies seeks to advance the cause of the disabled and promote social change by analyzing the present social formations that contribute to maintaining the walls of exclusion. Disability studies is thus a situated discourse and expresses a particular standpoint—that of the disabled" (9). Wilson and Lewiecki-Wilson's description of the aims of disability studies includes a careful recognition that such aims are political.

2. Neely, *Distracted Subjects.*

3. Ibid., 1–2.

4. Ibid., 2.

5. Ibid., 23.

6. Ibid., 16.

7. Stephen Dobranski, *Readers and Authorship in Early Modern England* (Cambridge: Cambridge University Press, 2005), 2–3, 15, and 11.

8. Louis A. Montrose, "Professing the Renaissance: The Poetics and Politics of Culture," in *The New Historicism*, ed. H. Aram Veeser (New York: Routledge, 1989), 15–36, and 20.

9. My emphasis here upon those for whom prayer book use resulted in authentic personal, devotional change is in contrast to Christopher Haigh's use of the term "parish Anglicans," those whom Haigh sees as essentially crypto-Catholic: individuals who focused upon remnants of the old faith in reformed liturgical service and rite. For a fuller discussion and definition of the term, see in particular Haigh's *English Reformations: Religion, Politics, and Society under the Tudors* (Oxford: Clarendon Press, 1993), 291–93.

10. Laura Schreibman, *The Science and Fiction of Autism* (Cambridge, MA: Harvard University Press, 2005), 111.

11. Christopher Haigh, *Reformation and Resistance in Tudor Lancashire* (Cambridge: Cambridge University Press, 1975); Judith Maltby, *Prayer Book and People in Elizabethan and Early Stuart England* (Cambridge: Cambridge University Press, 1998); and Ramie Targoff, *Common Prayer: The Language of Public Devotion in Early Modern England* (Chicago: University of Chicago Press, 2001).

12. *The Philosophical Writings of Descartes, Volume III: The Correspondence*, trans. John Cottingham, Robert Stoothoff, Dugald Murdoch, and Anthony Kenny (Cambridge: Cambridge University Press, 1991), 201.

13. Ibid.

14. Ibid.

15. Charles Taylor, *Sources of the Self: The Making of the Modern Identity* (Cambridge, MA: Harvard University Press, 1989), 144.

16. Ibid., 145.

17. Sutton, *Philosophy and Memory Traces*, 40.

18. Ibid.

19. Ibid. See Clark's quotation in its original context in Andy Clark, *Being There: Putting Brain, Body, and World Together Again* (Cambridge, MA: MIT Press, 1997), 163.

20. Schoenfeldt, *Bodies and Selves*, 6.

21. Paster, *Humoring the Body*, 14. See also her *Body Embarrassed* and Paster et al., *Early Modern Passions*.

22. It also should be noted, as Karen Zelan points out, that not all researchers into the autistic mind agree that ToM is a theory that should ultimately be confirmed as a definitive function. Citing the work of psychologist James Russell, she notes, "Russell and colleagues assert that it's not so much that a young autist's mind misses a theory of itself as it is that he cannot always act upon what he knows. It is the executive function that is impaired—the autist's control over action generally." See *Between Their World and Ours: Breakthroughs with Autistic Children* (New York: St. Martin's Press, 2003), 156. Russell's contention would direct researchers' attentions toward better understanding the substrates of executive function impairment and away from a theory that can be confirmed only by the fact of its absence in neurotypical individuals.

23. Simon Baron-Cohen, *Mindblindness: An Essay on Autism and Theory of Mind* (Cambridge: MIT Press, 1995), 51. For a fuller discussion of the relationship between ToM and the autistic brain, see especially chapter 5.

24. See Michael Tomasello, "Having Intentions, Understanding Intentions, and Understanding Communicative Intentions," in *Developing Theories of Intention: Social Understanding and Self-Control*, ed. P. D. Zelazo, J. W. Astington, and D. R. Olson (Mahwah, NJ: Erlbaum, 1999), 63–76.

25. *Diagnostic and Statistical Manual of Mental Disorders*, 4th ed. (DSM-IV) (Text Revision) (Washington, DC: American Psychological Association, 2000), 70.

26. Ibid. The full entry on autistic disorder is found on pp. 70–75 of the DSM-IV.

27. According to Majia Holmer Nadesan in her essay "Constructing Autism: A Brief Genealogy," in *Autism and Representation*, ed. Mark Osteen (London: Routledge, 1998), 78–95, misdiagnoses like these persisted even up through the late 1970s and early 1980s in the United States, and autism as a term did not achieve wide use in the medical community until the mid- to late 1980s. These facts concerning the diagnostic history of ASD are given further and provocative consideration in the collection *Foucault and the Government of Disability* (Ann Arbor: University of Michigan Press, 2005), edited by Shelley Tremain, in which a Foucauldian critique of the humanist subject is extended to the history of the disorder; see especially Nirmala Erevelles, "Signs of Reason: Rivière, Facilitated Communication, and the Crisis of the Subject," 51–52.

28. Erin D. Bigler et al., "Superior Temporal Gyrus, Language Function, and Autism," *Developmental Neuropsychology* 31 (2007): 218.

29. Ibid., 219.

30. Schreibman, *Science and Fiction*, 115.

31. Ibid., 115–16.

32. The fulfillment of steps in a process toward the completion of a task or plan is known in cognitive science as executive function. Individuals with ASD often demonstrate a marked lack of this ability and require visual aids to help them complete a great variety of tasks. Depending upon the severity of their ASD, and as these individuals age and mature, they may require less and less use of visual aids in order to complete tasks or to reach goals.

33. Patricia Howlin, *Autism and Asperger Syndrome: Preparing for Adulthood*, 2nd ed. (London: Routledge, 2004), 133.

34. Ibid., 128–29.

35. Carol Gray, *The New Social Story Book* (Arlington, TX: Horizons, 2000), v.

36. In modern liturgical practice, a collect is a carefully scripted back-and-forth exchange between the priest and the people. In the prayer book of 1559, for example, the collect is a short petition to God that is spoken by all the people, though there is no response from the priest.

37. John N. Wall, *Transformations of the Word: Spenser, Herbert, Vaughan* (Athens: University of Georgia Press, 1988), 27.

38. Charles Taylor has addressed this issue as well, noting "there are three things that get done in language: [1] making articulations, and hence bringing about explicit awareness; [2] putting things in public space, thereby constituting public space; [3] making the discriminations which are foundational to human concerns, and hence opening us to these concerns"; see *Philosophy and the Human Sciences: Philosophical Papers (Vol. 1)* (Cambridge: Cambridge University Press, 1985), 263.

39. For the most exhaustive and recent study of the compositional history of the Book of Common Prayer, see Diarmaid MacCulloch's *Thomas Cranmer: A Life* (New Haven, CT: Yale University Press, 1996), esp. 221–26, 410–53.

40. Targoff, *Common Prayer,* 17.

41. Ibid., 134n13.

42. Maltby, *Prayer Book,* 17.

43. Ibid.

44. John E. Booty, ed., *The Book of Common Prayer, 1559: The Elizabethan Prayer Book* (Washington, DC: Folger, 1978), 68.

45. Ibid., 77.

46. For more on this distinction, see Targoff, *Common Prayer,* chap. 1.

47. J. Eric Hunt, *Cranmer's First Litany, 1544 and Merbecke's Book of Common Prayer Notes, 1550* (London: SPCK, 1939), 86 (qtd. in Targoff, *Common Prayer,* 23).

48. Booty, *Book of Common Prayer,* 15.

49. Hunt, *Cranmer's First Litany,* 86 (qtd. in Targoff, *Common Prayer,* 23).

50. See, for example, Mark Turner, *The Study of English in the Age of Cognitive Science* (Princeton, NJ: Princeton University Press, 1991), and Sutton's *Philosophy and Memory Traces.*

51. Jerome Bruner, "The Narrative Construction of Reality," *Critical Inquiry* 18 (1991): 5–6.

52. Ibid., 7.

CHAPTER 10

Freedom and (Dis)Ability in Early Modern Political Thought

NANCY J. HIRSCHMANN

The history of early modern political thought is not just a history of particular figures—mostly "able-bodied" men—who wrote political and philosophical treatises but a history of concepts as well. The early modern era ushered in a way of thinking about humans' relationship to God, government, and each other that turned on new conceptions of obligation, duty, justice, equality, and freedom. The last of these concepts is arguably the most central. Indeed, one could say that modern political thought began with a thought experiment that centered on a first principle of natural freedom: the state of nature, from which men emerged to form civil society, postulates freedom as a first principle of human nature, a fundamental building block of the modernist definition of "human being." Starting humans in "a State of perfect Freedom to order their Actions, and dispose of their Possessions, and Persons as they think fit,"[1] social contract theorists, most notably Thomas Hobbes and John Locke, defined natural freedom in a very particular way that showcased the individual as divorced from culture, society, and natural relationships. This conception then became the foundation for all other Enlightenment concepts: obligation was defined by way of a "social contract" that involved people making free choices to give up their natural liberty in exchange for social order and political freedom; equality was defined as an equality of right, and an equality of freedom;

justice was defined by redressing unequal impositions on entitlement and rights, and thereby unequal restrictions of liberty. Putting liberty at the center of humans' moral universe, and this particular way in which freedom was conceptualized, was to retain a solid hold on the philosophical and political imagination for the centuries to follow, up to the present day.

This concept of freedom has particular implications for persons with disabilities, not just in the seventeenth century but today as well. This essay will show various ways in which Hobbes's and Locke's conceptions of freedom depend on a particular body with particular physical and mental capacities and orientations, a particular set of assumptions about what constitutes a human being, and a particular set of social relations that exclude disabled individuals from the role of political citizen. My aim is not to fault Hobbes's and Locke's views of disability per se, however. Rather, it is to shed light on a concept of freedom that derives from Hobbes and Locke but persists into twenty-first-century political theory and philosophy. This conception of freedom fails to appreciate the disability perspective and, in the process, takes a historically specific view of disability and turns it into a transhistorical universal. It not only fails to reflect the experience of disabled persons, however; it also implicitly draws on the disabled body to articulate the limiting conditions of freedom. While starting their conceptualizations from assertions about the universality and naturalness of freedom, they reveal a conceptual dependency on the abilities of particular bodies, and especially disabled bodies, as a way to illustrate the meaning of freedom: what the disabled body or mind can or cannot do shapes the parameters of what freedom can mean. The deployment of disability imagery in these early works, though often subtle, is nevertheless significant in pointing out the "ableism" in the assumptions we bring to our understanding of freedom today.

From the start such a project might seem anachronistic; as those who explore gender and race in leading canonical figures can attest, there is often so little material to work with that arguments can become weak, even distorting the original texts. Admittedly, Hobbes and Locke do not say a great deal about disability. Moreover, as Skinner, Pocock, and other historians of political thought have shown us, a theorist's use and meaning of concepts must always be situated in their specific historical and social contexts.[2] And the situation of disabled individuals in the seventeenth century was quite different from today. In the first place, there may have been far fewer disabled people then. As Rushton bemoans, the lack of consistent record-keeping makes a count of disabled people in the seventeenth century impossible to determine; most records that exist, for example, are concerned solely with "idiocy" and "lunacy."[3] But we can also surmise that, despite the troubled reputation of

"the medical model" in twentieth- and twenty-first-century disability studies, medical advances have resulted in vastly improved longevity for a wide
variety of disabling conditions, indeed making it possible for people with
certain conditions to live at all.[4] Second, much of the assistive technology
we have today was clearly not available then; though there is evidence of a
wheelchair dating to the sixth century B.C.E., and King Phillip II of Spain—
who was not disabled—had a wheelchair made for him at the very end of the
sixteenth century, it was not until the twentieth century that the wheelchair
as we know it came into common usage. Prosthetics were relatively crude,
and electronic assistive devices were obviously unavailable. Thus the limitations of the physical world may have been greater for disabled people in the
seventeenth century.

At the same time, we must acknowledge the probability that contemporary society, with its pollution, processed food, and stress, has likely produced many more disabilities and disabling diseases.[5] Furthermore, more
one-story living, no curbed sidewalks, and other manifestations of industrial
society, as well as the lack of stigma for those with "peg legs," eye patches,
and crutches may have meant that the seventeenth-century world was not
as disabling for certain impairments as it is today. Henri-Jacques Stiker's
history of disability suggests, in fact, that although the mentally and physically disabled were seen as struck by afflictions from God, which must be
borne by those individuals, whose families and communities cared for them
out of Christian charity, they were also—indeed thereby—fairly well integrated within the "normal" community throughout the seventeenth century.[6] Rushton's consideration of official court records suggests that although
some persons were put in jail and houses of correction, significant percent-
ages of cognitively disabled individuals lived in the custody of relatives,
while others "were left in virtual independence . . . with no hint of custody
or care by others."[7] Similarly, although Foucault dates "the great confinement" of the insane, which often included individuals with only physical
impairments, to the seventeenth century, Roy Porter maintains that in England the mentally disabled were not institutionalized in great numbers until
the late eighteenth and, more likely, nineteenth centuries.[8] Disabled individuals were thus both a commonplace and intimate part of the dominant
society and excluded from it in various ways. Locke and Hobbes therefore
must undoubtedly have encountered disabled people in their societies, even
if not explicitly discussing them at length in their theories. And as I will
show, their brief references to and invocations of various disabilities play a
subtle but significant role in defining who, or what, is an appropriate "subject" of freedom.

A final prefatory note: in this essay, I should note that I use the terms "disabled" and "disability" to refer to people with bodily and mental impairments. This should not be taken as an uncritical endorsement of a medical model approach to disability—though that would probably accurately describe the attitudes of the theorists I consider here. But the terms "impairment" and "handicap" are equally problematic and ambiguous, and since this essay focuses on the specific issue of freedom rather than the meaning of disability itself, I suggest that, fully cognizant of the social model of disability, we also must realize that seventeenth-century society was not particularly accessible to people with a wide range of non-normative conditions. Thus anyone with such conditions would be, by definition, "disabled." But the more important concern I have here is whether such people could also ever be "free," and what implications that has for the meaning of the concept itself.[9]

Thomas Hobbes: Ability as the Limit of Liberty

"*A* FREE-MAN *is he, that in those things, which by his strength and wit he is able to do, is not hindered to doe what he has a will to.*"[10] With these words, Thomas Hobbes arguably ushered in the modernist conception of freedom. It is generally accepted among historians of political theory that Thomas Hobbes was one of the first of the early modern figures to focus on liberty as a central element of his theory of human nature and of politics. Quentin Skinner notes that as Hobbes's work progressed throughout his life, he became more and more concerned with defining liberty as a key intellectual project, culminating in *Leviathan*.[11] But equally important is Hobbes's role as a founding figure in the modern conception of freedom, namely, the conception that we take for granted today. What Isaiah Berlin was later to call "negative liberty"—freedom as the absence of restraint, interference, and coercion, the most basic understanding of freedom today[12]—finds its most coherent articulation in Hobbes's famous definition, "By *liberty*, is understood, according to the proper signification of the word, the absence of externall impediments: which impediments, may oft take away part of man's power to do what he would. . . . Liberty, or freedom, signifieth (properly) the absence of Opposition; (by Opposition, I mean externall Impediments of motion)" (*Leviathan* 14, 189; 21, 261).

There are two parts to Hobbes's account. The first is the fact that obstacles must lie outside the self, they are "external"; second is the relationship between freedom and ability, or what Hobbes calls "power." Most contemporary theorists who write on Hobbes focus on the "hindrances" or restraints caused by "external impediments," but an equally important dimension of Hobbes's definition is ability or power: that "which by his strength and wit he is able to do." Both of these aspects are significant for disability theory, but it is arguably the case that the latter aspect of his definition is most significant, for it has become such an important assumption of contemporary freedom theory as to merit hardly any notice.

For Hobbes, this criterion of ability—like freedom itself—is applied to animate and inanimate beings alike.[13] Thus a stone that "lyeth still" is no more unfree than "a man . . . fastned to his bed by sicknesse," because both simply lack the ability to move (*Leviathan* 21, 262); it is as much the property of stones not to be able to move under their own force as it is for someone with a bad case of flu or a severe spinal injury to be unable to rise from her bed. What prevents them from motion lies within themselves, and freedom concerns the absence or presence of strictly external obstacles.

This invocation of illness is startling. The image that most harshly strikes the twenty-first-century disability scholar is the comparison of the disabled or ill person to a "stone"—not merely an inanimate object, but possibly the most inanimate of objects in the common imagination. In this, of course, twenty-first-century scholars will also note the collapsing of the two categories of illness and disability together, a move that is justified by the seventeenth-century view of disability and the profound lack of knowledge about the variety of specific disorders that produce specific impairments. But the point from Hobbes's perspective is that in his strictly descriptive account, if freedom presupposes ability, disabled individuals are not made unfree by their conditions. Instead, those conditions define the limiting condition of their freedom.

It might be suggested that what the sick man and stone lack is not ability but will; the man may be so ill as to not wish to arise, and the stone has no will at all. However, Hobbes's particular construal of the will rules this out, for he collapses will into desire. We are driven by appetites and aversions, and hence "No man can determine his own will. For the will is appetite; nor can a man more determine his will than any other appetite, that is, more than he can determine when he shall be hungry and when not. When a man is hungry, it is in his choice to eat or not eat; this is the liberty of the man. But to be hungry or not hungry, which is that which I hold to proceed from necessity, is not in his choice."[14] Will is the function of desire, and desire simply comes to us, it is not something that we choose. I choose only whether and how to fulfill (or deny) my desires, not whether to have them; "One can, in truth, be free to *act;* one cannot, however, be free to *desire.*"[15]

By the criteria of pursuing desire, we might want to argue that Hobbes is logically committed to the conclusion that disabled people, like nondisabled people, lack liberty insofar as "external impediments" prevent them from doing particular things; they cannot be "free" or "unfree" in general. Hobbes rejects the general notion of "a free man," despite his own use of this term throughout his writings, saying that we can really talk only about being free to do specific things. Hobbes does not envision, as contemporary freedom theorists do, humans having "life plans" or "projects" that define their being but rather a more discrete and temporal sense of life, perhaps based on his fearful account of human nature. Such an account might bode well for the freedom of disabled individuals; if I cannot walk across the room, that does not mean that I am not free to do other things. I am free to do whatever I *can* do.

But the logic of Hobbes's construal also suggests that if I cannot walk across the room, all I need is to not *want* to cross the room, and I would thereby be free. For in Hobbes's account, if my legs cannot support me, this fact of my body is likely to restructure my desires: that is, I may not want to endure the effort that would be required of me to cross the room. Returning to Stiker's argument that disability was seen as an affliction from God that must be borne, combined with the absence of many assistive technologies, the seventeenth-century disabled person would have had to adjust her sense of desire to the realm of what it was possible for her to do. This view meshes perfectly with Hobbes's: according to him, if I am torn between two desires, "deliberation" consists in a vacillation between "contrary appetites," and between appetite and aversion, weighing the balance of what would help me more or hurt me less. Thus in one of his more infamous examples, if a robber threatens to kill me if I refuse to hand over my wallet, I act freely in choosing to give up my money in order to save my life. Fear has only given me a reason for making a particular choice that expresses my immediate, or more intense, desire. "Extrinsical" factors that prevent me from doing what I want impede my liberty—such as when I push you away from the door and physically prevent you from leaving the room—but not those that cause me to change what I want—such as when my threat to hit you if you leave the room results in your deciding that you do not want to leave the room.

Additionally, freedom is an either/or proposition for Hobbes, not a matter of degree. I cannot be more or less free: either I can do what I want, or I cannot. And that "can" is strictly defined by the limits of my inherent ability; for me to complain that I am unfree because I want to walk across the surface of the ocean and cannot do so would involve a nonsensical use of the term "freedom." Humans are physically unable to walk on water, and therefore my desire is not the proper subject of the concept "liberty." Rather, it is the product of "fancy," "madnesse," or "lunacy." Similarly, if I am physically unable to walk across the room, my desire to do so is not the proper object of liberty. That does not mean that I am not free to *try* to cross the room by dragging myself across the floor, or supporting myself on my arms on a series of rails, for instance. Again, because such effort is more difficult, even dangerous, than the act of walking across the room is for an ambulatory person, we might think that the latter is intrinsically freer than the former; but Hobbes would disagree. If getting across the room is so difficult and tiring that I decide it is not worth the effort, then, Hobbes says, that shows that I just don't want to do it. My decision to sit where I am, therefore, is a free one. The disabled person might have a different number of things that he is free to do, but he does not thereby have lesser freedom. And if I think it is worth the effort but I fail, then that simply demonstrates that I am unable to do it, and therefore freedom does not enter the matter.

This distinction might seem simply semantic for most twenty-first-century readers, who will likely believe that the scope of freedom for the disabled person is more circumscribed than it is for the nondisabled person. There is a certain disingenuousness to the Hobbesian account of freedom from a twenty-first-century disability perspective, as he simply defines away the challenge that disability poses. But given the influence of Hobbes on contemporary thinking about freedom, we cannot simply dismiss it. Furthermore, we have to recall that this argument is coming from someone who thought that absolute monarchy was the surest way to escape the uncertainties of the state of nature, and that all men would rationally choose to give up much of their natural liberty to such a sovereign power: built into his conception of the social contract is a severe curtailment of the kinds of freedoms that we take for granted in contemporary liberal democracies, like the freedom to criticize the government. This curtailment was universal, not dependent on differences in various men's and women's abilities.[16]

The importance of being able to make the choices that Hobbes deems rational—to make the "right" choices, whether we realize it or not—suggests that Hobbes's text may relate more to cognitive disability than physical. In addition to the passage cited earlier of "a man . . . fastned to his bed by sicknesse," Hobbes makes reference to some physical impairments, such as "Epilepsie, or Falling-sickness," to serve as an analogy for academic religion's effect on the state (*Leviathan* 29, 371). He refers to lameness as an example of fraud: "two men conspiring, one to seem lame, the other to cure him with a charme" (37, 476); and again in discussing salvation, he refers to scriptural passages in which sickness and lameness are cured (38, 492). But his references to cognitive disabilities are more frequent, particularly to "Madnesse." He distinguishes madness from lunacy, which is a specific form of madness; he refers to "Lunatiques" in critiquing the inaccuracy with which people talk about "Evill Spirits . . . entered into men" (34, 441). But madness is a fairly universalizable concept for him, merely an overabundance of passion, which can be temporary (as in intense jealousy or rage) or longer lasting (leading to distraction). This condition is possible in all men, and indeed one could argue that Hobbes believes it was the main cause of the English civil war. Curbing this madness, this overabundance of passion, is the purpose of men's giving up natural liberty to an absolute monarch in Hobbes's account of the social contract.

But in curbing passion, we curb our freedom: passions are the primary motivating force for human action, but they paradoxically often interfere with our ability to choose what is in our best interest. If we are rational, thinking about our survival, we will consent to establish a sovereign power with absolute authority to rein in the passions and limit our natural liberty by creating law and punishing those, including ourselves, who break the law. Since this is the only rational choice that we can possibly make in the state of nature, those who fail to consent to the social contract must in fact have intended to consent to it whether they realize it or not; for anyone who chooses to violate his own interests "is not to be understood as if he meant it" (14, 192).[17] All such passions as vainglory, rage, jealousy, and so forth can be seen as instances of madness, thus justifying others to speak on his behalf: "Children, Fooles, and Madmen that have no use of Reason, may be Personated by Guardians, or Curators" (16, 219). Thus all are obligated to the contract regardless of whether they (think they) want to or not, for "as well he that Voted for it, as he that Voted against it, shall Authorize all the Actions and Judgements, of that Man, or Assembly of men, in the same manner, as if they were his own" (18, 229).

In other words, Hobbes defines freedom based on the assumption that many, perhaps most, men are driven by various forms of madness, and he constructs his social contract accordingly. This is the paradox of modern freedom; it is only by freely choosing to curtail our freedom that we can be free. And given the ease with which any of us can be mad temporarily, such as when we are in a jealous rage, or in a frenzy of "blind lust," Hobbes might be taken to be saying that disabled persons are not that different from nondisabled persons: we can all go into the depths of passion-driven madness, but the difference is the ease and speed with which some of us can "come back."

Indeed, Hobbes does not think that impairments—cognitive or physical—"disable" one from participating in the social contract or being a civil subject per se, because even if one is not capable of giving express consent, we can still infer it from the fact that all humans would rather not live in the "nasty, brutish, and short" state of nature. Furthermore, Hobbes even more explicitly grants civil status to disabled individuals when he argues that "whereas many men, by accident unevitable, become unable to maintain themselves by their labour; they ought not to be left to the Charity of private persons," running contrary to dominant views about the poor at this time; instead, the sovereign has a duty to provide economically for such individuals "by the Lawes of the Common-wealth," an early version of social welfare entitlements (*Leviathan* 30, 387). This strongly suggests that disabled people are civil subjects, entitled to civil recognition by the sovereign just as much as nondisabled ones, with the same civic freedom to act within the bounds of law.

So in one sense, disabled individuals are no less free than the nondisabled in Hobbes's view; they may have a different range of things that they may be free to do, but it is not necessarily a lesser range. Whether disabled people are free or not in Hobbes's view, however, may be less significant than the way in which he uses images of disability, such as madness and sickness, to demarcate the limits of liberty at the limits of ability. And in this the verdict is clearer: I must have a power in order to make its nonexercise a question of freedom. Insofar as disabled people lack certain powers, we cannot say that they are unfree to exercise them. We can only say that they are "unable." Indeed, given the extreme way in which Hobbes defines the concept, freedom is not even a relevant concern for such individuals, by definition. If freedom is at issue only when other people prevent me from doing what I otherwise could, then when my own impairments prevent me from doing something, they make me unable, not unfree. This semantic distinction, which seems rather disingenuous to twenty-first-century readers familiar with the social model of disability, is really a philosophical and political one in Hobbes's account, for it defines "the individual" as self-contained and contextless, and "freedom" as running contrary to the rational self-interest of such abstract individuals. Such assumptions can only lead to a political form of absolute monarchy. Moreover, his definitions of both freedom and madness suggest that freedom, while a central feature of humanity, is not actually an important quality for most people who are driven by passions. This is a troubling conclusion given Hobbes's influence on twenty-first-century ideas of freedom, but it shows the ways in which Hobbes's construction of freedom depends on his deployment of disability and the "able" body.

John Locke: Property, Reason, and Ability

John Locke, the other great seventeenth-century figure in the history of freedom theory, made a quite different assessment, though agreeing with Hobbes on many fundamentals. In his *Essay Concerning Human Understanding*, Locke makes a clear distinction between the terms "voluntary" and "free," the former referring to the will and desire, the latter to the physical conditions that permit or prevent my acting on my will. Locke says, much like Hobbes, that "Liberty is not an Idea belonging to Volition," for willing is different from acting on the will. But the theoretical meaning of not acting as one wills is not the reduction it is for Hobbes. For Locke, when "a Palsie" prevents my legs from moving me across the room when I want to move, "there is want of freedom."[18] This suggests that Locke allows for internal barriers to freedom; my own legs can prevent me from enacting my will. Although will may be a necessary condition for freedom to exist, it is not a sufficient condition; indeed, Locke says that "Liberty cannot be, where there is no Thought, no Volition, no Will; but there may be Thought, there may be Will, there may be Volition, where there is no Liberty" (*Essay* 2.21.8). Accordingly, "there is want of Freedom, though the sitting still even of a Paralytick, whilst he prefers it to a removal, is truly voluntary" (2.21.11). In other words, even if a "paralytick" doesn't want to move from where he is sitting, his inability to move demarcates a limitation on his freedom regardless of what he desires. The paralysis is, to all intents and purposes, a barrier to his freedom, though it may not be confounding his will.

Thus, contrary to Hobbes, Locke seems to believe that my will can be at odds with my freedom. Certainly, as with Hobbes, we still do not yet advance to the paradox posed by Rousseau, wherein following appetite is "slavery" and freedom entails following laws that I prescribe to myself.[19] But contrary to Hobbes, my own body—or rather its limitations—can serve as a "barrier" to my freedom, as in the case of the "paralytick." For both theorists, however, the particularities of one's body and one's ability constitute the limiting condition of freedom. For Hobbes, the disabled person's freedom concerns a more limited range of activities; for Locke, the disabled person is simply less free.

But in both cases, the universality of freedom is based on a set of assumptions about a very particular kind of body. As C. B. Macpherson has argued, it is a relatively wealthy body;[20] as feminists have shown, it is a male body;[21] as critical race theorists have argued, it is a white body.[22] But I suggest that it is also an "able" body: able to engage in certain kinds of physical action, particularly labor, and in rational thought. Labor is particularly important to Locke because it is central to property: God gives all humans "property in the person," and by adding my labor to things in nature, they become my property. This understanding of property is the engine that moves his entire theory, and property is the key to individual freedom.

At first glance the criteria of labor may seem to be negated by wealth. After all, a physically disabled property owner would be little different from a nondisabled one: both would hire laborers to work the land for them. But in order to be a free agent, the owner would have to engage in some sort of labor, either mental or physical. Locke was highly critical of wealthy people who squandered their inheritances and contributed nothing to enhancing the value of their estates. The connection—and distinction—between these two is reason. "Right reason" involves the full engagement of the mind, requiring the learning of Latin and mathematics, and thus could be developed by a wealthy but physically disabled son who could run his inherited estate as long as he had a foreman (or a younger brother) he could trust to tour the estate on a regular basis and make sure that the workers (who were inclined toward laziness) were doing what they should do.

By contrast to "right reason," reason *simpliciter* allows considerable gradation and is generally linked not merely to class, as Macpherson argued, but to the kind of labor associated with class. Hence, Locke says, "a country gentleman, who, leaving Latin and learning in the University, removes thence to his mansion house, and associates with neighbors . . . who relish nothing but hunting and a bottle" may become a judge or magistrate owing to "the strength of his purse and party." But he is still inferior in reason to "an ordinary coffee-house gleaner of the City," because the latter is being industrious, while the former dissipates his learning and his mind. And even within the working classes, there is gradation: "The day laborer in a country village has commonly but a small pittance of knowledge, because his ideas and notions have been confined to the narrow bounds of a poor conversation and employment; the low mechanic of a country town does somewhat outdo him; porters and cobblers of great cities surpass them." On the bottom were the unemployed, beggars, and those on parish relief.[23]

The majority of seventeenth-century physically disabled persons were likely to occupy the latter categories, as Locke's "Essay on the Poor Law" suggests. The point of his essay is the reform of the poor laws, urging the shift from outdoor parish relief (or direct payments to the poor), which was established by Elizabeth I, to work programs (or "indoor relief"). The disabled had been linked since the thirteenth century to the "deserving poor," who were willing but unable to work, contrasted to the "undeserving" poor who were simply social misfits or lazy. According to Anita Silvers, a category of "disabled" was designated that lumped together "persons with quite different disabilities into a single inferior class" to constitute the "deserving" poor.[24] In Locke's writings, this would seem to include three distinct categories of disability. The first is physical, and the one explicit recognition of physical disability causing an inability to work is found in his writings on the Irish linen trade, where Locke urged double the normal relief allowance for "any double wheel spinner" in the trade who became unable to work due to injury on the job.[25] The purpose of such provision was to make such work more attractive rather than any specific concern for "disability rights" or freedom, but such provisions indicate that Locke acknowledged the existence of the physically disabled and a social responsibility to provide for those with physical disability who were unable to work, particularly those who became disabled as a result of industrious labor, which signaled good "deserving" character.

The second category included the severely cognitively disabled. The few scholars who have discussed Locke in terms of disability have focused on his remarks on "ideots" and "lunaticks." As Stacy Clifford suggests, in Locke's work "idiocy reflects a deformed mirror image of the ideal citizen's rationality and freedom."[26] Though Locke talks at considerable length about "brutes, idiots and madmen" in terms of their relationship to reason, their comparison to "natural man" in the state of nature, and their ability to develop reason, he treats their relationship to freedom with efficient dispatch:

> if through defects that may happen out of the ordinary course of Nature, any one comes not to such a degree of Reason, wherin he might be supposed capable of knowing the Law [whether natural or positive] and so living within the Rules of it, he is never capable of being a Free Man, he is never let loose to the disposure of his own Will (because he knows no bounds to it, has not Understanding, its proper Guide) but is continued under the Tuition and Government of others, all the time his own Understanding is uncapable of that Charge. And so Lunaticks and Ideots are never set free from the Government of their Parents. (*Two Treatises* 2.60)

These two categories of disabled individuals constitute the "deserving poor," because they are dependent on others through no fault of their own. The "undeserving poor," however, posed a different kind of problem, and in fact I want to suggest they constitute a third kind of "disability" in the form of irrationality. Locke's essay, written during England's "seven barren years," from 1692 to 1699, when pauperism was extremely common and 2 percent of the British population owned 65 percent of the land,[27] nevertheless asserted that poverty resulted "not from scarcity of provisions, nor from want of employment for the poor, since the goodness of God has blessed these times with plenty," but rather from "the relaxation of discipline and corruption of manners; virtue and industry being as constant companions on the one side as vice and idleness are on the other."[28] Locke argued that poverty was caused by lack of reason—for why would anyone choose to be poor? Since economic opportunities were always available, those who were poor must be so because they simply did not understand the necessity of work; and as long as parish relief was offered, allowing such individuals to get something for nothing, that lack of understanding would persist.

But in contrast to "ideocy and lunacy," such irrationality could be "cured" by labor, as Locke the physician tacitly adopts a medical model approach to this particular form of cognitive disability. So Locke prescribed various forms of forced labor: those who asked for relief would be made to work for members of the parish "at a lower rate than is usually given" ("Essay" 188). Such an outcome, Locke believed, would quickly teach the rationally deficient poor that they should seek work on their own, since the pay would be better and there was no alternative of a free lunch. Begging was subject to even harsher treatment: adult male beggars served as enforced labor aboard sailing ships for three years; women would be assigned to forced labor locally for three months, and children for six weeks. But he also recommended permits for begging, claiming that some were "entitled" to beg, just as some were entitled to parish relief, because they were genuinely unable to work. Presumably these permits were to go to the first two categories of disabled people, as well as the "infirm," once again deploying the trope of the "deserving poor."

I postulate this not because Locke explicitly designated the "infirm" as unable to work but because almost everybody else was included in the rather large sweep of those who he claimed could work. For instance, Locke claimed that poor mothers should work, at least part time. Moreover, their children would be put into "working schools," which were basically wool factories, not only to free up the mothers' time for wage labor but also so the children could provide for their own upkeep and, most importantly, learn the lesson that working for your living is an important aspect of civil society. Elderly people, of course, worked until they could no longer do so. That left, for the most part, the physically and cognitively disabled. Moreover, given the harshness of his measures, with children as young as three in working schools, and his assumption that most beggars and requesters of parish relief were simply lazy, the level of disability that would entitle one to "deserve" parish relief, a begging permit, or a linen trade pension would have to be quite severe.

But in all three cases, disability, defined by the inability to work, links to freedom for Locke in a significant way: through rationality. In Locke's account, freedom has an intimate relationship to reason; hence in the previous quote that "ideots and lunaticks" are never "free from the Government of their Parents," Locke describes lack of freedom not on its own terms but rather by talking about reason, which is what leads to his abrupt conclusion. Freedom is about doing what I wish; but desire itself, what I wish, must be "within the bounds of the law of nature" and "reason . . . is that law" (*Two Treatises* 2.4, 2.6). Thus, insofar as cognitively disabled individuals are unable to utilize reason like "normal men," they are, according to Locke, unable to achieve freedom.[29]

Yet why the "Poor Law" essay, in particular, is so revealing is that, just as Hobbes's conception of madness could include most people, Locke's conceptualization of reason is one that might well exclude large numbers of "normal men" who are illiterate laborers. Indeed, Locke had fairly minimal hopes for the reason of the poor; getting them to understand the value of work would be about as much as could be hoped in the usual course. This was not necessarily because of inadequate natural capacity, however—since God provides all (or most) men with that—but rather because the circumstances of poverty prevent them from developing it; the "constant drudgery to their backs and their bellies"[30] means that laborers have insufficient time and energy to develop reason. This distinction did not apply to "ideots" because they simply lacked innate capacity. In this, "lunaticks" were better off; they had the capacity to reason. Their problem was that they applied their reason to faulty premises (e.g., believing "I am the king" when I am not). Locke seemed to believe, then, that "lunaticks" had the potential to regain their equilibrium, much as Hobbes seemed to believe about madmen.[31]

The average illiterate worker, however, insofar as Locke viewed him or her as disabled by irrationality, could be, as noted above, "cured" specifically through labor and reading scripture on Sundays.[32] But such "cure" was limited in his view: illiterate workers could never attain the "right reason" that seemed to be required of true citizens, those who could vote and hold office; they could only ever attain enough reason to obey the laws and work hard. Class mobility—the logical outcome of a "full cure" in the Lockean framework—was not yet commonplace in seventeenth-century capitalism and was therefore not something that Locke could readily employ in his argument, but working was nevertheless key to rationality. Though "God gave the World to Men in Common," he specifically "gave it to the use of the Industrious and Rational . . . not to the Fancy or Covetousness of the Quarrelsome and Contentious" (2.34). After all, land in its uncultivated state was useless; thus "God, when he gave the World in common to all Mankind, commanded Man also to labour, and the penury of his Condition required it of him" (2.32). God set things up in such a way that we were compelled to industry, as "Labour was to be his [man's] Title to" property and we needed property to stay alive. Hence, "God and his [i.e., man's] Reason commanded him to subdue the Earth" (2.34, 2.32). For those in whom rationality seemed insufficiently developed or, more specifically, those who seemed not to appreciate God's gift (whether they have a "defect in nature" or are "nurtured in vices" and "love the darkness"),[33] work would have to be coerced. Forcing people to work would enhance individuals' freedom by enhancing their basic rationality—at least, if their "defect in nature" was not too great. The implication that the poor are "disabled" because they lack rationality dovetails with the assumption that the way to enhance their rationality is to force them to work. Work is the cure for this particular form of potentially widespread disability, just as absolute obedience is the cure for Hobbes.

In all three cases, however—physical disability and the two kinds of cognitive disability, ranging from incurable "ideots" and lunaticks" to the lazy poor—we are left with the conclusion that disabled people are unfree in Locke's view. The improperly working bodies of the physically disabled prevent them from doing certain things, regardless of what they want, like the "paralytick" discussed earlier. And insofar as the physically disabled cannot participate in labor, the key to gaining property, their rationality will likely decline unless they find some other way to be useful and productive. Those disabled individuals who can work to support themselves, of course, are better off on this score. The cognitively disabled are similarly unfree because they lack the ability to reason altogether. To the extent that "lunaticks" have reason but use it wrongly, they are just as unfree as if they had no reason at all. People's reason and wills must be driven to the right choices: "change but a Man's view of these things; let him see that Virtue and Religion are necessary to his Happiness" (*Essay* 2.21.60). Such direction of the will is not constraint but liberty, for "The being acted by a blind impulse from without, or from within, is little odds" (2.21.67). In the third category, poor unemployed people who prefer begging or parish relief to hard work, who thereby demonstrate that they have faulty reasoning, Locke uses external force or constraint to remove internal blockage or compulsion because what is essential to attaining freedom is choosing well. To be an agent, we must not only think critically about our choices but also make the right choices—the path to which, Locke indicates, is clear, even if not everyone can see it. Disabled persons, then, are not the proper subjects of liberty in Locke's theory.

Embodied Individualism and the History of Freedom

From a disability perspective, this conclusion is disturbing enough. But when we consider the fact that both theorists end up including large numbers of people in the category—those who do not agree with absolute monarchy for Hobbes, large numbers of illiterate workers for Locke—the implications expand. It is a commonplace of twenty-first-century disability theory to point out the ways in which "we are all disabled"—if not now, eventually, as we age. But Hobbes and Locke present the flip side of that; for if the majority of individuals are disabled in some way, the theorists can still deploy ableist frameworks to dismiss that majority from the demos. In focusing on freedom in particular, we can see that disability constitutes a central element in the notion of "the individual" on which their conceptions depend. In the 1960s Marxist theorist C. B. Macpherson developed a famous notion of "possessive individualism," which he argued came out of seventeenth-century liberal thought and emerging market capitalism. It marked a conception of the individual as driven by the desire for wealth and property, with rationality directed to that end. Possessive individualism introduced to political theorists new ways of understanding what human nature meant in the modern era, situating our understanding of "man" in a specific historical context of emerging capitalism and private property.

A disability perspective shows us that this "possessive individual" was also an "embodied individual." That is, individuals were required to have a body with certain sorts of capacities that, like race and gender, fit into the social economy in very particular ways. These ways excluded those who, such as women and disabled people, supposedly were incapable of performing physical labor and therefore of owning property; and those who, such as women, the disabled, Africans, Caribbeans, and the poor, were deemed to lack the rational capacities required to see the logic and reason of the particular choices consistent with the liberal democratic state and market capitalism.[34] The representation of freedom and reason as "natural" that characterizes Enlightenment theories of freedom thus reflects particular kinds of bodies that are marked by class, gender, race, and other forms of typology, such as disability.

Hobbes's and Locke's conceptions of freedom, and many of their conceptual and theoretical fundamentals, form the essential foundation for twenty-first-century political theory, legal theory, and philosophy; and I suggest that the persistent individualization of disability in contemporary medical and political discourses stems from a long historical tradition that defines individualism, justice, rights, and freedom in terms of a particular notion of the able body that is socially located in a seventeenth-century conception of the individual. The centrality of this sort of imagery, and its use to circumscribe the limits of freedom, suggests that only a particular kind of person—a particular kind of body—is the appropriate subject of liberty. As illustrated by these two iconic figures, Hobbes and Locke, the distinction between freedom and ability confuses the natural with the socially constructed and historically specific, depends on a limited perspective of able-bodied men, and is built on a view of illness and disability that requires its designation as subhuman, more akin to "brutes" than to the rational, laboring man.[35] This individual, with his particular form of abilities, underlies the modern conception of the "man" and "citizen" who participated in the social contract and led to twenty-first-century understandings of the free agent and the democratic citizen.

Embodied individualism, as a result, affects contemporary understandings of what it means to be a human being and how social relations and institutions should be structured. These assumptions have had their clearest twentieth- and twenty-first-century articulations in Supreme Court decisions regarding application of the Americans with Disabilities Act to the workplace. These decisions are made possible only by a particular conception of the working citizen as "embodied individual," which from the start eliminates disabled people from the categories of both "citizen" and "individual." Indeed, this was so blatant that in 2008, the U.S. Congress passed the Americans with Disabilities Act Amendment Act in order to address problems in how the courts interpreted the original ADA on a highly individualistic medical model of disability, completely ignoring the social model's claim that disability is produced by a hostile physical environment. But they are also illustrated in a wide variety of other ethical values and choices. Though this issue is well beyond the scope of my essay in the space I have allocated to me, I suggest that tying contemporary conceptions of ability and disability to their underlying philosophical foundations enables an ethical and political argument that has potential for reorienting people's thinking about disability in both theory and public policy fora.

Notes

1. John Locke, *Two Treatises of Civil Government,* ed. Peter Laslett (New York: Cambridge University Press, 1960), 2.4. Subsequent references appear within the text with the standard citation of book and paragraph number.

2. See particularly the essays in James Tully, ed., *Meaning and Context: Quentin Skinner and His Critics* (Princeton, NJ: Princeton University Press, 1988), and J. G. A.

Pocock, *The Machiavellian Moment: Florentine Political Thought and the Atlantic Republican Tradition* (Princeton, NJ: Princeton University Press, 1975).

3. Peter Rushton, "Lunatics and Idiots: Mental Disability, The Community, and the Poor Law in North-east England, 1600–1800," *Medical History* 32 (1988): 34–50. Though Rushton does note that "perhaps we should be surprised by the number of adults [in the records], a possible sign that there was no familial policy of negligence or infanticide" (41).

4. This is hardly to deny the possible, even likely, "medicalization" of disability in the seventeenth century, though "social control" was more likely the intention behind institutionalization than "curing." Ibid., 43.

5. For one example, see Dan Hurley, *Diabetes Rising: How a Rare Disease Became a Modern Pandemic, and What to Do about It* (New York: Kaplan, 2010).

6. Henri-Jacques Stiker, *History of Disability* (Ann Arbor: University of Michigan Press, 1999), 167; see also Barbara Arneil, "Disability, Self Image, and Modern Political Theory," *Political Theory* 37, no. 2 (April 2009): 219.

7. Rushton, "Lunatics and Idiots," 43.

8. Michel Foucault, *Madness and Civilization: A History of Insanity in the Age of Reason* (New York: Vintage, 1988); Roy Porter, "Foucault's Great Confinement," *History of the Human Sciences* 3, no. 1 (1990): 47–54.

9. On the meaning of disability itself, and the medical and social models, I refer the reader to my other work for a fuller sense of my views. See particularly "Seeing, Being, Power: The Politics of Invisible Disability" in *Civil Disabilities: Theory, Citizenship and the Body*, ed. Nancy J. Hirschmann and Beth Linker (Philadelphia: University of Pennsylvania Press, forthcoming) and "Stem Cells, Disability, and Abortion: A Feminist Approach to Equal Citizenship," in *Gender Equality: Dimensions of Women's Equal Citizenship*, ed. Linda McClain and Joanna Grossman (Cambridge: Cambridge University Press, 2009).

10. Thomas Hobbes, *Leviathan*, ed. C. B. Macpherson (Harmondsworth, UK: Penguin, 1985), chap. 14, 186. Subsequent references appear within the text with the standard citation of chapter and page number.

11. Quentin Skinner, "Thomas Hobbes on the Proper Signification of Liberty: The Prothero Lecture," *Transactions of the Royal Historical Society* 40 (1990): 122.

12. Isaiah Berlin, "Two Concepts of Liberty," in *Four Essays on Liberty* (New York: Oxford University Press, 1971), 123.

13. In his "proper signification" of freedom, Hobbes refers to water that "falls freely" as an illustration of the meaning of the term (*Leviathan*, 14, 189; 21, 263).

14. Thomas Hobbes, "The Questions Concerning Liberty, Necessity, and Chance," in *Hobbes and Bramhall on Liberty and Necessity*, ed. Vere Chappel (New York: Cambridge University Press), 72.

15. Thomas Hobbes, *De Cive*, in *Man and Citizen: De Homine and De Cive*, ed. Bernard Gert (Indianapolis: Hackett, 1991), 46.

16. On women's abilities as different from or the same as men's, and the significance this has for their freedom in Hobbes's theory, see Nancy Hirschmann, *Gender, Class, and Freedom in Modern Political Theory* (Princeton, NJ: Princeton University Press, 2009), chap. 1.

17. See also Skinner, "Hobbes," 136, on the relationship between fear, will, and freedom.

18. John Locke, *An Essay Concerning Human Understanding,* ed. Peter H. Nidditch (Oxford: Clarendon Press, 1975), 2.21.8. Subsequent references appear within the text with the standard citation of book, chapter, and section.

19. Jean-Jacques Rousseau, *The Social Contract,* in *The Social Contract and Discourses,* trans. G. D. H. Cole, revised and augmented by J. H. Brumfitt and John C. Hall (London: Dent, 1973), book 1, chap. 8.

20. C. B. Macpherson, *The Political Theory of Possessive Individualism: Hobbes to Locke* (New York: Oxford University Press), 1962.

21. Nancy J. Hirschmann, *The Subject of Liberty: Toward a Feminist Theory of Freedom* (Princeton, NJ: Princeton University Press, 2003), chap. 2; Nancy J. Hirschmann and Kirstie M. McClure, eds., *Feminist Interpretations of John Locke* (University Park: Pennsylvania State University Press, 2007).

22. See particularly Charles Mills, *The Racial Contract* (Ithaca, NY: Cornell University Press, 1999).

23. John Locke, *Of the Conduct of the Understanding,* ed. Ruth Grant and Nathan Tarcov (Indianapolis: Hackett, 1996), sec. 3, para. 171–72.

24. Anita Silvers, "Reconciling Equality to Difference: Caring (f)or Justice for People with Disabilities," *Hypatia* 10, no. 1 (Winter 1995): 30–55.

25. Henry Richard Fox Bourne, *The Life of John Locke,* vol. 2 (Whitefish, MT: Kessinger, 2007), 367.

26. Stacy Clifford, "Indispensable Idiocy: Disability in the Development of John Locke's Thought," paper presented at the annual meeting of the Midwest Political Science Association, April 2010, Chicago, IL.

27. Bourne, *Life of John Locke,* 376; see also John Marshall, *John Locke: Resistance, Religion, and Responsibility* (New York: Cambridge University Press, 1994), 158.

28. John Locke, "An Essay on the Poor Law," in *Political Essays,* ed. Mark Goldie (New York: Cambridge University Press, 1997), 184. Subsequent references to this source appear within the text.

29. I say nothing about the gendered dimensions of freedom here, which are quite pronounced. See Hirschmann, *Gender, Class and Freedom,* chap. 2.

30. Locke, *Conduct of the Understanding,* sec. 7, para. 181.

31. Barbara Arneil takes a more severe view: "Because government requires rational consent, 'lunaticks' and 'ideots' are the opposite of 'freemen' and therefore ruled, according to Locke, under a perpetual (rather than limited) form of "government" within the private/domestic (rather than public) sphere. The disabled are thus most closely aligned with slaves in terms of their 'power,' as these are the only two groups of people in Locke's theory who are governed by unlimited patriarchal authority"; see "Disability," 222. But she overstates. In the first place, "ideot" children would be no more subject to arbitrary rule by their fathers than were all daughters, able-bodied or not, any more than women were to their husbands. The limits of the law of nature prevent *any* authority from being arbitrary, and in particular, fathers could not take the lives of their children, or husbands of their wives. In this, they are quite different from slaves, a much more complicated question for Locke; see *Two Treatises,* 2.182–83.

32. See Locke, *Conduct of the Understanding.*

33. John Locke, *Questions Concerning the Law of Nature,* ed. and trans. Robert Horwitz, Jenny Strauss Clay, and Diskin Clay (Ithaca, NY: Cornell University Press, 1990), 111, 109.

34. Though this rationality was as "cultivated" as it was "natural." In *Gender, Class, and Freedom,* chapter 2, I argue that Macpherson's claim that the poor had naturally inferior reason, like many feminists' similar assertions about Locke's view of women's rationality, is mistaken. Reason, for Locke, requires cultivation, and in several of his writings he seems to argue at least implicitly, and often explicitly, that reason *should not* be developed in women and laborers. It is unclear how physically disabled persons would fit into this schema, but clearly attempts to develop the reason of "ideots" would be wasted, though it might be worth trying to bring "lunaticks" back to sounder premises.

35. I have not taken up the theme of the "brute" because neither Locke nor Hobbes makes direct comparisons; but both Arneil and Clifford argue that at least Locke's remarks about the rational capacities of "ideots" and "lunaticks" tie closely to what he says about the reasoning of "brutes."

Shakespearean Disability Pedagogy

ALLISON P. HOBGOOD AND
DAVID HOUSTON WOOD

ntroducing disability studies to the early modern period might transform
not just our scholarship but our classroom practices as well. We invite
readers of this collection to imagine the essays herein as instruments of
an "enabling pedagogy" that conceives of, as Brenda Brueggemann writes,
"disability as insight."[1] Disability pedagogy understands and remarks upon
disability as inherent in human experience and hence universally crucial to
our students' educations. As one example of how teachers might integrate
disability into their classroom practices and conversations, we would like
to briefly narrate the trajectory of a course, "Shakespeare and Disability,"
that Allison Hobgood offered while teaching at Spelman College, a historically Black women's institution in Atlanta, Georgia. The goal of the course,
as Hobgood explained it to her undergraduates, was threefold: to introduce
disability studies as a critical approach, to imagine how contemporary disability theory might shape readings of Renaissance literature, and to uncover
new disability histories in the early modern period. Further, she framed the
academic venture with some basic questions: Where is the disabled body
located in Shakespeare's canon, and how is it figured? How and where do
both material and literary representations of disability appear in this period
more broadly? What traditions relating to disability did Shakespeare inherit,
and what early modern views inform our contemporary notions of differ-

ence? Lastly, and perhaps most importantly, what innovative critical interventions might we make by interrogating disability in Shakespeare?

In a seminar of twenty-five aspiring Shakespeareans, only one or two students identified as disabled, and even then, only timidly. Over time, though, many women began to see how their normative identities were constructed in relation to disability and how a subtle yet pervasive ableist discourse shaped their daily experiences and practices. Students began to notice a *lack* of disabled classmates at Spelman, for instance, and wondered about institutional support for disability. They found themselves identifying disability in close friends and family in ways they had never expected or noticed before. Most frequently, however, students teased out the intersections of disability, gender, race, and class, exploring, for example, how Aaron's blackness in *Titus Andronicus* could be "disabling" yet was not "disability."[2] Their own subject positions as predominately able-bodied, black women gave them unique insights into these intersections, especially in terms of exploring tensions between the materiality of the early modern body—its tangible pain or visible skin color—and its social construction. They began to see how, amidst their well-honed impulses to "decry racism, sexism, and class bias, it [had] not occurred to most of them," as Lennard Davis points out, "that the very foundations on which their information systems are built . . . are themselves laden with assumptions about . . . ability and disability in general."[3] Throughout the semester, students not only read Shakespeare to expose a new history of the early modern disabled body and to discover how that history was shaped, inflected, and complicated by other sorts of embodiment during the English Renaissance but also to shake up their complacent participation in a *modern* ableist hegemony that normatively insists on marking disabled individuals—and, indeed, all difference—as "other."

The course began fairly conventionally with readings by Stephen Greenblatt, Andrew Gurr, and Russ McDonald that outlined the fundamentals of early modern English theater—playhouse spaces, audience members, acting companies, and so on—as well as the historical contexts that surrounded playgoing.[4] Students then tackled Shakespeare's *Tragedy of Richard III* alongside Margaret Winzer's "Disability and Society before the Eighteenth Century."[5] This conjunction was meant to provide students with some background on disability throughout the ages, to remind them of its sociohistorical situatedness, and to coax them into discussion about disability more generally. In Shakespeare's depiction of a ruthless and "rudely stamped" king (1.1.16), *Richard III* confirms students' initial, somewhat narrow sense of disability as always both physical and visible. Richard is an accessible character who initiates a crucial, though rather predictable, conversation about early modern subjectivity: What is the correlation between exterior materiality and interior selfhood? Does Shakespeare's play suggest that Richard's disabled body betrays a corrupted soul punished for its sinfulness? Is Richard "naturally" evil or has his embodiment, and circumstantial responses to it, created his discontent? In this class, however, the play also provoked new insights about the junctures of class, disability, and even metaphor: for example, could Richard's representation as a "lump of foul deformity" (1.2.57) reflect his status as a third-born son? It also prompted musings about the play's portrayal of women as both more aware of and sensitive to the advantages and limitations of Richard's physical difference. As a counterpoint especially to this discussion of gender and disability in *Richard III,* students then read Shakespeare's *Titus Andronicus* and investigated Lavinia's rape and mutilation as a gendered disability performance. Again, however, the bodies in this particular play are characterized by *physical* difference—lost limbs and severed tongues abound—and hence are easily recognized and categorized by students as "disabled."

In the next section of the course, therefore, Hobgood encouraged class members to expand their notions of what disability "looks like" by asking them to conceive of chronic illness as disability. Students specifically took up Shakespeare's *Tragedy of Julius Caesar* in conjunction with Erving Goffman's *Stigma* and Lerita Coleman's "Stigma: An Enigma Demystified."[6] They spent time deconstructing Goffman and Coleman, grappling with the connections between physical and social stigma as well as the differences between stigma and stereotype. These conversations occurred in tandem with a reading of *Julius Caesar* and discussions of how disabilities such as epilepsy (as well as deafness) are often visually unidentifiable.[7] Caesar "passed," the students decided, as nondisabled for most of the play and hence embodied disability in a much more complex fashion than Shakespeare's Lavinia or Richard III. Students also identified, among other things, how this drama evidenced coincident, cultural disability narratives in the Renaissance; the narrative of Caesar's "falling sickness" is informed simultaneously by a latent medieval sense of the marvelous as well as a burgeoning early modern trend toward scientific rationalism.

The second half of the semester gained focus around Tobin Siebers's essay "Disability in Theory" and viewing of a video called "Talk" by the UK Disability Rights Commission.[8] This pairing was meant to throw into practical relief many of the theoretical issues students had addressed thus far and to remind them how much of their work in the course was explicitly historical.[9] "Talk" especially prompted conversation about how the scholarly activity of recovering disability histories was relevant to contemporary disability activism. The class then read *The Tragedy of King Lear* alongside Bradley Lewis's essay "A Mad Fight: Psychiatry and Disability Activism" and engaged disability and activism in the contexts of madness, "sanism," and ageism.[10] Could Lear be characterized as disabled? When does he begin to identify as such? Does his status as disabled have more to do with age or insanity? One young woman even went so far as to recognize other "disabling" instances in *King Lear,* positing Edmund's illegitimacy as a very broad form of impairment in the play. She imagined Edmund's blood as deviant, as the invisible physical marker of his stigma and bastardization. Edmund's biology, according to her logic, rendered him less able to function in a society that refused to acknowledge positively his unconventional kinship ties and mottled blood lineage.

These discussions of Lewis and *King Lear* were followed closely by an investigation of representations of the "freak" in early modern literature. Students first read Shakespeare's long poem *Venus and Adonis* and explored Venus as embodying freakishness.[11] They combined more traditional readings of gender inversion, homoeroticism, and androgyny in this epyllion with a disability narrative about Venus's Amazonian size and strength.[12] Specifically, a number of students conceived of what previously has been imagined as Venus's transgressive gender and sexuality instead as the poem's exploitation of her physical difference: Venus as freakishly super-abled.[13] The catalyst for this interesting reading was Rosemarie Garland-Thomson's chapter "The Cultural Work of American Freak Shows" from her influential book *Extraordinary Bodies: Figuring Physical Disability in American Literature and Culture.*[14] The challenge of using this particular essay lay in reminding students of the specificity of Garland-Thomson's argument and helping them resist an ahistorical collapsing of her narrative onto Shakespeare's work. Carefully, then, students worked to clarify representations of freakishness in both *Venus and Adonis* and in the final play of the semester, *The Tempest.* They put into fruitful conversation three texts widely disparate in their geographical and historical interests but similar in their understanding of the sometimes tragic and yet always seductive spectacle that is human variation.[15]

As even this very brief review of Hobgood's undergraduate course attests, early modern disability studies, in *all* its iterations, develops from a flexible array of historicist and presentist methodologies and textual- and performance-related concerns that work together to examine difference, selfhood, and identity in the Renaissance. *Recovering Disability in Early Modern England* thus serves as an initiating example of how we might complicate and deepen current work on disability and an illustration of how Renaissance studies informs disability studies and vice versa. Training ourselves to pursue non-normativity and its various manifestations in the full breadth of early modern English literature allows us to understand as new that which we have presumed to be settled. Reading and thinking from a disability perspective can usefully recondition us—and our students—not only to the historicized ways in which early modern writing once meant, but also to the multivalent ways in which it continues to do so.

Notes

1. Brenda Brueggemann, "An Enabling Pedagogy," in Snyder et al., *Disability Studies,* 321.

2. William Shakespeare, *The Most Lamentable Tragedy of Titus Andronicus,* in Greenblatt et al., *Norton Shakespeare,* 371–434. While Hobgood encouraged intellectual risk-taking, she cautioned students against an uncritical collapsing of the disability category onto race and gender systems. Following Rosemarie Garland-Thomson's logic, she explained that "one must be vigilant not to conflate them [race, gender, and disability] so as to suggest that racial categorization, for example, is the same thing as disability, but simply in another form;" see Davis, "Integrating Disability Studies into the Existing Curriculum," *Disability Studies Reader,* 1st ed., 305.

3. Davis, *Enforcing Normalcy,* 4–5.

4. Stephen Greenblatt, "General Introduction," *Norton Shakespeare,* 1–24; Andrew Gurr, "The Shakespearean Stage," *Norton Shakespeare,* 3281–88; and Russ McDonald, "Performances, Playhouses, and Players," *The Bedford Companion to Shakespeare: An Introduction with Documents,* 2nd ed. (Boston: Bedford/St. Martin's, 2001), 40–73.

5. Winzer, "Disability and Society," 75–109; and William Shakespeare, *The Tragedy of Richard III,* in Greenblatt et al., *Norton Shakespeare,* 507–600.

6. See again Davis, *Disability Studies Reader,* 1st ed., 203–15 and 216–31, respectively.

7. William Shakespeare, *The Tragedy of Julius Caesar,* in Greenblatt et al., *Norton Shakespeare,* 1525–90.

8. Tobin Siebers, "Disability in Theory: From Social Constructionism to the New Realism of the Body," in Davis, *Disability Studies Reader,* 2nd ed., 173–84. As described online by the Disability Rights Commission, "'Talk' is an award-winning 12 minute film which challenges misconceptions about disability in a creative and entertaining way. Starring TV heart-throb Jonathan Kerrigan of BBC's 'Casualty' fame, 'Talk' portrays a society in which non-disabled people are a pitied minority and disabled people live full and active lives. Kerrigan plays a business executive, whose negative preconceptions of disability are dramatically shattered. 'Talk' was screened at numerous independent UK film festivals, at the Palm Springs Film Festival, USA, the Osnabruck Film Festival, Austria and the 2002 Maui Film Festival, Hawaii, and won the Short Film Award at the Third Rushes Soho Shorts Film Festival in August 2001. As part of 'Citizenship and Disability,' a classroom resource for teachers at Key Stages 3 and 4, 'Talk' has been sent free to schools throughout England, and is used as part of the National Curriculum." Access the video in two parts via YouTube at the following links:

Part 1: http://www.youtube.com/watch?v=FZfOVNwjFU0&feature= related

Part 2: http://www.youtube.com/watch?v=A9a2ZqLhuAw&feature=related

9. We would also recommend screening with students *Vital Signs: Crip Culture Talks Back*, dir. David T. Mitchell and Sharon Snyder (Brace Yourselves Productions, 1997).

10. William Shakespeare, *The Tragedy of King Lear: A Conflated Text*, in Greenblatt et al., *Norton Shakespeare*, 2479–554; Bradley Lewis, "A Mad Fight: Psychiatry and Disability Activism," in Davis, *Disability Studies Reader*, 2nd ed., 339–54.

11. William Shakespeare, *Venus and Adonis*, in Greenblatt et al., *Norton Shakespeare*, 601–34.

12. See Katherine Schwarz, *Tough Love: Amazon Encounters in the English Renaissance* (Durham, NC: Duke University Press, 2000) for more on early modern Amazons.

13. For more on desire and sexuality in this poem, see Richard Rambuss, "What It Feels Like for a Boy: Shakespeare's *Venus and Adonis*," in *A Companion to Shakespeare's Works, Volume IV: The Poems, Problem Comedies, Late Plays*, ed. Richard Dutton and Jean E. Howard (Malden, MA: Blackwell, 2003), 240–58; James Schiffer, "Shakespeare's *Venus and Adonis:* A Lacanian Tragicomedy of Desire," in *Venus and Adonis: Critical Essays*, ed. Philip Kolin (New York: Garland, 1997), 359–76; and Goran Stanivukovic, "Troping Desire in Shakespeare's *Venus and Adonis*," *Forum for Modern Language Studies* 33, no. 4 (October 1997): 289–301.

14. Garland-Thomson, *Extraordinary Bodies*, 55–80.

15. Caliban is described by Trinculo as "Legged like a man, and his fins / like arms" (2.2.31–32), a "monster of the isle with four legs" (62), and a "moon-calf" (100). Trinculo also alludes to the wealth and fame that Caliban's exploitation might offer back in England: "Were I in England now, / as I once was, and had but this fish painted, not a holiday-fool / there but would give a piece of silver. There would this mon- / ster make a man" (26–29); see William Shakespeare, *The Tempest*, in Greenblatt et al., *Norton Shakespeare*, 3055–107.

WORKS CITED

Acker, Paul. "Dwarf-Lore in Alvissmal." In *The Poetic Edda,* edited by Paul Acker and Carolyne Larrington, 213–28. New York: Routledge, 2002.

Adelson, Betty. *The Lives of Dwarfs: Their Journey from Public Curiosity toward Social Liberation.* New Brunswick, NJ: Rutgers University Press, 2005.

Ainscow, Mel, and Memmenasha Haile-Giorgis. "Educational Arrangements for Children Categorized as Having Special Needs in Central and Eastern Europe." *European Journal of Special Needs Education* 14, no. 2 (1999): 103–21.

Albrecht, Gary L. "Disability Humor: What's in a Joke?" *Body and Society* 5, no. 4 (1999): 67–74.

Alciato, Andrea. *Emblemata: Lyons, 1550.* Translated by Betty I. Knott. Brookfield, VT: Ashgate-Scholar, 1996.

Alpers, Paul J. *The Poetry of* The Faerie Queene. Princeton, NJ: Princeton University Press, 1967.

Anderson, Judith H. *Translating Investments: Metaphor and the Dynamic of Cultural Change in Tudor-Stuart England.* New York: Fordham University Press, 2005.

[Armstrong, Archie]. *A Banquet of Jeasts; Or Charge of Cheare.* London, 1630.

———. *A Choice Banquet of Witty Jests, Rare Fancies, and Pleasant Novels.* London, 1660.

Arneil, Barbara. "Disability, Self Image, and Modern Political Theory." *Political Theory* 37, no. 2 (April 2009): 218–42.

Bacon, Francis. *The Essays.* Edited by John Pitcher. Harmondsworth, UK: Penguin Books, 1985.

Baines, Barbara J. "*Antonio's Revenge:* Marston's Play on Revenge Plays." *Studies in English Literature* 23, no. 2 (1983): 277–94.

Baker, Naomi. "'To make love to a Deformity': Praising Ugliness in Early Modern England." *Renaissance Studies* 22, no. 1 (2007): 86–109.

Bakhtin, M. M. *Rabelais and His World.* Cambridge, MA: MIT Press, 1968.

193

Barasch, Moshe. *Blindness: The History of a Mental Image in Western Thought.* New York: Routledge, 2001.

Barkan, Leonard. *Nature's Work of Art: The Human Body as Image of the World.* New Haven, CT: Yale University Press, 1975.

Barnes, Colin, Mike Oliver, and Len Barton. *Disability Studies Today.* Cambridge, UK; Malden, MA: Polity Press in association with Blackwell Publishers, 2002.

Baron-Cohen, Simon. *Mindblindness: An Essay on Autism and Theory of Mind.* Cambridge, MA: MIT Press, 1995.

Barrough, Philip. *The Methode of Phisicke Conteyning the Causes, Signes, and Cures of Invvard Diseases in Mans Body from the Head to the Foote. Vvhereunto Is Added, the Forme and Rule of Making Remedies and Medicines, Which Our Phisitians Commonly Vse at This Day, with the Proportion, Quantitie, & Names of Ech [Sic] Medicine.* Imprinted at London: By Thomas Vautroullier dwelling in the Blacke-friars by Lud-gate, 1583.

Barton, Len. *Disability and Society: Emerging Issues and Insights.* Longman Sociology Series. London; New York: Longman, 1996.

Barton, Len, and Michael Oliver. *Disability Studies: Past, Present, and Future.* Leeds: Disability Press, 1997.

Basse, William. *A Helpe to Discourse. Or, A Miscellany of Merriment.* London, 1619.

Behn, Aphra. *The Works of Aphra Behn.* 3 vols. Edited by Janet Todd. London: William Pickering, 1995.

Berger, Harry, Jr. "Displacing Autophobia in *The Faerie Queene.*" *English Literary Renaissance* 28 (March 1998): 163–82.

Berlin, Isaiah. "Two Concepts of Liberty." In *Four Essays on Liberty.* New York: Oxford University Press, 1971.

Bevington, David, ed. *The Complete Works of Shakespeare.* 5th ed. New York: Pearson/Longman, 2003.

———, ed. *English Renaissance Drama.* London: Norton, 2002.

Bicks, Caroline. "Stones like Women's Paps: Revising Gender in Jane Sharp's *Midwives Book.*" *Journal for Early Modern Cultural Studies* 7, no. 2 (2007): 1–27.

Bigler, Erin D., Sherstin Mortensen, E. Shannon Neeley, Sally Ozonoff, Lori Krasny, Michael Johnson, Jeffrey Lu, Sherri L. Provencal, William McMahon, and Janet E. Lainhart. "Superior Temporal Gyrus, Language Function, and Autism." *Developmental Neuropsychology* 31 (2007): 217–38.

Bolt, David, Julia Miele Rodas, and Elizabeth J. Donaldson. *The Madwoman and the Blindman: Jane Eyre, Discourse, Disability.* Columbus: The Ohio State University Press, 2012.

Booty, John, ed. *The Book of Common Prayer, 1559: The Elizabethan Prayer Book.* Washington, DC: Folger, 1978.

Bordo, Susan. "The Body and the Reproduction of Femininity." In Conboy et al., *Writing on the Body,* 90–110.

Bourne, Henry Richard Fox. *Life of John Locke.* 2 vols. Whitefish, MT: Kessinger, 2007.

Bowers, Fredson. *Elizabethan Revenge Tragedy, 1587–1642.* Princeton, NJ: Princeton University Press, 1940.

Bragg, Lois. *Oedipus Borealis: The Aberrant Body in Old Icelandic Myth and Saga.* Madison, NJ: Fairleigh Dickinson University Press, 2004.

Braidotti, Rosi. "Mothers, Monsters, and Machines." In Conboy et al., *Writing on the Body,* 59–79.

Breckenridge, Carol A., and Candace Volger. "The Critical Limits of Embodiment: Disability's Criticism." *Public Culture* 13, no. 3 (2001): 349–58.

Breitenberg, Mark. *Anxious Masculinity in Early Modern England.* Cambridge: Cambridge University Press, 1996.

Brewer, Derek. "Prose Jest-Books Mainly in the Sixteenth to Eighteenth Centuries in England." In *A Cultural History of Humor: From Antiquity to the Present Day,* edited by Jan Bremmer and Herman Roodenburg, 90–111. Cambridge: Polity, 1997.

Bright, Timothie. *A Treatise, Vvherein Is Declared the Sufficiencie of English Medicines, for Cure of All Diseases, Cured with Medicines. Whereunto Is Added a Collection of Medicines Growing (for the Most Part) within Our English Climat, Approoued and Experimented against the Iaundise, Dropsie, Stone, Falling-Sicknesse, Pestilence.* London: Printed by H[umphrey] L[ownes] for Tho. Man, 1516.

Brown, Georgia. "Disgusting John Marston: Sensationalism and the Limits of a Post-Modern Marston." *Nordic Journal of English Studies* 4, no. 2 (2005): 121–42.

Brown, Jonathan. *Velázquez: The Technique of Genius.* New Haven, CT: Yale University Press, 1998.

Brożyna, Martha A. *Gender and Sexuality in the Middle Ages: A Medieval Source Documents Reader.* Jefferson, NC: McFarland, 2005.

Bruner, Jerome. "The Narrative Construction of Reality." *Critical Inquiry* 18 (1991): 1–21.

Bryson, Anna. *From Courtesy to Civility: Changing Codes of Conduct in Early Modern England.* New York: Oxford University Press, 1998.

Burton, Robert, and Floyd Dell. *The Anatomy of Melancholy. Now for the First Time with the Latin Completely Given in Translation and Embodied in an All-English Text.* New York: Tudor Pub. Co., 1948.

Butler, Judith. *Bodies That Matter: On the Discursive Limits of Sex.* New York: Routledge, 1993.

Campbell, Lily B. *Shakespeare's Tragic Heroes, Slaves of Passion.* Cambridge: The University Press, 1930.

———. "Theories of Revenge in Renaissance England." *Modern Philology* 38 (1931): 281–96.

Carroll, William. *Fat King, Lean Beggar.* Ithaca, NY: Cornell University Press, 1996.

Casasanto, Daniel. "Embodiment of Abstract Concepts: Good and Bad in Right- and Left-Handers." *Journal of Experimental Psychology: General* 138, no. 3 (August 2009): 360.

Castiglione, Baldessare. *The Courtyer of Count Baldessar Castilio divided into Foure Books.* Translated by Thomas Hoby. London, 1561.

Cavanagh, Sheila T. *Wanton Eyes and Chaste Desires: Female Sexuality in* The Faerie Queene. Bloomington: Indiana University Press, 1994.

[Chamberlain, Robert]. *The Booke of Bulls, Baited with two Centuries of bold Jests and Nimble Lies.* London, 1636.

Cheu, Johnson. "Performing Disability, Problematizing Cure." In Sandahl and Auslander, *Bodies in Commotion,* 135–46.

Chivers, Sally, and Nicole Markotić, eds. *The Problem Body: Projecting Disability on Film.* Columbus: The Ohio State University Press, 2010.

Clare, Eli. *Exile and Pride: Disability, Queerness, and Liberation.* Cambridge, MA: South-End, 1999.

Clark, Andy. *Being There: Putting Brain, Body, and World Together Again.* Cambridge, MA: MIT Press, 1997.

Clark, Stuart. *Vanities of the Eye: Vision in Early Modern European Culture.* Oxford: Oxford University Press, 2009.

Clifford, Stacy. "Indispensable Idiocy: Disability in the Development of John Locke's Thought." Paper presented at the annual meeting of the Midwest Political Science Association, April 2010, Chicago, IL.

The Cobler of Caunterburie. London, 1590.

Cohen, Jeffrey Jerome. *Of Giants: Sex, Monsters, and the Middle Ages.* Minneapolis: University of Minnesota Press, 1999.

Coleman, Lerita. "Stigma: An Enigma Demystified." In Davis, *Disability Studies Reader,* 1st ed., 216–31.

Collinson, Patrick. *The Religion of Protestants: The Church in English Society, 1559–1625.* Oxford: Oxford University Press, 1984.

A Compleat Collection of Remarkable Tryals of the most Notorious Malefactors, at the Sessions-House in the Old Baily, for near Fifty Years Past. 4 vols. London, 1718–21.

Conboy, Katie, Nadia Medina, and Sarah Stanbury, eds. *Writing on the Body.* New York: Columbia University Press, 1997.

[Copley, Edward]. *Wits, Fits, and Fancies: Or, a generall and serious Collection, of the Sententious Speeches, Answers, Jests and Behaviours, of all sortes of states, From the Throane to the Cottage.* London, 1614.

Crisp, Peter. "Allegory: Conceptual Metaphor in History." *Language and Literature* 10 (2001): 5–19.

Croft, Pauline. "The Reputation of Robert Cecil: Libels, Political Opinion and Popular Awareness in the Early Seventeenth Century." *Transactions of the Royal Historical Society,* 6th ser., I (1991): 43–69.

Crooke, Helkiah. *Mikrokosmographia. A Description of the Body of Man. Together Vvith the Controversies and Figures Thereto Belonging. Collected and Translated out of All the Best Authors of Anatomy, Especially out of Gaspar Bauhinus, and Andreas Laurentius.* 2nd ed. London: W. Iaggard, 1618.

The Cuckold's Calamity, Or the Old Usurer Plunder'd out of his Gold by His Young Wife, Pepys Ballads 5.256 (n.d.). http://ebba.english.ucsb.edu/ballad/22091/image.

Cunningham, Merrilee. "The Interpolated Tale in Spenser's *Faerie Queene* Book I." *South Central Bulletin* 43, no. 4 (1983): 99–104.

"Czech Republic: Country Reports on Human Rights Practices—2002." Released by the Bureau of Democracy, Human Rights, and Labor (the U.S. Department of State): http://www.state.gov/g/drl/rls/hrrpt/2002/18361.htm.

Dasenbrock, Reed Way. "Escaping the Squires' Double Bind in Books III and IV of *The Faerie Queene." Studies in English Literature* 26, no. 1 (Winter 1986): 25–45.

D'Avenant, William. *Salmacida Spolia.* English Verse Drama Full-Text Database. Cambridge: Chadwycke-Healey, 1994.

Davidson, Michael. *Concerto for the Left Hand: Disability and the Defamiliar Body.* Ann Arbor: University of Michigan Press, 2008.

Davies, Telory. *Performing Disability: Staging the Actual.* Saarbrücken, Germany: VDM Publishing, 2009.

Davis, Lennard J. *Bending over Backwards: Disability, Dismodernism, and Other Difficult Positions.* New York: New York University Press, 2002.

———, ed. *The Disability Studies Reader.* 1st ed. New York: Routledge, 1997.

————, ed. *The Disability Studies Reader.* 2nd ed. New York: Routledge, 2006.

————. *Enforcing Normalcy: Disability, Deafness, and the Body.* London: Verso, 1995.

della Casa, Giovanni. *Galateo of Maister John Della Casa.* Translated by Robert Peterson. London, 1576.

Descartes, René. *The Philosophical Writings of Descartes. Volume III: The Correspondence.* Translated by John Cottingham, Robert Stoothoff, Dugald Murdoch, and Anthony Kenny. Cambridge: Cambridge University Press, 1991.

Diagnostic and Statistical Manual of Mental Disorders. 4th ed. (Text Revision). Washington, DC: American Psychological Association, 2000.

Dickie, Simon. *Cruelty and Laughter: Forgotten Comic Literature and the Unsentimental Eighteenth Century.* Chicago: University of Chicago Press, 2011.

————. "Hilarity and Pitilessness in the Mid-Eighteenth Century: English Jestbook Humor." *Eighteenth-Century Studies* 37, no. 1 (2003): 1–22.

Dobranski, Stephen. *Readers and Authorship in Early Modern England.* Cambridge: Cambridge University Press, 2005.

Dolan, Frances E. *Marriage and Violence: The Early Modern Legacy.* Philadelphia: University of Pennsylvania Press, 2008.

Dollimore, Jonathan. *Radical Tragedy: Religion, Ideology and Power in the Drama of Shakespeare and His Contemporaries.* 3rd ed. New York: Palgrave, 2004.

Douglas, Mary. *Purity and Danger: An Analysis of Concepts of Pollution and Taboo.* New York: Routledge and Kegan Paul, 1966.

Drout, Michael D. C. *J. R. R. Tolkien Encyclopedia: Scholarship and Critical Assessment.* London: Routledge, 2006.

Dugaw, Dianne. *Warrior Women and Popular Balladry, 1650–1850.* Chicago: University of Chicago Press, 1996.

Duprat, Anne. "*Stultitia loquitur:* Fiction and Folly in Early Modern Literature." *Comparative Critical Studies* 5, nos. 2–3 (2008): 141–51.

Eiesland, Nancy L. *The Disabled God: Toward a Liberatory Theology of Disability.* Nashville: Abingdon Press, 1994.

Enderle, Alfred, Dietrich Meyerhofer, and Gerd Unverfehrt, eds. *Small People—Great Art: Restricted Growth from an Artistic and Medical Viewpoint.* Bremen: Artcolor Verlag, 1994.

English Broadside Ballad Archive. University of California, Santa Barbara. http://ebba. english.ucsb.edu.

Erasmus, Desiderius. *The Praise of Folly.* Edited and translated by Clarence H. Miller. 2nd ed. New Haven, CT: Yale University Press, 2003.

Erevelles, Nirmala. "Signs of Reason: Riviere, Facilitated Communication, and the Crisis of the Subject." In Tremain, *Foucault and the Government of Disability,* 45–64.

Evans-Wentz, W. Y. *The Fairy-Faith in Celtic Countries* [1911]. Introduction by Carl McCollman. Franklin Lakes, NJ: New Page Books, 2004.

Eyler, Joshua. *Disability in the Middle Ages: Rehabilitations, Reconsiderations, Reverberations.* Burlington, VT: Ashgate, 2010.

Farmer, John S., ed. *Jacob and Esau.* New York: AMS, 1970.

Fiedler, Leslie. *Freaks.* New York: Simon and Schuster, 1978.

Ford, John. *'Tis Pity She's a Whore.* In Bevington, *English Renaissance Drama,* 1912–67.

Foucault, Michel. *The Birth of the Clinic.* Trans. A. M. Sheridan Smith. New York: Vintage Books, 1973.

————. *Discipline and Punish.* New York: Vintage, 1979.

———. *Madness and Civilization: A History of Insanity in the Age of Reason.* New York: Vintage, 1988.

———. *The Order of Things: An Archaeology of the Human Sciences.* New York: Vintage, 1970.

———. *Power/Knowledge: Selected Interviews and Other Writings, 1972–1977.* Edited by Colin Gordon. New York: Pantheon Books, 1980.

Foyster, Elizabeth A. *Manhood in Early Modern England: Honour, Sex and Marriage.* London: Longman, 1999.

Franko, Mark. *Dance as Text: Ideologies of the Baroque Body.* Cambridge: Cambridge University Press, 1993.

Fudge, Erica. "Monstrous Acts: Bestiality in Early Modern England." *History Today* 50, no. 8 (2000): 20–25.

Fumerton, Patricia. "'Secret' Arts: Elizabethan Miniatures and Sonnets." *Representations* 15 (Summer 1986): 57–97.

Galen. *On the Usefulness of the Parts of the Body.* Translated by Margaret Tallmadge May. Ithaca, NY: Cornell University Press, 1968.

Garber, Marjorie B. *Vested Interests: Cross-dressing and Cultural Anxiety.* New York: Routledge, 1991.

Garland, Robert. *The Eye of the Beholder: Deformity and Disability in the Graeco-Roman World.* London: Duckworth, 1995.

Garland-Thomson, Rosemarie. "Beauty and the Freak." In *Points of Contact: Disability, Art, and Culture,* edited by S. Crutchfield and M. Epstein, 181–96. Ann Arbor: University of Michigan Press, 2000.

———. "Dares to Stares: Disabled Women Performance Artists and the Dynamics of Staring." In Sandahl and Auslander, *Bodies in Commotion,* 30–41.

———. *Extraordinary Bodies: Figuring Physical Disability in American Literature and Culture.* New York: Columbia University Press, 1997.

———. "Integrating Disability Studies into the Existing Curriculum." In Davis, *Disability Studies Reader,* 1st ed., 295–306.

———. "Misfits: A Feminist Materialist Disability Concept." *Hypatia* 26, no. 3 (Summer 2011): 591–609.

———. *Staring: How We Look.* Oxford: Oxford University Press, 2009.

———, ed. *Freakery: Cultural Spectacles of the Extraordinary Body.* New York: New York University Press, 1996.

Geertz, Clifford. "Centers, Kings, and Charisma: Reflections on the Symbolics of Power." In *Rites of Power: Symbolism, Ritual, and Politics since the Middle Ages,* edited by Sean Wilentz, 13–40. Philadelphia: University of Pennsylvania Press, 1985.

Goffman, Erving. "Selections from *Stigma.*" In Davis, *Disability Studies Reader,* 1st ed., 203–15.

———. *Stigma: Notes on the Management of Spoiled Identity.* Englewood Cliffs, NJ: Prentice-Hall, 1963.

Goodey, C. F. "'Foolishness' in Early Modern Medicine and the Concept of Intellectual Disability." *Medical History* 48 (2004): 289–310.

———. *A History of Intelligence and 'Intellectual Disability': The Shaping of Psychology in Early Modern Europe.* Farnham, Surrey; Burlington, VT: Ashgate, 2011.

Gowing, Laura. *Common Bodies: Women, Touch and Power in Seventeenth-century England.* New Haven, CT: Yale University Press, 2003.

Gray, Carol. *The New Social Story Book.* Arlington, TX: Horizons, 2000.

Greenblatt, Stephen. "The False Ending in *Volpone*." *Journal of English and Germanic Philology* 75 (1976): 90–104.

———. *Shakespearean Negotiations: The Circulation of Social Energy in Renaissance England*. Oxford: Clarendon Press, 1988.

Greenblatt, Stephen, Walter Cohen, Jean E. Howard, Katharine Eisaman Maus, and Andrew Gurr, eds. *The Norton Shakespeare*. 1st ed. New York: W. W. Norton, 1997.

Griffiths, Paul. *Lost Londons: Change, Crime and Control in the Capital City, 1550–1660*. Cambridge: Cambridge University Press, 2008.

Haigh, Christopher. *English Reformations: Religion, Politics, and Society under the Tudors*. Oxford: Clarendon Press, 1993.

———. *Reformation and Resistance in Tudor Lancashire*. Cambridge: Cambridge University Press, 1975.

Hakewill, George. *The Vanitie of the Eye First Beganne for the Comfort of a Gentlewoman Bereaved of Her Sight, and since Vpon Occasion Enlarged & Published for the Common Good. By George Hakewill Master of Arts, and Fellow of Exeter Coll. in Oxford, Second Edition Augmented by the Author*. Oxford: Joseph Barnes, 1608.

Hall, Kim F. *Things of Darkness: Economies of Race and Gender in Early Modern England*. Ithaca, NY: Cornell University Press, 1995.

Hallett, Charles A., and Elaine S. Hallett. *The Revenger's Madness: A Study of Revenge Tragedy Motifs*. Lincoln: University of Nebraska Press, 1980.

Hamilton, A. C., ed. *The Spenser Encyclopedia*. New York: Routledge, 1991.

Hay, William. *Deformity: An Essay*. Edited by Kathleen James-Cavan. Victoria, BC: University of Victoria, 2004.

Henderson, Bruce, and Noam Ostrander, eds. *Understanding Disability Studies and Performance Studies*. New York: Routledge, 2010.

Henley, Pauline. *Spenser in Ireland*. 1928; reprint, New York: Russell and Russell, 1969.

Hicks, William. *Coffee-House Jests*. London, 1677.

———. *Oxford Jests, Refined and Enlarged*. London, 1671.

Hirschmann, Nancy J. *Gender, Class, and Freedom in Modern Political Theory*. Princeton, NJ: Princeton University Press, 2008.

———. *The Subject of Liberty: Toward a Feminist Theory of Freedom*. Princeton, NJ: Princeton University Press, 2003.

Hirschmann, Nancy J., and Beth Linker, eds. *Civil Disabilities: Theory, Citizenship and the Body*. Philadelphia: University of Pennsylvania Press, forthcoming.

Hirschmann, Nancy J., and Kirstie M. McClure, eds. *Feminist Interpretations of John Locke*. University Park: Pennsylvania State University Press, 2007.

Hobbes, Thomas. "De Cive." In *Man and Citizen: De Homine and De Cive*, edited by Bernard Gert. Indianapolis: Hackett, 1991.

———. *Leviathan*. Edited by Richard Tuck. Cambridge: Cambridge University Press, 1991.

———. *Leviathan*. Edited by C. B. Macpherson. Harmondsworth UK: Penguin, 1985.

———. "The Questions Concerning Liberty, Necessity, and Chance." In *Hobbes and Bramhall on Liberty and Necessity*, edited by Vere Chappel, 69–90. New York: Cambridge University Press, 1999.

Hobby, Elaine. "'The Head of This Countefeit Yard Is Called Tertigo' or, 'It Is Not Hard Words That Perform the Work': Recovering Early-Modern Women's Writing." In *Women's Writing, 1550–1750*, 13–23. Bundoora, Australia: Meridian, 2001.

———. "'To God Alone Be All Praise and Glory' or 'Serving Mine Own Sex First'?

Nicholas Culpepper, Jane Sharp, and the Restoration Midwifery Manual." In *The Female Wits: Women and Gender in Restoration Literature and Culture*, 249–63. Huelva, Spain: Universidad de Huelva, 2006.

Hobgood, Allison, and David Houston Wood. "Disabled Shakespeares." *Disability Studies Quarterly* 29, no. 4 (Fall 2009): n.p. http://dsq-sds.org/article/view/991/1183.

Holland, Daniel. "Grass Roots Promotion of Community Health and Human Rights for People with Disabilities in Post-communist Central Europe: A Profile of the Slovak Republic." *Disability and Society* 18, no. 2 (2003): 133–43.

Horden, Peregrine, ed. *Music as Medicine: The History of Music Therapy since Antiquity.* Aldershot, UK: Ashgate, 2000.

Howlin, Patricia. *Autism and Asperger Syndrome: Preparing for Adulthood.* 2nd ed. London: Routledge, 2004.

Hrdličková, Martina. "Richard III: Jan Potměšil nehraje neřest v moralitě." *Reflex* 47 (2000): 87.

Hughes, Bill. "What Can a Foucauldian Analysis Contribute to Disability Theory?" In Tremain, *Foucault and the Government of Disability*, 78–92.

———. "Wounded/Monstrous/Abject: A Critique of the Disabled Body in the Sociological Imaginary." *Disability & Society* 24, no. 2 (2009): 399–410.

Hunt, J. Eric. *Cranmer's First Litany, 1544 and Merbecke's Book of Common Prayer Notes, 1550.* London: SPCK, 1939.

Hurley, Dan. *Diabetes Rising: How a Rare Disease Became a Modern Pandemic, and What to Do about It.* New York: Kaplan, 2010.

Inahara, Minae. *Abject Love: Undoing the Boundaries of Physical Disability.* Saarbrücken, Germany: VDM Verlag Dr. Müller, 2009.

Jackson, Kenneth. *Separate Theaters: Bethlem ("Bedlam") Hospital and the Shakespearean Stage.* Newark: University of Delaware Press, 2005.

Jeníková, Eva. "Potměšilovi slouží vozík jako exkluzivní rekvizita." *Zemské Noviny: Kultura,* 25 September 2000.

———. "Richard Třetí odráží stav české politiky." *Zemské Noviny: Kultura,* 22 April 2000.

Johnson, Mark. *The Body in the Mind: The Bodily Basis of Meaning, Imagination, and Reason.* Chicago: University of Chicago Press, 1987.

Jones, Vivien, ed. *Women in the Eighteenth Century: Constructions of Femininity.* New York: Routledge, 1990.

Jonson, Ben. *Volpone.* Edited by Brian Parker and David Bevington. Manchester: Manchester University Press, 1999.

———. *Works.* Edited by C. H. Herford, Percy Simpson, and Evelyn Simpson. Oxford: Clarendon Press, 1925–52.

Kleege, Georgina. *Sight Unseen.* New Haven, CT: Yale University Press, 1999.

Kostihová, Marcela. *Shakespeare in Transition.* New York: Palgrave Macmillan, 2010.

Kövecses, Zoltán. *Metaphor: A Practical Introduction.* 2nd ed. New York: Oxford University Press, 2010.

Kristeva, Julia. *The Powers of Horror: An Essay on Abjection.* New York: Columbia University Press, 1982.

Kříž, Jiří P. "Prahou zní: Království za koně." *Právo,* 29 September 2000.

Kudlick, Catherine J. "Disability History: Why We Need Another 'Other.'" *American Historical Review* 108, no. 3 (2003): 763–93.

Kuppers, Petra. *Disability and Contemporary Performance: Bodies on Edge*. New York: Routledge, 2003.

———. *Disability Culture and Community Performance: Find a Strange and Twisted Shape*. New York: Palgrave Macmillan, 2011.

———. *The Scar of Visibility: Medical Performances and Contemporary Art*. Minnesota: University of Minnesota Press, 2007.

Kyd, Thomas. *The Spanish Tragedy*. In Bevington, *English Renaissance Drama*, 3–73.

Lake, Peter. *Anglicans and Puritans? Presbyterianism and English Conformist Thought from Whitgift to Hooker*. New York: HarperCollins, 1988.

Lakoff, George, and Mark Johnson. *Metaphors We Live By*. Chicago: University of Chicago Press, 1980.

Lakoff, George, and Mark Turner. *More Than Cool Reason: A Field Guide to Poetic Metaphor*. Chicago: University of Chicago Press, 1989.

Lane, Harlan. "Construction of Deafness." In Davis, *Disability Studies Reader*, 2nd ed., 82–83.

Le Strange, Nicholas. *Merry Passages and Jeasts: A Manuscript Jestbook of Sir Nicholas Le Strange (1603–1655)*. Edited by H. F. Lippincott. Salzburg: Institut für Englische Sprache und Literatur, Universität Salzburg, 1974.

Linton, Simi. *Claiming Disability: Knowledge and Identity*. New York: New York University Press, 1998.

———. *My Body Politic: A Memoir*. Ann Arbor: University of Michigan Press, 2006.

Locke, John. *An Essay Concerning Human Understanding*. Edited by Peter H. Nidditch. Oxford: Clarendon Press, 1975.

———. "An Essay on the Poor Law." In *Political Essays,* ed. Mark Goldie, 182–200. New York: Cambridge University Press, 1997.

———. *Of the Conduct of the Understanding*. Ed. Ruth Weissbourd Grant and Nathan Tarcov. Indianapolis: Hackett, 1996.

———. *Questions Concerning the Law of Nature*. Edited and translated by Robert Horwitz, Jenny Strauss Clay, and Diskin Clay. Ithaca, NY: Cornell University Press, 1990.

———. *Two Treatises of Government*. New York: Cambridge University Press 1960.

Longmore, Paul K. *Why I Burned My Book and Other Essays on Disability*. Philadelphia: Temple University Press, 2003.

Lund, Roger. "Laughing at Cripples: Ridicule, Deformity and the Argument from Design." *Eighteenth-Century Studies* 39, no. 1 (2005): 91–114.

MacCulloch, Diarmaid. *Thomas Cranmer: A Life*. New Haven, CT: Yale University Press, 1996.

MacDonald, Michael. *Mystical Bedlam: Madness, Anxiety, and Healing in Seventeenth-Century England*. Cambridge: Cambridge University Press, 1981.

Macpherson, C. B. *The Political Theory of Possessive Individualism: Hobbes to Locke*. Oxford: Clarendon Press, 1962.

Mairs, Nancy. *Waist-High in the World: A Life among the Nondisabled*. Boston: Beacon Press, 1997.

Maltby, Judith. *Prayer Book and People in Elizabethan and Early Stuart England*. Cambridge: Cambridge University Press, 1998.

Manning, John, and Alistair Fowler. "The Iconography of Spenser's Occasion." *Journal of the Warburg and Courtauld Institutes* 39 (1976): 263–66.

Marlowe, Christopher. *The Jew of Malta*. In Bevington, *English Renaissance Drama*, 293–348.

Marshall, John. *John Locke: Resistance, Religion, and Responsibility*. Cambridge: Cambridge University Press, 1994.

Marston, John. *Antonio's Revenge*. Edited by W. Reavley Gair. Manchester: University of Manchester Press, 1978.

Maus, Katharine Eisaman. *Inwardness and Theater in the English Renaissance*. Chicago: University of Chicago Press, 1995.

McClain, Linda C., and Joanna L. Grossman. *Gender Equality: Dimensions of Women's Equal Citizenship*. Cambridge: Cambridge University Press, 2009.

McClimens, Alex. "lost in translation." *Learning and Disability Practice* 8, no. 6 (July 2005): 34–35.

McDonald, Russ. "Performances, Playhouses, and Players." In *The Bedford Companion to Shakespeare: An Introduction with Documents*, 2nd ed., 40–73. Boston: Bedford/St. Martin's, 2001.

McManaway, James G. "'Occasion,' *Faerie Queene* II.iv.4–5." *Modern Language Notes* 49, no. 6 (1934): 391–93.

McRuer, Robert. "Compulsory Able-Bodiedness and Queer/Disabled Existence." In Snyder et al., *Disability Studies*, 88–99.

Melville, Lewis. *Society at Royal Tunbridge Wells in the Eighteenth Century—and After*. London: Eveleigh Nash, 1912.

Mendelson, Sara, and Patricia Crawford. *Women in Early Modern England*. New York: Oxford University Press, 1998.

Metzler, Irina. *Disability in Medieval Europe: Thinking about Physical Impairment during the High Middle Ages, c. 1100–1400*. London: Routledge, 2006.

Microphilus [Master Slater]. *The new-yeeres gift presented at court, from the lady Parvula to the Lord Minimus, (commonly called Little Jefferie) Her Majesties servant, with a letter as it was penned in short-hand: wherein is proved little things are better then* [sic] *great*. London, 1636.

Middleton, Thomas. *The Revenger's Tragedy*. In Bevington, *English Renaissance Drama*, 1303–67.

Miller, Jacqueline. "The Courtly Figure: Spenser's Anatomy of Allegory." *Studies in English Literature* 31 (1991): 51–68.

Miller, William Ian. *The Anatomy of Disgust*. Cambridge, MA: Harvard University Press, 1997.

Mills, Charles W. *The Racial Contract*. Ithaca, NY: Cornell University Press, 1999.

Mitchell, David T., and Sharon Snyder. *Cultural Locations of Disability*. Chicago: University of Chicago Press, 2006.

———. *Narrative Prosthesis: Disability and the Dependencies of Discourse*. Ann Arbor: University of Michigan Press, 2001.

Montaigne, Michel de. "On not pretending to be ill." In *The Complete Essays*, edited by M. A. Screech, 781–83. New York: Penguin, 2003.

Montrose, Louis A. "Professing the Renaissance: The Poetics and Politics of Culture." In *The New Historicism*, edited by H. Aram Veeser, 15–36. New York: Routledge, 1989.

The Moral Play of Everyman. In *Everyman and Medieval Miracle Plays*, edited by A. C. Cawley, 195–225. London: J. M. Dent/Everyman, 1993.

Morris, Jeffrey B. "To (Re)Fashion a Gentleman: Raleigh's Disgrace in Spenser's Legend of Courtesy." *Studies in Philology* 94, no. 1 (1997): 38–58.

Murdoch, John, and V. J. Murrell. "The Monogramist DG: Dwarf Gibson and His Patrons." *Burlington Magazine* 123, no. 938 (May 1981): 282–91.

Nadesan, Majia Holmer. "Constructing Autism: A Brief Genealogy." In *Autism and Representation*, edited by Mark Osteen, 78–95. London: Routledge, 2008.

Neely, Carol Thomas. *Distracted Subjects: Madness and Gender in Shakespeare and Early Modern Culture*. Ithaca, NY: Cornell University Press, 2004.

Newman, Steve. *Ballad Collection, Lyric, and the Canon: The Call of the Popular from the Restoration to the New Criticism*. Philadelphia: University of Pennsylvania Press, 2007.

Nichols, Tom. "The Vagabond Image: Depictions of False Beggars in Northern Art of the Sixteenth Century." In *Others and Outcasts in Early Modern Europe: Picturing the Social Margins*, 37–60. Aldershot, UK: Ashgate, 2007.

Nohrnberg, James. *The Analogy of 'The Faerie Queene.'* Princeton, NJ: Princeton University Press, 1976.

Nussbaum, Felicity. "Dumb Virgins, Blind Ladies, and Eunuchs: Fictions of Defect." In *Defects: Engendering the Modern Body*, edited by Helen Deutsch and Felicity Nussbaum, 31–53. Ann Arbor: University of Michigan Press, 2000.

———. *Torrid Zones: Maternity, Sexuality, and Empire in Eighteenth-Century English Narratives*. Baltimore: Johns Hopkins University Press, 1995.

Oliver, Michael. *Understanding Disability: From Theory to Practice*. New York: St. Martin's Press, 1996.

Oliver, Michael, Colin Barnes, and Michael Oliver. *The New Politics of Disablement*. Houndmills, Basingstoke ; New York, NY: Palgrave Macmillan, 2012.

Orso, Stephen. *Velázquez, "Los Borrachos," and Painting at the Court of Philip IV*. Cambridge: Cambridge University Press, 1993.

Otto, Barbara. *Fools Are Everywhere*. Chicago: University of Chicago Press, 2001.

Otway, Thomas, and Pre-1801 Imprint Collection (Library of Congress). *Friendship in Fashion. A Comedy, as It Is Acted at His Royal Highness the Dukes Theatre*. London: Printed by E. F. for Richard Tonson, at his Shop within Grays-Inn-Gate, next Grays-Inn-Lane, 1678.

The Oxford English Dictionary. 2nd ed. Oxford: Oxford University Press, 1989.

Page, Nicholas. *Lord Minimus: The Extraordinary Life of Britain's Smallest Man*. London: HarperCollins, 2001.

Paré, Ambroise. *On Monsters and Marvels*. Edited and translated by Janis L. Palliser. Chicago: University of Chicago Press, 1982.

Park, Katherine, and Lorraine Daston. "Unnatural Conceptions: The Study of Monsters in Sixteenth- and Seventeenth-Century France and England." *Past and Present* 92 (1981): 20–55.

———. *Wonders and the Order of Nature, 1150–1750*. New York: Zone Books, 1998.

Pasquil's Jestes, Mixed with Mother Bunches Merriments. London, 1609.

Paster, Gail Kern. *The Body Embarrassed: Drama and the Disciplines of Shame in Early Modern England*. Ithaca, NY: Cornell University Press, 1993.

———. *Humoring the Body: Emotions and the Shakespearean Stage*. Chicago: University of Chicago Press, 2004.

Paster, Gail Kern, Katherine Rowe, and Mary Floyd-Wilson, eds. *Reading the Early Modern Passions: Essays in the Cultural History of Emotion*. Philadelphia: University of Pennsylvania Press, 2004.

Pearman, Tory Vandeventer. *Women and Disability in Medieval Literature (the New Middle Ages)*. New York: Palgrave Macmillan, 2010.

Pepys, Samuel. English Broadside Ballad Archive. University of California, Santa Barbara. http://emc.english.ucsb.edu/ballad_project.

Pinkethman, William. *Pinkethman's Jests, Or, Wit Refin'd.* 4th ed. London, 1735.

Pocock, J. G. A. *The Machiavellian Moment: Florentine Political Thought and the Atlantic Republican Tradition.* Princeton, NJ: Princeton University Press, 1975.

Poor Robin's Jests: Or, the Compleat Jester. London, 1672.

Porter, Roy. "Foucault's Great Confinement." *History of the Human Sciences* 3, no. 1 (1990): 47–54.

Pratt, Mary Louise. "Arts of the Contact Zone." In *Profession* 91, 33–40. New York: MLA, 1991.

Putna, Martin C. "Shakespeare a klid na práci." *Mladá Fronta Dnes,* 25 September 2000.

Puttenham, George. *The Art of English Poesy.* Edited by Frank Whigham and Wayne A. Rebhorn. Ithaca, NY: Cornell University Press, 2007.

Quayson, Ato. *Aesthetic Nervousness: Disability and the Crisis of Representation.* New York: Columbia University Press, 2007.

Rambuss, Richard. "What It Feels Like for a Boy: Shakespeare's *Venus and Adonis.*" In *A Companion to Shakespeare's Works, Volume IV: The Poems, Problem Comedies, Late Plays,* edited by Richard Dutton and Jean E. Howard, 240–58. Malden, MA: Blackwell, 2003.

Rathbone, Isabel E. "The Political Allegory of the Florimell-Marinell Story." *English Literary History* 12, no. 4 (1945): 279–89.

Ricoeur, Paul. *The Rule of Metaphor: Multi-disciplinary Studies of the Creation of Meaning in Language.* Translated by Robert Czerny with Kathleen McLaughlin and John Costello. Toronto: University of Toronto Press, 1977.

Roberts, Hannah. "Mental Health Care Still Poor in Eastern Europe." *The Lancet* 360 (17 August 2002): 552.

Rousseau, Jean-Jacques. *The Social Contract; And, Discourses; Translation [From the French] and Introduction by G. D. H. Cole, Revised and Augmented by J. H. Brumfitt and John C. Hall.* London: Dent, 1973.

Row-Heyveld, Lindsey. "The Lying'st Knave in Christendom: The Development of Disability in the False Miracle of Saint Albans." *Disability Studies Quarterly* 29, no. 4 (2009): n.p. http://www.dsq-sds.org/article/view/994/1178.

Rushton, Peter. "Lunatics and Idiots: Mental Disability, the Community, and the Poor Law in North-East England, 1600–1800." *Medical History* 32 (1988): 34–50.

Salgādo, Gāmini. *Cony-Catchers and Bawdy Baskets: An Anthology of Elizabethan Low Life.* Harmondsworth, UK: Penguin, 1972.

Sandahl, Carrie. "The Tyranny of Neutral: Disability and Actor Training." In Sandahl and Auslander, *Bodies in Commotion,* 255–68.

Sandahl, Carrie, and Philip Auslander, eds. *Bodies in Commotion: Disability and Performance.* Ann Arbor: University of Michigan Press, 2005.

Sawday, Jonathan. *The Body Emblazoned: Dissection and the Human Body in Renaissance Culture.* New York: Routledge, 1995.

Scarry, Elaine. *The Body in Pain.* Oxford: Oxford University Press, 1985.

Schiffer, James. "Shakespeare's *Venus and Adonis:* A Lacanian Tragicomedy of Desire." In *Venus and Adonis: Critical Essays,* edited by Philip Kolin, 359–76. New York: Garland, 1997.

Schleiner, Winfried. "Justifying the Unjustifiable: The Dover Cliff Scene in *King Lear.*" *Shakespeare Quarterly* 36, no. 3 (1985): 337–43.

Schoenfeldt, Michael C. *Bodies and Selves in Early Modern England: Physiology and Inwardness in Spenser, Shakespeare, Herbert, and Milton.* New York: Cambridge University Press, 1999.

Schreibman, Laura. *The Science and Fiction of Autism.* Cambridge, MA: Harvard University Press, 2005.

Schwarz, Katherine. *Tough Love: Amazon Encounters in the English Renaissance.* Durham, NC: Duke University Press, 2000.

Schweik, Susan M. "Dissimulations." In *The Ugly Laws: Disability in Public,* 108–40. New York: New York University Press, 2009.

The Second Maiden's Tragedy. Charleston: Nabu, 2010.

Shakespeare, Tom. *Disability Rights and Wrongs.* New York: Routledge, 2006.

———. "Joking a Part." *Body and Society* 5, no. 4 (1999): 47–52.

Shakespeare, William. *The Complete Works of Shakespeare.* Edited by David Bevington. 5th ed. New York: Pearson Longman, 2003.

———. *Richard III.* In *The Riverside Shakespeare,* 2nd ed., edited by G. Blakemore Evans, J. J. M. Tobin, Herschel Baker, Anne Barton, Frank Kermode, Harry Levin, Hallett Smith and Marie Edel, 748–804. Boston: Houghton Mifflin, 1997.

Sharp, Jane. *The Midwives Book.* London, 1671. Available through the Brown Women Writers Project: http://www.wwp.brown.edu.

Shepard, Alexandra. *Meanings of Manhood in Early Modern England.* Oxford: Oxford University Press, 2003.

Sidney, Philip. *Sir Philip Sidney's Defense of Poesy,* ed. Lewis Soens (Lincoln: University of Nebraska Press, 1970), 25.

Siebers, Tobin. *Disability Aesthetics.* Ann Arbor: University of Michigan Press, 2010.

———. "Disability as Masquerade." *Literature and Medicine* 23, no. 1 (2004): 1–22.

———. *Disability Theory.* Ann Arbor: University of Michigan Press, 2008.

Siena, Kevin. *Venereal Disease, Hospitals, and the Urban Poor.* Rochester, NY: University of Rochester Press, 2004.

Silvers, Anita. "Reconciling Equality to Difference: Caring (f)or Justice for People with Disabilities." *Hypatia* 10, no. 1 (1995): 30–55.

Skinner, Quentin. "Thomas Hobbes on the Proper Signification of Liberty: The Prothero Lecture." *Transactions of the Royal Historical Society* 40 (1990): 122.

Snyder, Sharon. "Unfixing Disability in Lord Byron's 'The Deformed Transformed.'" In Sandahl and Auslander, *Bodies in Commotion,* 280–91.

Snyder, Sharon, Brenda Brueggemann, and Rosemarie Garland-Thomson, eds. *Disability Studies: Enabling the Humanities.* New York: Modern Language Association of America, 2002.

Snyder, Sharon L., and David T. Mitchell. "Afterword—Regulated Bodies: Disability Studies and the Controlling Professions." In Turner and Stagg, *Social Histories,* 175–89.

———. *Cultural Locations of Disability.* Chicago: University of Chicago Press, 2006.

Sontag, Susan. *Illness as Metaphor and AIDS and Its Metaphors.* New York: Picador, 1989.

Southworth, John. *Fools and Jesters at the English Court.* London: Sutton, 1998.

Špalek, Jakub. "*Richard III.*" Divadelní spolek Kašpar, Divadlo v Celetné, 20 September 2000.

Spenser, Edmund. *The Faerie Queene.* Ed. A. C. Hamilton; text ed. Hiroshi Yamashita and Toshiyuki Suzuki. Revised 2nd edition. Harlow, UK: Pearson Education, 2001.

Spinrad, Phoebe S. "The Sacralization of Revenge in *Antonio's Revenge.*" *Comparative Drama* 39, no. 2 (2005): 169–85.

Sprunger, David A. "Depicting the Insane: A Thirteenth-Century Case Study." In *Marvels, Monsters, and Miracles: Studies in the Medieval and Early Modern Imaginations,* edited by Timothy S. Jones and David A. Sprunger, 223–41. Kalamazoo: Western Michigan University Press, 2002.

Stallybrass, Peter, and Allon White. *The Politics and Poetics of Transgression.* Ithaca, NY: Cornell University Press, 1986.

Stanivukovic, Goran V. "Troping Desire in Shakespeare's *Venus and Adonis.*" *Forum for Modern Language Studies* 33, no. 4 (October 1997): 289–301.

Stewart, Susan. *On Longing: Narratives of the Miniature, the Gigantic, the Souvenir, the Collection.* Baltimore: Johns Hopkins University Press, 1984.

Stiker, Henri-Jacques. *A History of Disability.* Ann Arbor: University of Michigan, 1999.

Stříbrný, Zdeněk. *The Whirligig of Time: Essays on Shakespeare and Czechoslovakia.* Edited by Lois Potter. Newark: University of Delaware Press, 2007.

Strier, Richard. "Against the Rule of Reason: Praise of Passion from Petrarch to Luther to Shakespeare to Herbert." In Paster et al., *Early Modern Passions,* 23–42.

Suttie, Paul. *Self-interpretation in 'The Faerie Queene.'* London: D. W. Brewer, 2006.

Sutton, John. *Philosophy and Memory Traces: Descartes to Connectionism.* Cambridge: Cambridge University Press, 1998.

Swan, Jim. "Disabilities, Bodies, Voices." In Snyder et al., *Disability Studies,* 283–95.

"Talk." UK Disability Rights Commission, 2001. http://www.celebratingthejourney.org/talk-videos.asp.

Targoff, Ramie. *Common Prayer: The Language of Public Devotion in Early Modern England.* Chicago: University of Chicago Press, 2001.

Tave, Stuart M. *The Amiable Humorist: A Study in the Comic Theory and Criticism of the Eighteenth and Early Nineteenth Centuries.* Chicago: University of Chicago Press, 1960.

Taylor, Charles. *Philosophy and the Human Sciences: Philosophical Papers (Vol. 1).* Cambridge: Cambridge University Press, 1985.

———. *Sources of the Self: The Making of the Modern Identity.* Cambridge, MA: Harvard University Press, 1989.

Thiher, Allen. *Revels in Madness: Insanity in Medicine and Literature.* Ann Arbor: University of Michigan Press, 1999.

Thomas, Keith. "The Place of Laughter in Tudor and Stuart England." *Times Literary Supplement,* 21 January 1977, 77–81.

Tichý, Zdeněk A. "Kašpar by měl s námi i vymřít, míní Špalek." *Mladá Fronta Dnes: Kultura,* 20 September 2000.

———. "Potměšil tasí meč jako Richard III." *Mladá Fronta Dnes: Kultura,* 20 September 2000.

———. "U Kašparů může být i zlo fascinující." *Mladá Fronta Dnes,* 13 October 2000.

Tilmouth, Christopher. *Passion's Triumph over Reason: A History of the Moral Imagination from Spenser to Rochester.* Oxford: Oxford University Press, 2007.

Tomasello, Michael. "Having Intentions, Understanding Intentions, and Understanding Communicative Intentions." In *Developing Theories of Intention: Social Understanding and Self-Control,* edited by P. D. Zelazo, J. W. Astington, and D. R. Olson, 63–76. Mahwah, NJ: Erlbaum, 1999.

Torrey, Michael. "'The Plain Devil and Dissembling Looks': Ambivalent Physiognomy and Shakespeare's *Richard III.*" *English Literary Renaissance* 30, no. 2 (2000): 123–53.

Toufar, Ivo. "Ríjen: Divadelní Blázinec." *Hospodářské Noviny,* 13–15 October 2000.

Tourneur, Cyril. *The Atheist's Tragedy.* In *Four Revenge Tragedies,* edited by Katharine Eisaman Maus, 93–173. Oxford: Oxford University Press, 2008.

Tremain, Shelley, ed. *Foucault and the Government of Disability.* Ann Arbor: University of Michigan Press, 2005.

———. "On the Subject of Impairment." In *Disability/Postmodernity: Embodying Disability Theory,* edited by Marian Corker and Tom Shakespeare, 32–47. London: Continuum, 2002.

Trevor, Douglas. *The Poetics of Melancholy in Early Modern England.* Cambridge: Cambridge University Press, 2004.

Tuan, Yi-Fu. *Dominance and Affection: The Making of Pets.* New Haven, CT: Yale University Press, 1984.

Tully, James. *Meaning and Context: Quentin Skinner and His Critics.* Princeton, NJ: Princeton University Press, 1988.

Turner, David M. *Disability in Eighteenth-Century England: Imagining Physical Impairment.* New York and London: Routledge, 2012.

Turner, David M., and Kevin Stagg. *Social Histories of Disability and Deformity.* New York: Routledge, 2006.

Turner, Mark. *Death Is the Mother of Beauty: Mind, Metaphor, Criticism.* Chicago: University of Chicago Press, 1987.

———. *The Study of English in the Age of Cognitive Science.* Princeton, NJ: Princeton University Press, 1991.

Turner, Victor. *Dramas, Fields, and Metaphors: Symbolic Action in Human Society.* Ithaca, NY: Cornell University Press, 1974.

Tyacke, Nicholas. *Anti-Calvinists: The Rise of English Arminianism c. 1590–1640.* New York: Oxford University Press, 1987.

Tyson, Brian F. "Ben Jonson's Black Comedy: A Connection between *Othello* and *Volpone.*" *Shakespeare Quarterly* 29 (1978): 60–66.

U.S. Department of Justice, Americans with Disabilities Act of 1990, www.usdoj.gov/crt/ada/pubs/ada.txt.

Vaught, Jennifer C. *Masculinity and Emotion in Early Modern English Literature.* Aldershot, UK: Ashgate, 2008.

Vidali, Amy. "Seeing What We Know: Disability and Theories of Metaphor." *Journal of Literary & Cultural Disability Studies* 4, no. 1 (2010): 33–54.

Villa, J. Moreno. *Locos, enanos, negros y niños palaciegos.* Mexico: La Casa de España en Mexico, Editorial Presencia, 1939.

Vital Signs: Crip Culture Talks Back. Directed by David T Mitchell and Sharon Snyder. Brace Yourselves Productions, 1997. Film.

Wainwright, Martin. "Richard III: Could the skeleton under the car park be the king's? Remains at church near Bosworth Field battle site show signs of violent death and severe curvature of the spine." *The Guardian* online, 12 September 2012. http://www.guardian.co.uk/science/2012/sep/12/richard-skeleton-king-remains-bosworth.

Wall, John N. *Transformations of the Word: Spenser, Herbert, Vaughan.* Athens: University of Georgia Press, 1988.

Watt, Tessa. *Cheap Print and Popular Piety, 1550–1640.* Cambridge: Cambridge University Press, 1991.

Webster, John. *The Duchess of Malfi.* In Bevington, *English Renaissance Drama,* 1755–1830.

Wheatley, Edward. *Stumbling Blocks before the Blind: Medieval Constructions of a Disability.* Ann Arbor: University of Michigan Press, 2010.

White, Paul Whitfield, ed. *The History of Jacob and Esau.* In *Reformation Biblical Drama in England: An Old-spelling Critical Edition.* New York: Garland, 1992.

Wilson, F. P. "The English Jestbooks of the Sixteenth and Early Seventeenth Centuries." *Huntington Library Quarterly* 2, no. 2 (1938): 121–58.

Wilson, James C., and Cynthia Lewiecki-Wilson. "Disability, Rhetoric, and the Body." In *Embodied Rhetorics: Disability in Language and Culture,* edited by James C. Wilson and Cynthia Lewiecki-Wilson, 1–24. Carbondale: Southern Illinois University Press, 2001.

Wiltenburg, Joy. *Disorderly Women and Female Power in the Street Literature of Early Modern England and Germany.* Charlottesville: University of Virginia Press, 1992.

Wood, David Houston. "'Fluster'd with flowing cups': Alcoholism, Humoralism, and the Prosthetic Narrative in Othello." *Disability Studies Quarterly* 29.4 (2009): n.p. http://dsq-sds.org/article/view/998/1182.

———. *Time, Narrative, and Emotion in Early Modern England.* Literary and Scientific Cultures of Early Modernity. Farnham, England; Burlington, VT: Ashgate, 2009.

Woods-Marsden, Joanna. "A Vision of Dwarfs." *Dreams and Visions: Presenting the Past,* ed. Nancy Van Deusen (Leiden: Brill, 2010), 325–37.

World Health Organization. *Disabilities.* Geneva: World Health Organization, 2010. http://www.who.int/topics/disabilities/en.

Wright, Thomas. *The Passions of the Minde in Generall. A Reprint Based on the 1604 Edition.* Urbana: University of Illinois Press, 1971.

Würzbach, Natascha. *The Rise of the English Street Ballad, 1550–1650.* Cambridge: Cambridge University Press, 1990.

Yates, Julian. *Error, Misuse, Failure: Object Lessons from the English Renaissance.* Minneapolis: University of Minnesota Press, 2003.

Young, Elizabeth V. "De-Gendering Genre: Aphra Behn and the Tradition of English Verse Satire." *Philological Quarterly* 81 (2002): 185–205.

Zall, P. M. *A Hundred Merry Tales and Other Jestbooks of the Fifteenth and Sixteenth Centuries.* Lincoln: University of Nebraska Press, 1963.

Zelan, Karen. *Between Their World and Ours: Breakthroughs with Autistic Children.* New York: St. Martin's Press, 2003.

EMILY BOWLES currently serves as a Senior Lecturer in Women's Studies at the University of Wisconsin-Fox Valley and as the Assistant to the Chairs for the UW Colleges. She has published on Aphra Behn, Henry Fielding, and Frances Brooke. Her current research interests include satiric representations of femininity and sexuality in Mary Wortley Montagu's poetry.

SIMONE CHESS is an Assistant Professor of English and Women's Studies at Wayne State University. Her research interests are in Early Modern literary and cultural studies, with an emphasis on gender and sexuality. She has published articles and book chapters on the topics of bathroom activism, on ballads and Shakespeare, and on the role of oath-making in "murderous wife" ballads. She is currently completing a book project titled "Where's your man's heart now": Male to Female Crossdressing in Early Modern Literature.

LAUREN COKER is a doctoral candidate in English at Saint Louis University. She is currently completing her dissertation. The project, tentatively titled "Metatheatricality and 'Disability Drag': Performing Bodily Difference on the Renaissance Stage," examines theatrical constructions of feigned disability in various early modern English dramas.

RACHEL E. HILE is an Associate Professor in the Department of English & Linguistics at Indiana University–Purdue University Fort Wayne, where she also serves as editor of *Clio: A Journal of Literature, History, and the Philosophy of History.* She is the author of various articles on Renaissance poetry and drama, and editor [as Rachel Hile Bassett] of the collection *Parenting and Professing: Balancing Family Work with an Academic Career* (Vanderbilt University Press, 2005). She is currently working on a book about Edmund Spenser's influence on satirical poetry written in the 1590s and early 1600s in England.

NANCY J. HIRSCHMANN is Professor of Political Science at The University of Pennsylvania and Vice-President of the American Political Science Association. She is the author of many articles and books including *Gender, Class, and Freedom in Modern Political Theory, The Subject of Liberty: Toward a Feminist Theory of Freedom,* and *Rethinking Obligation: A Feminist Method for Political Theory.* She is also coeditor with Beth Linker of *Civil Disabilities: Theory, Citizenship and the Body* (forthcoming). She has held fellowships from American Council of Learned Societies, The Institute for Advanced Study, the National Endowment for the Humanities, and the Princeton University Center for Human Values.

ALLISON P. HOBGOOD serves as Assistant Professor of English and Women's and Gender Studies at Willamette University. Her fields of interest are Shakespeare and Early Modern literature, women's and gender studies, and disability studies. She has published articles in *Shakespeare Bulletin, European Romantic Review,* and *Disability Studies Quarterly,* a journal for which she coedited the special issue "Disabled Shakespeares." She is currently completing a book, *Passionate Playgoing in Early Modern England,* which investigates the feeling of spectatorship in English Renaissance theater.

MARCELA KOSTIHOVÁ is Associate Professor of English at Hamline University, where she teaches a range of courses in literary, cultural, gender, and film studies. Her research investigates changing structures of identity formation in central-eastern Europe represented in the postcommunist cultural sphere, ranging from literature, to theater, to film. She has published in national and international journals, and her first book, *Shakespeare in Transition: Political Appropriations in the Post-communist Czech Republic,* was published by Palgrave Macmillan in 2010.

MARDY PHILIPPIAN, JR., earned his Ph.D. at Purdue University and is currently Associate Professor of English at Simpson University, where he also serves as the Writing Center Director. He has published in the journals *Literature and Film Quarterly, Film Criticism, Prose Studies,* and *Forum for World Literature Studies,* and in the *Companion to Pre-1600 British Poetry.* In fall 2010 he joined the editorial board of *The Oswald Review: An International Journal of Undergraduate Research and Criticism in the Discipline of English,* published at the University of South Carolina Aiken.

LINDSEY ROW-HEYVELD is Assistant Professor of English at Canisius College. She has published articles on disability in early modern drama and is currently at work on a book titled *Dissembling Disability in Early Modern England,* which explores fraudulent performances of the nonstandard body on and off the stage.

DAVID M. TURNER is Reader in History at Swansea University. He has written widely on the society and culture of early modern Britain and is the author of *Fashioning Adultery: Gender, Sex and Civility in England 1660–1740* (Cambridge University Press, 2002); he is also coeditor (with Kevin Stagg) of *Social Histories of Disability and Deformity* (Routledge, 2006). His most recent book, *Disability in Eighteenth-Century England: Imagining Physical Impairment* (Routledge, 2012), was the winner of the Disability History Association Outstanding Publication Award 2012.

SARA VAN DEN BERG is Professor of English at Saint Louis University. Her publications include *The Divorce Tracts of John Milton,* coedited with W. Scott Howard (2010); *Language, Culture, and Identity: The Legacy of Walter J. Ong, S.J.,* coedited with Thomas M. Walsh (2011); and essays on Milton, Jonson, and Shakespeare. Her current book project is a study of the cultural meanings of the dwarf body from 1500 to the present. She teaches courses in medical humanities, disability studies, and Early Modern English literature.

DAVID HOUSTON WOOD serves as Honors Program Director and Associate Professor of English at Northern Michigan University, where he focuses on sixteenth-century literature and culture. His recent work includes a monograph titled *Time, Narrative, and Emotion in Early Modern England* (Ashgate, 2009); a coedited collection of essays titled "Disabled Shakespeares," published in the journal *Disability Studies Quarterly* 29, no. 4 (Fall 2009); and numerous essays in journals such as *Shakespeare Yearbook, Renaissance Drama,* and *Prose Studies.*